# Urban Sociology, Capitalism and Modernity

## SOCIOLOGY FOR A CHANGING WORLD
Series Editors: Janet Finch and Graham Allan
Founding Editor: Roger King

This series, published in conjunction with the British Sociological Association, evaluates and reflects major developments in contemporary sociology. The books focus on key changes in social and economic life in recent years and on the ways in which the discipline of sociology has analysed those changes. They reflect the state of the art in contemporary British sociology, while at the same time drawing upon comparative material to set debates in an international perspective.

*Published*

Rosamund Billington, Annette Fitzsimons, Lenore Greensides and Sheelagh Strawbridge, *Culture and Society*
Lois Bryson, *Welfare and the State*
Frances Heidensohn, *Crime and Society*
Glenn Morgan, *Organizations in Society*
Mike Savage and Alan Warde, *Urban Sociology, Capitalism and Modernity*
Andrew Webster, *Science, Technology and Society*

*Forthcoming*

Prue Chamberlayne, Brian Darling and Michael Rustin, *A Sociology of Contemporary Europe*
Angela Glasner, *Life and Labour in Contemporary Society*
Marilyn Porter, *Gender Relations*
John Solomos and Les Back, *Racism in Society*
Claire Wallace, *Youth and Society*

**Series Standing Order**
If you would like to receive future titles in this series as they are published, you can make use of our standing order facility. To place a standing order please contact your bookseller or, in case of difficulty, write to us at the address below with your name and address and the name of the series. Please state with which title you wish to begin your standing order. (If you live outside the United Kingdom we may not have the rights for your area, in which case we will forward your order to the publisher concerned.)

Customer Services Department, Macmillan Distribution Ltd
Houndmills, Basingstoke, Hampshire RG21 2XS, England

# URBAN SOCIOLOGY, CAPITALISM AND MODERNITY

Mike Savage and Alan Warde

MACMILLAN

First published 1993 by
THE MACMILLAN PRESS LTD
Houndmills, Basingstoke, Hampshire RG21 2XS
and London
Companies and representatives
throughout the world

ISBN 0–333–49163–7 hardcover
ISBN 0–333–49164–5 paperback

A catalogue record for this book is available
from the British Library.

Reprinted 1994

Printed in China

# Contents

# Acknowledgements

It is extremely rewarding, though also frustrating, to write a book when the field is changing so fast. This is a book that changed many times in the making, and which made us read and think until the last minute. Many thanks to all those who have helped us by talking to us, making comments, and giving general advice. In particular Mike Savage would like to thank students on his workshop at Keele University on urban sociology in 1990 for helping him to realise some of the limitations of existing work (and textbooks!) in the field.

Frances Arnold, our publishing editor, has been very supportive. Janet Finch helped to commission the volume, and she and Graham Allan commented helpfully on drafts. The following people have commented on the whole or parts: Peter Dickens; Helen Hills; Brian Longhurst; Chris Pickvance; Greg Smith; Gerry Stoker; Adam Tickell; John Urry; and Paul Watt. Versions of Chapter 2 were presented by Mike Savage to the Urban and Regional Studies Seminar, University of Sussex, December 1990, and by Alan Warde to the Department of Sociology, University of Melbourne, at Easter 1991. Versions of Chapter 6 were presented by Mike Savage to the Urban Change and Conflict Conference at Lancaster University, September 1991, and to the Department of Sociology, University of Salford, May 1992. Many thanks for the comments received.

Finally, on a personal note, Mike Savage would like to thank Helen Hills for her love and support. Virtually our first conversation was about our mutual interest in urbanism, and it led to fine things.

MIKE SAVAGE
ALAN WARDE

The authors and publishers are grateful to the following for permission to reproduce copyright material: *Urban Studies* for a table from G. Bentham, 'Socio-tenurial polarisation', vol. 23, no. 2 (April 1986); The University of Chicago Press for a diagram from R. E. Park, E. W. Burgess and R. D. McKenzie, *The City* (1967); Pergamon Press Ltd for a table from A. Heath *et al.*, *Understanding Political Change* (1991); HMSO for Central Statistical Office material from *Social Trends*, © Crown copyright 1989; The American Academy of Political and Social Science for a figure from C. D. Harris and E. L. Ullman, 'The Nature of Cities', vol. 2 (1945), *The Annals of the American Academy of Political and Social Science*.

Every effort has been made to contact all the copyright-holders, but if any have been inadvertently omitted the publisher will be pleased to make the necessary arrangements at the earliest opportunity.

# 1 Introduction

Consider one view of why the experience of the modern city is so fascinating and compelling:

> the great buildings of civilisation; the meeting places, the libraries and theatres, the towers and domes; and often more moving than these, the houses, the streets, the press and excitement of so many people, with so many purposes. I have stood in many cities and felt this pulse: in the physical differences of Stockholm and Florence, Paris and Milan: this identifiable and moving quality: the centre, the activity, the light. Like everyone else I have also felt the chaos of the metro and the traffic jam: the monotony of the ranks of houses, the aching press of strange crowds . . . this sense of possibility, of meeting and of movement, is a permanent element of my sense of cities . . .
>
> (Williams, 1973, pp. 14–15)

Many people will recognise elements of Raymond Williams's feelings in their own encounters with cities – for he repeats a cultural stereotype which pervades modern societies. This book, a critical reflection on the nature of urban life and experience in the context of social change, evaluates the extent to which this view of the city can be sustained sociologically.

The problem of urban sociology can be discerned initially in the short extract above: its scope is potentially enormous – from the architecture of cities to traffic congestion, the experience of urban life, the behaviour of crowds, housing, planning and so forth. The experience of urban life seems so all-encompassing that it is difficult to distinguish what might not be the domain of urban sociology. The definition of the subject has often been a source of despair to its practitioners and advocates. The recurrent worry was how to define 'the urban', to specify distinctive and unique properties of the city that provided the focus for specialised scholarly

1

attention. Thus, as far back as 1955, Ruth Glass pointed out that 'there is no such subject [as urban sociology] with a distinct identity of its own' (Glass, 1989, p. 51). She continued, 'in a highly urbanised country such as Great Britain, the label "urban" can be applied to almost any branch of current sociological study. In the circumstances, it is rather pointless to apply it at all' (Glass, 1989, p. 56).

Nevertheless, urban sociologists continued to research and write about life in cities, undaunted by the prospect of contributing to a subject whose boundaries could not be delimited. We have written this book in the belief that there is no solid definition of the urban; approaching matters from the point of view of a definition of the 'urban' produces very oblique appreciations of the role and achievements of urban sociology. The label 'urban' sociology is mostly a flag of convenience. However, the fact that the urban cannot be defined in a general way does not mean that important things cannot be said about specific processes in particular cities! This text therefore isolates the actual contribution of the subdiscipline, in order to identify the common elements explaining its persistence.

Looking at the textbooks published over the past thirty years, it would be hard to isolate a core to the subject, for their principal organising themes are extraordinarily various. Some are about planning improvement of life in cities, others describe urban forms and structures; some offer histories of urban growth while others seek the biological or ecological bases of urban behaviour; some are theoretical treatises on the quality of the urban experience, others epistemological reflections on the concept of the urban (e.g. respectively, Greer, 1962; Pahl, 1970; Reissman, 1964; Dickens, 1990; Smith, 1980; Saunders, 1981). This prompts our view that the history of urban sociology is discontinuous, unamenable to an account of its linear evolution around a single theme (cf. Saunders, 1981). Yet, although there is no cumulative tradition, there are a number of recurrent threads and themes around which urban sociology revolves.

Themes examined within urban sociology and the types of topics which we discuss include:

1. what it feels like to live in a modern city and whether there is a unitary or universal 'urban' experience. Defining characteristics have been sought, e.g. anonymity – being just another face in a vast crowd; the uncertainty and unpredictability of events in complex urban environments; the senses of possibility and danger induced by cities;
2. whether, by contrast, places are distinctive, what makes for attach-

ment to particular neighbourhoods or cities, given that people certainly perceive places to have their own identity and characteristics;

3. how urban life is affected by the features of local social structure, e.g.
class position, gender, ethnic group, housing situation, and so forth;

4. how informal social bonds develop and to what extent the nature of
affective relationships – with kin, neighbours, friends and associates –
are determined by the external social context and environment, much
discussion having been devoted to whether different kinds of settlement engender concomitant types of social ties;

5. how to explain the history of urbanisation and the concentration of
population in towns, cities and conurbations;

6. what are the basic features of the spatial structure of cities and whether
different spatial arrangements generate distinctive modes of interaction;

7. what is the nature of, and what are the solutions to, 'urban' problems
like congestion, pollution, poverty, vagrancy, delinquency and street
violence;

8. how urban political affairs are conducted, what influences political
participation and what impact the different agencies of the local state
have on daily life.

Urban sociologies oscillate in their focus as they select among themes
and try to reconcile divergent concerns. In this book we argue that a
coherent programme for urban sociology would be concerned with the
mutual impact of two analytically separate entities, *capitalism* and *modernity*. Moreover, past achievements too are best appreciated as an extended
enquiry into the relationship between modernity and capitalism.

Definitions of modernity are highly contested. A glut of recent literature, focused on a putative transition to post-modernity, has caused
intensive re-examination of what is meant by the term 'modernity' (for a
summary see Smart, 1992). We prefer to reserve the concept modern to
describe a particular mode of experience. One insightful formulation is
that of Berman (1983) who makes 'the experience of modernity' a central
organising principle of his study of Western aesthetic reflections on life
in cities:

There is a mode of vital experience – experience of space and time, of
self and others, of life's possibilities and perils – that is shared by men
and women all over the world today. I will call this body of experience
'modernity'. To be modern is to find ourselves in an environment that

promises us adventure, power, joy, growth, transformation of ourselves and the world – and, at the same time, that threatens to destroy
everything we have, everything we know, everything we are. Modern
environments and experiences cut across all boundaries of geography
and ethnicity, of class and nationality, of religion and ideology: in this
sense, modernity can be said to unite all mankind. But it is a paradoxical unity, a unity of disunity; it pours us all into a maelstrom
of perpetual disintegration and renewal, of struggle and contradiction,
of ambiguity and anguish. To be modern is to be part of a universe in
which, as Marx said, 'all that is solid melts into air' (Berman, 1983,
p. 1).

The ambivalent experience of modernity contrasts with traditional
ways of life, which were socially more secure and predictable because less
open and manipulable. Most urban sociologists, and particularly the early
ones, were fascinated by this experience of modernity. Yet this dominant
preoccupation has always existed in tension with another, the way in
which capitalist economic structures affect urban life.

Capitalism refers to the economic order of Western societies in which
production is organised around the search for profit. The private ownership of the means of production – land, tools, machines, factories and
suchlike – entails that their owners ultimately retain profits, and those
who do not share ownership are forced to work as employees. These
economic relations of exploitation generate social class inequality, an
inherent feature of capitalist societies. The search for profit leads also to
a dynamic, competitive, conflictual, economic system prone to crisis.
These powerful economic forces cannot but affect the nature of cities and
in the 1960s and 1970s urban sociologists, influenced by the revival of
Marxist political economy, concentrated attention on the capitalist roots
of urban conditions.

Today the tide is turning again and urban sociology is once more
being focused on issues of modernity, sometimes in the current guise of
debate about post-modernity. Rather than condone wholeheartedly this
intellectual shift, we submit that urban sociology needs to synthesise the
best elements of the political economy of capitalism with more cultural
analyses of modernity, realigning the subject near the heart of the sociological discipline as well as illuminating urban experiences.

The book contains six substantial chapters. Each deals with a different
set of issues and body of literature; each body of literature, for purposes
of study, may be read separately. However, there is also a sustained

argument running throughout the book about the nature and functions of urban sociology and how the analysis of the interacting mechanisms of capitalism and modernity constitute differential urban experiences.

Chapter 2 provides a brief history of urban sociology, primarily as practised in Britain and the USA. In the 1970s and 1980s older work was heavily criticised and radical new approaches were promulgated. Much of value in the older tradition was prematurely condemned as inquiry into the social conditions of modernity was discarded. We recommend that contemporary urban sociology should reintegrate older and newer approaches.

Chapter 3 explores economic theories of urban development and decline. Here we show how recent analyses of capitalism have used the concept of uneven development to explore the differentiation of cities in varying parts of the globe. Instead of a uniform process of urbanisation, where all cities grow according to the same logic, attention to uneven development identifies variation in accordance with location within the capitalist world system. We also argue that such theories are insufficient to express the cultural dimensions of modernity.

Chapter 4 examines urban manifestations of the inherent inequalities of capitalism which powerfully affect the spatial and social organisation of cities. We discuss processes which produce inequalities within cities, such as gentrification, suburbanisation, and household divisions. Hence we argue that the experience of modernity is not a universal one, its costs and benefits are differentially felt.

Chapter 5 shifts the focus directly onto the city and modernity. We consider the classic works of Georg Simmel and Louis Wirth, in search of a 'generic' urban culture. Is there an urban way of life, which can be defined in terms which apply, in some way, to all cities? We examine Wirth's attempt to show that urban ways of life could be contrasted with rural ways of life and Simmel's endeavours to specify the city as the locus of modernity. Protracted investigation, we contend, has failed to provide a convincing demonstration of the existence of an urban way of life.

Chapter 6 therefore considers how places gain different meanings. We argue that no account of urban culture is adequate unless it takes seriously personal, unique, experiences of urban life, but that this occurs in the context of broader cultural forces. It is suggested that the work of Walter Benjamin offers a series of valuable beginnings for this project. His ideas implicitly criticise the fashionable claim that an era of post-modernity has emerged.

Chapter 7 surveys analyses of urban politics, showing their responsiveness to changing political agendas and the impact of the forces of capitalism and modernity. We examine, in particular, the importance of state welfare and the politics of consumption, the significance of local economic policy, urban protest, the urban bases of political alignments, and the policing of cities.

# 2   The Roots of Urban Sociology

In this chapter we present a brief and selective survey of the history of urban sociology. Section 2.1 deals with the concerns of urban sociology in its 'golden age' between 1910 and the 1930s, when it was central to the development of the discipline. We focus on the Chicago School and identify elements in its legacy which are relevant for analysis today. We contrast the development of urban sociology in the UK to indicate some of the specific strengths of the British tradition of urban research. After the Second World War urban sociology became more marginal to sociology, and in section 2.2 we indicate some of the reasons for this. The pressing sense of social turmoil and political unrest which had earlier generated an interest in cities was replaced by more complacent political attitudes in which it was assumed that economic growth and social harmony were destined to be permanent features of capitalist welfare states. The rise of functionalist and structuralist social theory altered the terrain of sociological inquiry. By the middle of the 1970s most commentators were contemptuous of the contribution of the Chicago School and of urban sociology more generally. However, in section 2.3 we argue that this dismissive evaluation was misplaced and that the theoretical approaches favoured in the 1970s left a series of serious conceptual problems. We consider in particular the influential Marxist critique of urban sociology of Castells and elements of its subsequent development as 'the new urban sociology'. In conclusion we suggest that aspects of the research agenda of contemporary sociology signify a return to some broad objectives of urban sociology implicit in the work of Georg Simmel and the Chicago School, where the study of urban life is seen as integrally linked to an investigation of 'modernity'.

## 2.1   The development of urban sociology 1900–30

At first glance our claim that the early twentieth-century was a 'golden age' for urban sociology may seem strange. Modern sociology frequently traces its roots back to three leading theorists – Karl Marx, Max Weber, and Emile Durkheim – all of whom (Weber partly excepted) were relatively uninterested in urban phenomena (Giddens, 1971; Alexander, 1982). These three were preoccupied with analysing other principal characteristics of new industrial societies of the nineteenth century (Kumar, 1978; Lee and Newby, 1982). For Marx these were new capitalist societies, divided between the property-owning bourgeoisie and the property-less working class, racked by class conflict and division. Weber on the other hand emphasised the decline of traditional authority and the rise of rational, bureaucratic authority. Durkheim had a rather more optimistic view, in which people would learn to cooperate as they came to realise that they all depended upon each other in societies with a highly elaborate division of labour.

None of these writers were particularly preoccupied with the specific character of modern urban life. Indeed Saunders (1986) claimed that they all advanced rather different arguments in support of the view that in modern societies cities had lost any distinctive properties they might once have possessed. Whilst in ancient societies the distinction between town and countryside was socially significant, and in feudal Europe cities had distinctive social and political autonomy from the rule of rural landlords, by the nineteenth-century this was no longer true. In modern societies there are no social activities which happen only in cities or only in the countryside. In an age of high geographical mobility, in which people travel long distances to work, in which they frequently migrate, in which the mass media transmit messages across vast areas, and in which goods and services are moved to many different locations, it does not make sense, argued Saunders, to treat the city and the countryside as self-contained social orders, detached from each other.

If the 'founders' of sociology were uninterested in urban phenomena, how could urban sociology be of prime importance to the discipline in its early days? The paradox is more apparent than real, since the influence of Marx, Weber and Durkheim on early sociology was not as marked as is sometimes suggested in later accounts. Marx never claimed to be a sociologist, and his work was rarely taken seriously within Western sociology until the 1960s, being at most a position which was criticised as deterministic and mistaken. Weber, although an academic (unlike Marx) was also seen, until the 1930s, primarily as a specialised historical sociologist and his methodological writings, which have influenced later sociologists, were not especially well-known until Parsons popularised them in the 1930s (see Parsons, 1937). Of the three only Durkheim had a strong influence on the development of sociology as an academic discipline, helping to found one of the earliest sociological journals, *L'Année Sociologique*, in 1896. Even so he was important in only one of the two French sociological schools which emerged at the end of the nineteenth century, and the other, strongly based on the work of Frederic Le Play and the journal, *La Science Sociale*, arguably had a more important short-term impact.

Thus, irrespective of the theoretical writings of Marx, Weber and Durkheim, sociology emerged in the early twentieth century as a discipline primarily concerned with the nature of urban life and the analysis of what might loosely be termed 'urban problems' – unemployment, poverty, social unrest, rootlessness, congestion and so forth. The sociology of cities dominated early sociological work, both in Britain and America, and it proved of particular value in examining social relationships in an individualised and fragmented society.

## 2.1.1  The Chicago School

The Chicago School played a particularly important role in the establishment of urban sociology. The University of Chicago was founded in 1892 and the Department of Sociology soon came to have a commanding influence in the USA, partly because the leading journal, *American Journal of Sociology*, was based there. By the First World War the concern with urban life had been made apparent by Robert Park's publication of his article on 'The City', which laid down an exhaustive research agenda for urban sociology. The School subsequently produced two distinctive bodies of work: one is associated with the ecological mapping of the so-called 'natural areas' of Chicago, the other with a series of ethnographies of diverse social groups in the city.

The Chicago School is often best-known for Burgess's model of urban form, based on patterns of land-use in 1920s Chicago, which attempted to delineate the basic patterns of social segregation in modern cities. This, the concentric zone model (see Figure 2.1), was an ideal-type representation of city growth, assuming the absence of natural features like waterfronts and hills. It postulated the existence of a Central Business District (CBD), in the middle of the city, and then, further out, a zone of

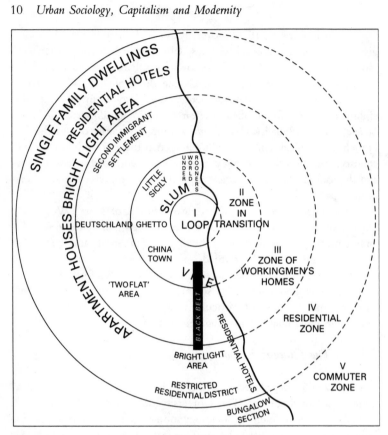

**Figure 2.1**    *Urban areas*
*Source:* R. E. Park, E. W. Burgess and R. D. McKenzie (eds), *The City* (University of Chicago Press, 1967) p. 55.

transition characterised by urban decay, which was 'invaded' by business and industry. This made it unattractive to residents who, when they had the resources, moved outwards either to the zone of working-men's homes or, if they could afford it, to the suburbs, where the middle classes tended to predominate. Burgess saw this model as testifying to the importance of ecological processes: as cities expanded so successive waves of 'invasion' took place as people spilled out of their areas into others, leading to competition between differing communities, and a changing urban form. Corroboration and qualification of this model eventually resulted in considerable, statistically based, research, involving mapping land-use, the distribution of particular populations and the incidence of social pathologies like suicide and crime.

The other, ethnographic, strand of Chicago School research has been less well-known within urban sociology, although its influence on urban anthropology has been great (see Hannerz, 1980). From the 1920s a series of famous ethnographies on different aspects of Chicago life began to emerge in response to some of the questions raised by Park (see the summary of these in Hannerz, 1980). These ethnographies were all detailed studies of particular facets of urban life in Chicago, and tended to focus on the disadvantaged, insecure, and transient. The most famous of these included: *The Gang* (Thrasher, 1927) – a detailed study of 1313 gangs in different parts of Chicago; *The Hobo* (Andersen, 1923) – a study of migrants and tramps; *The Taxi-Hall Dancers* (Cressey, 1932) – a study of women who danced with men in return for payment, and of the men who bought female company in this way; and *The Gold Coast and the Slum* (Zorbaugh, 1929) – a study of social relationships in two adjacent areas of central Chicago.

These ethnographies were all written from field research based on participant observation. They were written by researchers who sought to gain access to the people they were researching, examining the motivations and attitudes guiding the actions of gang-members, tramps, slum-dwellers and so forth. They began to contribute to a project suggested by Park: 'anthropology, the science of man, has been mainly concerned up to the present with the study of primitive peoples. But civilised man is quite as interesting an object of investigation' (Park, 1967, p. 3). Hannerz (1980) sees them as the first attempts to carry out micro-research using anthropological techniques in modern societies.

The key themes still relevant today that can be extracted from the Chicago School do not concern formalised ecological theory nor early versions of urban ethnographic method, but are three interconnected substantive elements: sociation, its changing modes within modernity, and social reform.

## Sociation

The first and most general of these is an interest in the nature and patterns of social interaction and processes of social bonding. Questions included why people associated with particular others, how social groups, bonds and loyalties developed, and how they changed. This concern drew upon the insights of Simmel, who was highly influential for the Chicago

School, and for whom the main focus of sociology was to account for patterns of 'sociation' (Frisby, 1984). Simmel argued that:

> just as the differentiation of the specifically psychological from object-ive matter produces psychology as a science, so a genuine sociology can only deal with what is specifically societal, the form and forms of sociation (quoted in Frisby, 1984, p. 52).

The concept of sociation is not an easy one, and Simmel develops it by contrast with 'society'. Society consists of 'permanent interactions . . . crystallised as definable, consistent structures such as the state and family . . .' (Simmel, 1950, p. 9). Sociation however comprises the 'less conspicuous' ties which bind people together: 'that people look at one another and are jealous of one another: that they exchange letters or dine together; that irrespective of all tangible interests they strike one another as pleasant or unpleasant . . . the whole gamut of relations that play from one person to another and that may be momentary or permanent, conscious or unconscious, ephemeral or of grave consequence, all these tie men (sic) incessantly together' (Simmel, 1950, p. 10). Sociation is concerned with the informal ordering of social life, the moral codes and conventions underlying apparently haphazard and incoherent forms of human action. Forms of social action which may appear meaningless, volatile or anarchic nonetheless have a meaning when situated in spatial and social context. For instance, Thrasher showed that gangs were not simply groups of hot-headed adolescents, beyond control and bent on violence and law-breaking, but had their own moral codes and meanings. Cressey's study of the taxi-hall dancers showed how they and their customers became involved in the activity, despite its rough reputation, by paying particular attention to the values they used to justify it.

## Sociation's changing modes within modernity

The interest in patterns of sociation was related to a second main issue, a more empirical question of how processes of sociation were changing in contemporary America in the early twentieth century. Park, in his re-search agenda written in 1915, laid out the issues clearly enough. Eco-nomic growth, he wrote, breaks down or modifies:

> the older social and economic organisation of society, which was based upon family ties, local associations, on culture, caste and status, and to substitute for it an organisation based on occupational and vocational

interests, division of labour, the concentration of industries and groups or special tasks have continually changed the material conditions of life, and in doing this have made readjustment to novel conditions increasingly necessary (Park, 1967, pp. 13, 19).

Here is the empirical concern of the Chicago School: understanding the importance of the rise of modern industrialism and its impact on processes of sociation. Modernity, for Park, involved the breaking down of formal, structural bases of human action, and the growth of informal social life. Park's view was that the division of labour meant that work and occupation tended to fragment social bonds (e.g. Park, 1967). The only way in which social ties could be built up lay in the rise of neighbourhood solidarities. He argued that families and what he termed 'primary attachments' had been eroded in modern cities. His concern was with the nature of other social bonds, to see how they might, or might not, build up collective organisation. Many Chicago studies focused upon the unattached – those without primary bonds – to see whether they were forming other sorts of social ties. Hence the interest in people who inhabited the lonely world of the taxi-hall dancer, the hobo, and the tramp.

The work of the Chicago School is best seen as an extended empirical inquiry into the nature of social bonding in the modern, fragmented, city. The city interested them for empirical, rather than conceptual reasons. It was where the division of labour was most elaborate and developed, and hence where the fragmentary nature of modern life could most profitably be studied. Moreover, in Chicago as in other American cities, the extent of immigration also posed a challenge to the establishment of orderly and comprehensible social relationships.

## Social reform

A third important characteristic of the Chicago School's work was its directly political concern. As Smith (1988) argues, what bound the Chicagoans together was less a common theoretical position than shared liberal political ideals and the desire to translate them into political practice. He maintained that 'they believed American democracy, properly functioning, should enable men and women to achieve the satisfactions embodied in what has become known as the American dream' (Smith, 1988, p. 5). The School accepted the basic parameters of a capitalist economy and a liberal democratic electoral system – which partly explains their relative lack of interest in employment or the state –

but were concerned with how cooperative sorts of interaction could be developed to replace the fragmenting forms evident in contemporary Chicago. The Chicagoans believed in a reformist politics, involving experimenting with social institutions to examine how they might affect the character of sociation in specific environments.

Each of these three areas of concern was stimulated by puzzlement about social integration in a rapidly urbanising context. All three addressed issues of potential social disorganisation that arose from handling a rapid influx of people, strangers of many kinds, into a swiftly expanding city. The contemporary problem was how individuals could deal with the disorienting, exciting, unstable, insecure, disembedded, polyvalent and anomic conditions that an industrial city like Chicago posed. These scholars confronted the intellectual and practical problems associated with what we would now describe as the experience of modernity.

Despite the novelty of their approach, and the diversity of their empirical research, the Chicago School lacked any clear theoretical orientation. This is not to say that various Chicago writers did not write theoretical papers or speculate on social theory. This they most certainly did, albeit largely in article form. But, whilst it is possible to use these theoretical speculations to attempt to discern a 'Chicago' position, most of the propositions based on it are not actually followed in the empirical research presented in the ethnographies.

The theoretical position of the Chicago School is usually seen as its endorsement of 'human ecology' and its attempt to adapt biological ideas to the study of cities. Saunders, for instance, argues that the Chicago School developed a form of 'human ecology', in which patterns of urban life were seen as driven by principles similar to those evidence in plant ecology, where different species of plant competed to gain dominance in a particular habitat. A recent champion of the Chicago School, Peter Dickens (1990), has even defended the contribution of the Chicagoans precisely because of this. However, since forms of biological reductionism are generally considered completely unsustainable, most urban sociologists have used such interpretations as grounds for dismissing Chicago's contemporary relevance.

Park used human ecology to indicate the importance of processes of conflict and competition within cities for scarce resources. The social structure of cities showed that different communities – of ethnic groups, or social classes – tended to concentrate in differing areas. This was not a static or unchanging pattern however, and just as types of plants moved from area to area, so did different urban communities. Park referred to this process as one of 'succession', which went through a cycle of competition (between groups, for instance, different ethnic groups in one area), dominance (as one ethnic group gains the upper hand and the other begins to move out), succession (as the new group establishes itself as the sole group in that area), and invasion (as it then expands into another area, so beginning the cycle all over again). By using this ecological perspective it seemed that the Chicago School were taking the emphasis away from processes of racism and class conflict, instead seeing patterns of settlement in urban areas as the product of evolutionary processes of 'the survival of the fittest'.

Although there is no doubt that these 'ecological' themes were evident in the work of Park, and other Chicago School writers, this was not the sole theoretical preoccupation of the Chicago School, and neither should evaluation of the whole school rest upon this one idea. Park himself had other ideas too, tending to emphasise cultural factors in social life, being quite explicit that cultural factors could modify ecological processes (Lal, 1990, pp. 28–9). Smith (1988, ch. 7) argues that Park only attempted to systematise his ecological arguments after he retired, his strongest statements of ecological principles being written in the 1930s (e.g. Park 1938), well after most of the Chicago ethnographies had been written and when he was no longer especially influential within Chicago. In his first and most important paper, 'The City: Suggestions for the Investigation of Human Behaviour in the Urban Environment', written in 1915, which set the research agenda for the ethnographers, Park mentions the ecological approach only briefly, at the beginning, and even here he sees it as only one of four approaches to the city: the others being 'the geographic', the economic, and the cultural. Most of his article concentrates on the economic aspect of urban change, especially – echoing Durkheim – on the sociological significance of the division of labour.

One should not assume that human ecology is necessarily a form of biological determinism. Many commentators have asserted the weaknesses of drawing parallels between natural and human ecology, among the first and most elaborate being Alihan's (1938) demonstration of the inconsistencies and absurdities involved in the Chicago School's use of concepts like environment, sustenance, competition and succession. Yet Park's writing needs to be treated carefully. He frequently refers to the way in which sociologists study 'human nature'. Today the term 'human nature' is taken to mean a fixed biological essence and is treated with suspicion by social scientists, but for Park the term does not have these connotations: 'human nature, as we have begun to conceive it in recent years, is largely a product of social intercourse; it is therefore, quite as much as society itself, a subject for sociological investigation' (Park, 1921, p. 172). As Donna Harraway (1989) has shown, ecological ideas, rather than being biologically derived, were largely forms of evolutionary social theory imported into the study of animals. In later years the ecological research was simply taken to refer to a particular method of gathering data about certain areas, rather than to any explicit link with biological arguments.

As Harvey (1987) argued, the 'Chicago School' was actually rather diverse. Other Chicago writers drew upon ecological arguments hardly at all. W.I. Thomas, for instance, saw social life as driven by 'four wishes' – the needs for new experience, security, response and recognition – an observation which emphasised the specifically human dynamics of social life and tended to undermine any simple association of human and plant life. Indeed Thomas was seen by contemporaries (Ellwood, 1927) as being concerned to develop a rounded account of the role of 'culture' in social life which proved difficult to square with biological reductionist views.

If we focus on the heart of the Chicago research – the ethnographies of Chicago life carried out in the 1920s – it is clear that many of them explicitly criticise reductionist arguments. In one of the most famous of these, Thrasher's *The Gang*, the writer spends some considerable time criticising the idea that there is a 'gang instinct', and emphasises how gangs emerge for social reasons, paying particular attention to the way they might emerge out of youthful play groups. This idea shows signs of being influenced by Cooley's (1909) stress on the importance of socialisation processes in affecting social life – again an idea which is not linked to biological arguments.

It is sometimes argued that ecological arguments were developed through Burgess's formulation of ecological principles in the concentric zone model of the city. However, whatever its value, it was of only marginal importance to the Chicago ethnographies. Virtually all writers mention this model as a point of reference, but nearly always to show that the subject of interest to them could not be fitted easily into its dimensions. Thrasher argued that Chicago gangs were located in 'interstitial' sites between the main zones discussed by Burgess, whilst Cressey's taxi-hall dancers were not located in any particular site within a city. The ethnographies were primarily interested in the unattached, lonely worlds of the migrant, transient population, which almost by definition evaded being mapped fixedly to a particular place within the city.

The ecological model of concentric zones developed by Park and Burgess was used largely metaphorically by Chicago writers. Rather than actually arguing that patterns of urban life were the same as those of plant life (which a moment's thought tells us is a ridiculous argument) the biological arguments are used as analogies, in order to show how comparison with biology might throw light on urban life. Human ecology, as Smith (1988, pp. 136–7) writes, was 'at best a loose framework of ideas oriented to both measurement and meaning which drew upon the borrowed prestige of the natural sciences'. The development of a more explicit ecological approach in the 1930s was caused by the need to attempt to systematise what had previously been loose notions into an apparently scientific statement which could satisfy the increasingly positivist climate of the times.

The Chicago School's most valuable legacy was its conception of sociology as concerned with forms of interaction in the contemporary city and its vision of the sociologist as a promoter of cooperative relationships. They were analysts of what recent sociologists have termed 'modernity', the specific experience of living in a modern world where any overriding social customs and values have been swept away. Furthermore, it was the combination of these three elements within a distinctive research programme based on the empirical, ethnographic study of inter-war Chicago which marked out the School. Any one of these elements, taken alone, led away from any distinctive urban sociology towards a rather different focus. The interest in sociation alone could lead to the development of symbolic interactionism and ethnomethodology. The Chicago School were not interested in analysing the general or formal properties of social action in the manner of Garfinkel (1967) or Goffman (1959). The School's interest was always in studying patterns of social bonding in a given historical situation and in particular spatial settings – the American city in the early twentieth century. Their other two main interests, taken alone, might also have led them away from urban issues: the interest in the characteristics of contemporary society alone could lead to the rediscovery of Marx, Weber and Durkheim on the nature of modern societies; political engagement alone could feed through to the liberal views characteristic of forms of sociological thought, like that of Parsons. What marked out the Chicago contribution was interconnection of these three elements: the concern with studying the contemporary nature of social interaction in the context of a broad set of reformist political concerns.

The city was thus of interest because it allowed their three focal concerns to be reconciled and elaborated. The city was interesting not for anything intrinsic to cities *per se*, but because it was where economic development and hence the modern division of labour was best-established, because it was where diverse types of social interaction took place, and because it was the scene of major local political interventions in inter-war America. This explains Park's frequent evocation of the idea that cities were a 'social laboratory' (e.g. Park, 1967, p. 46). There were good methodological reasons for studying cities, given the concerns of the Chicago writers:

> a great city tends to spread out and lay bare to the public view in a massive manner all the human characters and traits which are ordinarily obscured and suppressed in smaller communities . . . [this] justifies the view that would make of the city a social laboratory or clinic in which human nature and social processes may be conveniently and profitably studied (Park, 1967, pp. 45–6).

Before turning to consider how this ambitious research programme in urban sociology declined after the 1930s, we consider the case of early British work in the area, which also had some distinctive strengths.

## 2.1.2   British urban sociology before the Second World War

In Britain academic sociology was much slower to develop than in the USA, and it was not until the 1960s that it became a widely taught subject in higher education. Nonetheless, there was a long tradition of social research in Britain, as in the USA, preoccupied with the nature, causes and consequences of 'urban problems and issues'.

This was especially true in what Halsey, Heath and Ridge (1980) have called the 'political arithmetic' tradition of Victorian social research of Henry Mayhew, Charles Booth, and Seebohm Rowntree. They were primarily concerned to measure the extent of poverty in urban areas. Mayhew, in the 1850s, spent considerable time interviewing the poor in London, publishing his findings as newspaper articles. The style was not ethnographic in the Chicago sense, being more akin to in-depth journalism, but what marked out Mayhew from other contemporary reporters was his attempt to understand theoretically the causes of poverty, which he saw as stemming from low pay resulting from the cyclical nature of production in many urban handicraft trades, rather than from individual defects of the poor themselves (Thompson and Yeo, 1971; Kent 1981).

His successors, Charles Booth and Seebohm Rowntree had similar concerns, but abandoned Mayhew's style of interviewing in favour of more rigorous statistical surveys. In an extensive study of London, carried out in the 1880s, Booth tried to enumerate the causes of poverty by distinguishing the effects of individual habits from those of specific types of employment, a concern also taken up by Rowntree in his studies of poverty in York.

There were major differences between British and American traditions of urban research. In Britain there was less concern with the transient and rootless, more with issues of poverty and social class. Booth developed an elaborate classification of social classes, which he used to construct the social geography of London. When his work was drawn upon by Chicago writers, it was to bring out the significance of class as a social force (see Pfautz, 1967). Pfautz argued that Booth was one of the first sociologists to show systematically how social class affected urban social segregation and involvement in institutional life, like religious activity. This concern with class was to give a distinctively British flavour to some urban sociology, in contrast to the Americans' greater interest in race and ethnicity. Moreover, in this, the central tradition of urban surveys, work, unemployment, poverty and associational activities were the substantive focus of attention. The principal research instrument was a steadily more sophisticated version of the sample survey, cultivated by sociologists seeking professional accreditation and by social reformers of the liberal and Fabian types.

Institutionally, another tradition of early British sociology was based on the Sociological Society, founded in 1903 (Abrams, 1968). This Society developed a direct interest in the study of towns and cities. Branford (1926), discussing the intellectual lineage of the Sociological Society, saw it as drawing upon the two French sociological schools of Durkheim and Le Play. Nonetheless, Le Play, rather than Durkheim, was the more important figure for the Sociological Society. Branford criticised Durkheim for his neglect of historical processes, claiming that he abandoned Comte's theory of:

> the social heritage, which is the very core of Comte's sociology, systematically built around the concept of history as an interplay of

temporal and spiritual powers acting through the perennial but changing social types of chiefs and peoples, emotionals and intellectuals
(Branford, 1928, p. 334).

The stress on Le Play is instructive. Le Play was no theorist, but
focused upon the role of sociology as a survey-based discipline which
investigated the relationships between what he termed 'Place, Work and
Folk'. He argued that sociologists needed to examine households in their
regional context in order to investigate the reciprocal relationship between environment and society. For Branford this formula, which we
maintain remains useful, allowed sociology to unite otherwise disparate
disciplines. 'Through the master [sic] concept', wrote Branford, 'that
place determines work and work in turn conditions family life and folk
organisation, his [Le Play's] observations become alive with the breath
of unity' (Branford, 1928, p. 335).

Branford saw the attempt to unite the Durkheimian and Le Play
traditions as occurring:

> more especially by applying the characteristic methods of each towards
> studying the evolution of cities and their regions. For this school (i.e.
> the Sociological Society) it is living cities and their regions which most
> fully offer to the plain, scientific student, as well as to the plain man,
> the directly observable aspects of civilisation (Branford, 1926, p. 315).

The research instrument chosen by Branford and Geddes was the 'regional survey', not to be confused with the sample surveys of Booth.
Geddes, an idiosyncratic scholar, originally biologist, sometime geo-
grapher, sociologist, propagandist and educationalist before becoming
influential in the town-planning movement, advocated this method. His
was a much more totalising sense of the term 'survey', for it included
considering the natural environment and the history of a place as well as
the activities of its current inhabitants. He genuinely sought to incorp-
orate the insights of natural science, geography, economics and anthropology, all of which, being influenced by Comte, he thought might be
subsumed as sociology. He persuaded many groups of people in different
places to undertake such surveys, for reasons of self-education and civic
awareness as well as for scientific purposes. They were undertaken by
amateurs in the towns and villages of Britain in the quarter century after
Geddes's own pioneering survey of Dunfermline in 1903. Most later
commentators (e.g. Abrams, 1968, p. 118; Mellor, 1989, p. 136) think
Geddes contributed little, agreeing with Glass that:

His failure to devise an adequate method for urban sociology and his premature diversion into planning propaganda and educational projects were critical. They discredited urban sociology among sociologists and they established an essentially non-sociological use of the social survey among planners (Glass, 1989, p. 120).

Branford maintained that sociology could only proceed by the inductive generalisation of facts from a regional survey. In 1928 he wrote that 'Regional Surveys . . . are now in progress throughout Britain . . . thus arises the need and practicability of a social observatory for each city, with departments of study on all the . . . levels with their various outlooks (Branford, 1928, p. 337).

We have seen that the Chicago School saw urban sociology as involving three general concerns: sociation in the modern city; the nature of modernity; and a liberal political project. Britain was somewhat different. The interest in 'sociation' was almost entirely absent. Whilst the Chicagoans focused upon the social life of the neighbourhood, gang or informal social group, the British mainstream focused upon the household survey, probing issues based on household income and expenditure, and were not especially concerned with the extent of wider social bonds. The British tended to assume that social class identities provided social bonds, even in otherwise diverse urban settings.

The British were, nevertheless, interested in the nature of 'contemporary' life and were also politically involved. Geddes's ideas were central to the Town Planning and Garden City movements, also associated with Ebenezer Howard, which argued that most urban problems could be resolved by planning cities more rationally. It is interesting to speculate whether it was the Utopian and visionary aspects of Geddes thought that led to his lack of acceptability within British social science. But he and Branford also added a dimension missing in the Chicago school. From Le Play they adopted the idea that sociology was vitally concerned with the context and environment of social life. For Branford the main viewpoint was 'that of the essential interconnexion of all main aspects of any given community and its civilisation' (Branford, 1926, p. 317). The regional focus allowed them to show how it was impossible to abstract individuals from their wider social environment, and that sociology was a contextual discipline, concerned not to partition social action into a series of subdisciplines but to integrate different aspects of social activity. They showed the way to examine the total configuration of forces that provided the basis of everyday activities in different places.

Through the 1930s more local surveys were accomplished. Foremost among these were the Merseyside Survey, published in 1934, the New London Survey of London Life and Labour (1930) and the York survey (1936). The two last-mentioned were follow-up surveys of earlier research, and concentrated on assessing the extent to which poverty levels had changed. Their success began to suggest that cumulative sociological knowledge could be developed. The emerging hegemony of the sample survey influenced by statistical ideas such as random sampling, was perhaps indicated by the largely adverse reaction to the appearance of Mass Observation (Kent, 1981). This social movement of 'observers', instead of conducting interviews using a pre-designed schedule, employed basic ethnographic techniques, including the use of direct observation of social activities in certain towns. Although the techniques were rather closer to those of the ethnographers of Chicago, its project of 'a science of ourselves' received little attention in British academia.

## 2.2   The decline of urban sociology: the post-war years

In both Britain and the USA, until the 1930s, urban sociology was scarcely a specialised sub-branch of the discipline. Rather, empirical sociological issues revolved around urban conditions: mass immigration, poverty, social pathologies, conflict groups and social bonding. Sociologists were thus directly concerned with the environments and contexts which generated social action. Developments after the 1930s displaced the urban focus of sociology and, hence, its contextual logic.

Most generally, sociology began to be organised around a different set of intellectual problems. The main theoretical concern of the reconstructed sociology was the nature of social order. Talcott Parsons, in his book, *The Structure of Social Action*, published in 1937, introduced Pareto, Weber and Durkheim as the key figures in sociological thought, the first two having been largely ignored earlier. His subsequent *The Social System* (1951) fixed the problem of order at the centre of American sociology. In European sociology the study of inequality and social control remained prominent but, particularly because of the increasing legitimacy of statistically based research methods, the contextual focus characteristic of urban research was diminished.

The Parsonian conception of social order had no place in the older sociology in America or Europe. One of the few points of agreement within the Chicago School was a belief that there was no social order in the modern city, but only an uncoordinated struggle for resources and survival. The question of social order was seen as a political, rather than a sociological issue, as something that might be achieved through political engagement, but which did not presently exist. Whilst not uninterested in inequality, the prime focus was on the bonds within, rather than between, social groups and classes.

The influence of Parsons's normative functionalism to some extent reflected the new political climate after 1945. The Chicagoans had conceived the city as fragmented and chaotic, a site of social unrest:

> cities, particularly the great cities, are in unstable equilibrium. The result is that the vast casual and mobile aggregations which constitute our urban populations are in a state of perpetual agitation, swept by every new wind of doctrine, subject to constant alarms, and in consequence the community is in a chronic condition of crisis (Park, 1967, p. 22).

This apocalyptic view of social disorganisation seemed increasingly out of place in the post-war, planned, Keynesian era of steady economic growth, declining mass migration and muted social conflict. In the new age, the vitality of urban sociology was lost; its theoretical relevance diminished and its political concerns grew more parochial.

Of course, urban sociology never ceased to exist in the USA and specialist scholars continued to work in the field. However, technically, inquiry became increasingly positivistic and issues of urban planning seemed to predominate. Louis Wirth's article 'Urbanism as a Way of Life' (1938), discussed in detailed in Chapter 5, proved an influential starting-point for comparing urban and rural social relations by observing measurable differences. His distinction between urban and rural ways of life fuelled nostalgic debates about 'the decline of community' (e.g. Stein, 1964) and investigation of the personality types of urban dwellers (e.g. Riesman, 1950). Both concerns were infused by the mass-society thesis which, despite some affinity to depictions of the experience of modernity and its prominence in American social science in the 1950s and 1960s, added little to sociological insight. In addition the techniques of urban analysis that in part emerged from the statistical wing of the Chicago School – the ecological analysis of Hawley (1950) for example – while providing useful descriptive material about segregation in American cities, subdued many of the appealing aspects of the pre-war period. Post-war urban sociology in many ways resolved the methodological debate in Chicago between case studies and survey methods in favour of the latter (Bulmer, 1984). Though there continued to be some fascinating ethnographic studies of areas of cities, working-class communities and suburbs mostly, (e.g. Suttles, 1968; Gans, 1962 and 1968a qualitative research became less prestigious and less widely practised than statistical methods.

The substance of urban research became more the investigation of ways of dealing with urban problems, though as an issue of management rather than political reform. Textbooks (e.g. Greer, 1962) and urban manifestos (e.g. Jacobs, 1961) were concerned with improving life in cities, and this was often considered in terms of enhancing community and neighbourliness. However, in America, political developments, in particular the urban riots of the mid-1960s, disturbed the academic *status quo* and brought some insistent questions of justice and order to the fore. Subsequently, analysing conflictual political behaviour became a major endeavour, contributing to dissatisfaction with Parsonian theory.

In Britain, too, changes in preferred methods of investigation coincided with new concerns. In place of contextual study of the interaction between people and their environment came an overriding interest in occupational stratification. In post-war empirical sociology social class, rather than region or neighbourhood, became the central concept integrating sociological subdisciplines. By the 1970s it was joined by a growing concern with gender and racial inequality. Rather than examining how social actions were rooted in specific places, social practices were related to the operations of common, national, class (and later, gender and race) systems. Thus key concerns of pre-war urban sociology receded.

The immediate post-war period saw the proliferation of community studies, increasingly influenced by the concerns of anthropology, a discipline stronger than sociology in the UK. The community-study approach owed relatively little to the 'regional survey' tradition and became concerned predominantly with the internal mechanics of social relationships within small geographical areas. Though deeply and rightly concerned with sociation, research was framed, as in the USA, largely by the contrast between rural order and urban anomie and the project of re-establishing a lost sense of community (see Frankenberg, 1966). Those most interested in social bonding and identity primarily chose rural settlements for their ethnographies – Luogh and Rynamona in County Clare, Ireland, Llansaintffraid Glynceiriog in Wales, Gosforth in England (Arensberg and Kimball, 1940; Frankenberg, 1957; Williams, 1956). The call by Mass

Observation for 'a science of ourselves' (evocative because the British anthropological tradition had previously been largely devoted to exotic peoples of the Empire) was thus to some degree answered. Much good work was done, but it was relatively little appreciated, typically being criticised from a positivist viewpoint for being non-cumulative, unverifiable, and parochial (see Chapter 5).

These inquiries did contribute to a more theoretically informed interest in social class, though the local focus was used simply as a frame. This was true of Stacey's (1960) work on Banbury and also particularly true of the famous study *Coal is Our Life* (Dennis et al., 1956). This report of a Yorkshire colliery village showed how the culture of the miners was rooted in their work and community. In many ways it was a classic example of Le Play's axiom that cultures emerged out of people's relationship to nature in specific geographical milieux. Nonetheless, class, rather than place, was the organising focus of the book.

Stacey and Dennis et al, like other British sociologists, concentrated on the abstract nature of social groups, organisations and institutions, rather than their contextual, spatial and environmental aspects. Before the 1950s social classes had been studied only in specific social settings. Research was on the working class in London, or poverty in York. The new approaches to social class abstracted from the particular places in which people lived. Social mobility research was an early example. David Glass and his associates (Glass, 1954) reoriented sociological interest towards analyses of the mobility between classes at the national level, using national surveys. This trend was not instantaneous. Still in the mid-1960s social mobility was frequently related to spatial mobility. Likewise, David Lockwood's influential explanation of variations in 'working-class images of society' emphasised the importance of community as a vital determinant of people's values (Lockwood, 1966). Workers living in one-industry towns tended to be more class-conscious and oppositional than those living in new housing estates alongside the middle classes. It was symbolic, however, that the famous 'affluent worker' study of the 1960s (Goldthorpe et al., 1968, 1969), which examined the social and political attitudes of car workers in Luton, was interpreted as applying to affluent workers anywhere, the evidence rarely being put in its particular local context.

By the 1970s social environment played little or no part in analyses of social class. Moreover, in social theory, a structuralist analysis inspired by the French Marxist, Althusser, emerged, maintaining that class analysis should be focused not upon people but upon the forces affecting class positions – the 'empty slots' into which people were fitted. Social class became more closely related to purely economic processes affecting the nature of work and employment relations than to wider social milieux of everyday life, social networks and residence. Structuralism left a legacy in many branches of empirical sociology. In social mobility research John Goldthorpe's (1980) influential analysis depended entirely upon a national random sample, collected in the early 1970s, without concern for regional variation or spatial mobility (see also Payne, 1987).

The achieved supremacy of the sample survey and its associated statistical techniques undermined contextual accounts of class. It is not accidental that histories of empirical sociology in Britain tend to write Whiggish accounts of the survey method, a story of its development and triumph as a tool of professional, scientific sociologists who need no longer have truck with the vague, expansive and amateurish activities of a Geddes or of Mass Observation (e.g. Abrams, 1968; Kent, 1981).

The same tendency is apparent in the British sociology of the family, originally an offshoot of community studies. Young and Willmott of the Institute of Community Studies, set out to examine in the 1950s how family relationships were affected by migration from inner London to an Essex suburb. Their research involved detailed investigation of specific local communities, to see how family organisation was related to the social and environmental milieux, thus following clearly in the Le Play tradition. In related work by Elizabeth Bott (1957) the social networks of marriage partners in the neighbourhood were the primary influences on relationships within the household. Where couples were strongly integrated into networks outside the household, gender roles inside the household were more segregated.

This research suggested that families and households could best be understood in relationship to their encompassing, external, social environment. In the 1960s this view began to be undermined. Willmott and Young argued that the social environment was not, in fact, especially significant in shaping family structures. Apparent differences in family type in old working-class areas and on newer estates could be explained simply because traditional social arrangements had not had time to re-emerge. For them, whilst social environment seemed relatively unimportant, class became vital, hence their contrast between extended working-class and nuclear middle-class families. Willmott and Young later became even less interested in the neighbourhood context of family life, adopting random-sample-surveys designs for their *Symmetrical Family* inquiry (Young and Willmott, 1975). As with social mobility research, the survey replaced the local case study. Specific urban contexts became incidental.

One of the crucial concerns of both the Chicago School and the early British urban sociologists was their sense of political engagement. On both sides of the Atlantic social research continued to be wedded to a politics of social democratic reform, by and large supporting state intervention to ameliorate the position of those to whom the market offered least. However, increasingly, sociologists found themselves agitating less at the local level and becoming more concerned to lobby central government. Whilst the Chicago School was preoccupied by thinking about how to reform the city of Chicago and had a very close association with leading local politicians, and whilst inter-war British urban sociologists attempted to improve local communities, the post-war sociologists deemed national reports the most effective way to pressurise central government. Local studies might be dismissed as unrepresentative, while national survey research carried more weight, especially since Government Departments tended to hold statistical knowledge in highest esteem.

By the late 1960s the sociological wheel had turned full circle. Georg Simmel, in his account of 'The Field of Sociology' had argued that sociology should not simply concern itself with 'definable, consistent structures such as the state and the family, the guild and the church, social classes and organisations based on common interests' (Simmel, 1950, p. 9) but rather should make the study of 'sociation' central. By the 1960s, however, mainstream sociology had returned almost exclusively to these institutions. Urban context and the moral order implicit in everyday actions were consequently neglected. National studies of class structures based on sample surveys replaced local studies of inequality and social interaction. With prospects for urban sociology bleak, the 1970s and 1980s saw an attempt at its reconstitution to fit the revised state of the social sciences. Thus emerged 'the new urban sociology.'

## 2.3   The 'new urban sociology'

Urban sociology survived, in the USA especially, despite being out of step with post-war theoretical developments in sociology. Much of its output consisted of statistical description of urban conditions, offering some informative basis for addressing urban problems. It also continued to explore questions of city growth and, particularly, to explore a contrast between urban and rural life. Despite some exceptional studies, urban sociology became something of an intellectual backwater. This tranquil existence was fractured by a series of devastating critiques of its theoretical failings. The most famous and original was the Marxist critique of Manuel Castells in *The Urban Question* (1977), which condemned the older traditions of urban sociology and sought to reconstitute it on an alternative basis. Castells's critique coincided with the resurgence and widespread adoption of Marxist analysis in Europe. Once again, general trends in social theory propelled urban studies onto new terrain. The concerns of neo-Marxism included isolating the specifically capitalist aspects of economic life, stressing the role of classes as historical agents and a critical rejection of the way in which welfare arrangements were socially incorporating the working class without significant redistribution of wealth or power. The particular version of neo-Marxism associated with the French philosopher, Louis Althusser, proved most influential in the attempt to develop a more rigorous and theoretical 'new urban sociology'. This provided a starting-point not only for Marxists but also for some Weberians, including Peter Saunders in his book *Social Theory and the Urban Question* (1981). He, too, sought to pull down the final curtain on the older traditions of urban sociology.

The starting-point of the critique was the argument that a scientific discipline needed to have a proper 'theoretical object'. In this claim both Castells and Saunders were heavily indebted to Althusser, who argued that what distinguished scientific from 'ideological' works was the way that the latter began with taken-for-granted notions whilst the former constituted their concerns theoretically. The creation of a scientific discipline required a distinct 'theoretical object' specific to it. Within this framework it was argued that all existing urban sociology was ideological since it began with commonsense concepts such as community, the city, or urban problems, which it was unable to ground theoretically.

Urban sociology proved an easy target for criticism from this epistemological viewpoint. What was the specific 'theoretical object' of urban sociology? Was it the city? If so, there were distinctive problems in specifying social activities which only took place in cities. Forms of industry, patterns of interaction, leisure activities, class conflict, and so forth could be seen in the city and the countryside. What possible reason was there then, for distinguishing the city from the countryside?

Perhaps, instead, the theoretical object of urban sociology might be a concern with 'space', and the way in which spatial arrangements affected social life? But it proved very difficult to show how space itself – taken as physical distance between natural and social objects – could really help sociological explanation. To give a simple example, close physical proximity to others may make you very fond of them, or heartily tired of them. The mere fact of physical proximity seems far less important in explaining people's actions than the type of social and personal relationships between them.

The critique developed by Castells and Saunders was extremely powerful. Urban sociology has no theoretical object, and it is difficult to know how one might be constructed. Castells attempted to reconstruct urban sociology by integrating it with his analysis of the contradictions of capitalist societies. He argued that in late capitalism cities had a distinctive role not in the process of production, the usual Marxist emphasis, but rather as centres of 'collective consumption'. Collective consumption referred to forms of services collectively provided, usually by the state – mass housing, transport, health facilities, and so forth. Because collective consumption is geared to people living within a certain spatial radius, it has a spatial referent. Moreover, the provision of such services was identified as a source of political mobilisation, as it spawned urban social movements, protest groups aiming to improve urban conditions through contesting the existing pattern of collective consumption. Castells maintained that because these protests were linked to the reproduction of labour power, they might have revolutionary potential if linked into working-class movements.

Castells's account initially appeared to solve some problems both for urban sociology and for Marxist political practice. Urban sociology acquired a theoretical object, collective consumption, while Marxism was nourished by the notion that disparate urban protests of the 1970s, squatters' movements, tenants' movements, and the like, were connected to class struggle. Academically, the analysis of cities specifically as sites for the reproduction of labour power became the distinctive feature of 'the new urban sociology'. Symptomatic was a new journal, the *International Journal of Urban and Regional Research*, launched in 1977 and heavily influenced by Castells and French Marxism, though open also to other materialist theoretical perspectives. Various trend reports around 1980 (e.g. Zukin, 1980; Lebas, 1982) perceived enormous potential in the Marxist approach of Castells as a way to reinvigorate urban sociology. Castells was a vehement critic of culturalist approaches to the city like that of Wirth, of evolutionary accounts of urban development and of spatially determinist theories. His alternative emphasised the changing nature of economic production and the contemporary role of the state in organising consumption. His concern with urban social movements, as vehicles for social opposition, had practical political ramifications. Above all it promised a theoretically coherent framework for urban studies.

Ultimately Castells's arguments raised as many problems as they solved. Politically, urban social movements proved difficult to fuse with Marxist politics, at least outside the developing countries. Throughout Europe, communist parties failed to mobilise on the basis of urban social movements and, in his later work, Castells (1983) repudiated the vision of an association between class struggle and urban protest. Although Castells did help to introduce Marxist concepts to urban sociology, in the course of the 1980s production processes, rather than collective consumption, became the focus of Marxist scholarship and the new urban sociology subsided. David Harvey, Doreen Massey, Dick Walker, Allen Scott and others developed a Marxist-informed political economy in which the concept of collective consumption played little part.

Castells's formulation of the concept of collective consumption proved more popular in Britain amongst non-Marxist writers like Patrick Dunleavy and Peter Saunders, though they appropriated it critically. As Saunders pointed out, collective consumption is not a purely 'urban' process. The collective consumption of education and health services occurs in both city and countryside. Furthermore, Saunders observed, not all the consumption practices within cities are collective, many are private, purchased by individuals. Saunders, following Dunleavy, used this distinction as a way of identifying social groups possessing distinctive material and political interests by virtue of the extent to which they depended upon either collective or private consumption. Hence Saunders proposed that the correct focus of urban sociology should be consumption in all its forms, and that it should lose any residual spatial reference. This raised another question, however. Why not abandon urban sociology entirely and develop a new subdiscipline, the 'sociology of consumption', for such a project seemed not to require the ideas, empirical findings or theories of earlier urban sociology?

The 'new urban sociology' was very challenging and it did manage to inspire empirical study and theoretical analysis of some of the most pressing political issues of the 1970s and 1980s. The concept of collective consumption implicitly addressed the role of, and changes within, the welfare state, the declining quality and recommodification of services being probably the major social issue of the period. It directed attention to urban movements and the mobilisation of political actors around issues of urban planning. Because of its Marxist derivation it also encouraged a much deeper analysis of the relationship between city life and capital accumulation. Nevertheless, it consciously renounced the intellectual traditions of urban sociology, which contain more of value than was appreciated. In particular, while accepting that it is not possible to constitute 'the urban' as a theoretical object, excessive concern with defining 'the urban' distorted the history of urban sociology. For, in fact, few urban sociologists ever claimed that the city was a theoretical entity. Park, for instance, was quite clear about this when stating that the city 'was a laboratory, or clinic, in which human nature and social processes may be profitably studied' (Park, 1967, p. 46). He and his colleagues were concerned with social bonds in a fragmented world, and cities were arenas in which such a topic might be examined. What motivated the Chicago School and the early British sociologists was, rather, a broad set of social and political concerns about the nature of contemporary social life.

## 2.4 Conclusion

The critique on which the new urban sociology was based is, therefore, both true and misleading. Urban sociology does not have a clear theoretical object, and it is not simply the study of cities, understood as physical units with large populations. Instead it should be conceived as a broader inquiry into the nature of contemporary social relations in their contextual settings. It has been part of a sociological venture that concentrates on the ways in which institutions and practices combine in a totalising fashion. The attempt has been to explore the interrelationship between institutional domains: 'place, work and folk' for the admirers of Le Play; 'production, consumption and exchange' for the Marxists; perhaps race, class and family for many of the American empirical urbanists. It was not the particular characteristics of urban spaces that justified such inquiries; rather, it was the appropriateness of urban areas as sites of research where sociologists could examine in considerable detail the interdependence of the social institutions that form everyday experience. In many ways synthetic theories were being formulated and tested empirically in confined areas where context could be appreciated.

Because urban sociology brings the study of different kinds of institutions, mechanisms and structures together, in empirical exploration, it has remained a valuable, if ambivalent and discontinuous, field of knowledge. Schematically, its oscillations can be considered as responses to external changes in social theory and contemporary political issues which intersect with an internal technical dynamic.

In our view, the core concerns have been pursued primarily in the process of investigating abstract theories of modern society. More than many other subdisciplines, the rhythm of development of urban sociology has been determined by the concerns of social theory, particularly the attempt to understand the nature of modern, individual and collective, experience. Urban sociology recurrently responds to developments in social theory. This is one sense in which the city may be considered as a sociological laboratory, for it is regularly used to address, to some degree empirically, particularly those matters concerned with the experience of modernity.

Urban sociology has also responded regularly to changing political agendas and priorities. This is partly because abstract social theory itself is also guided by the vagaries of contemporary political predicaments. In the time of the Chicago School emphasis was on the political problems emanating from explosive industrial-city growth, mass migration, and the concentration of apparently rootless, and dangerous, people. Simultaneously in the UK, urbanists depicted urban poverty and inequality during the years of the Depression, advocating state intervention, planning and the preservation of community as political remedies. In the post-war era the priority seemed to become more one of effective planning, management and control of urban living. Urban managerialist approaches, for instance, explored issues regarding the routines of state administration and what an interventionist commitment can do to mitigate inequality and inadequate standards of living. This was disrupted in the USA initially by the civil rights movement and violent urban protest which brought 'the urban question' to the fore as politicians sought some response. At this stage urban sociology took a much closer interest in urban conflict, the actors and the social movements involved in promoting urban change. Subsequently, the issue of the future of welfare provision and debates about the merits of privatisation *versus* state intervention became a key contemporary issue. The new urban sociology of the 1970s offered a diagnosis of the pacifying influence of welfare, the stifling of dissent and the faltering progress of class struggle.

The field of political programmes and commitments raises the question of the relationship between urban sociology and urban studies. Urban studies is a sphere of rather disconnected interdisciplinary inquiries into various aspects of city organisation. We see its limited coherence arising as an ineradicable consequence of the institutional structure of local government. In most countries including the UK and the USA, cities and towns are political jurisdictions with considerable numbers of citizens who have certain shared concerns. Problems arise in coordinating·

and facilitating an irreducible level of often impersonal social interaction in urbanised societies. This is the sphere of urban studies which cannot be eliminated precisely because cities are themselves political institutions requiring understanding and systematic knowledge collection in order to facilitate the management of social life at a localised level. One distinctive attribute of urban sociology is that it tries to introduce some theoretical themes that make some sense of these practices, their determinants and their effects. The mission is a totalising one. The urban sociologist is the intermediary between social theory and the urban problem.

There is also a subdued, but nevertheless discernible internal dynamic to urban sociology that arises from technical developments in modes of social investigation. We have argued that changes in the prestige of different kinds of method are an important factor explaining the history of urban sociology. Before the Chicago School urban investigations were either based on histories of cities or on simple observation. The Chicago School pioneered both systematic urban ethnography and statistical methods of ecological analysis. There has been some oscillation ever since between case-study approaches, including community studies, and statistical approaches, increasingly of the sample-survey type. Currently greater confidence has been expressed in the use of imaginative description and hermeneutic interpretation of meanings. Despite the variety of methods deployed there have developed aspects of what Kuhn would describe as 'normal science', where specialised techniques for inquiring into social segregation and patterns of sociability have steadily improved providing the basis for reliable analysis. These are pursued constantly and are regularly redeployed to deal with pressing political issues of urban inequality and social or cultural disorganisation. Chapters 4 and 7 deal with the former, 5 and 6 with the latter.

It is our contention, then, that the contribution of older forms of urban sociology has been somewhat misunderstood and that there are a number of themes within it, particularly in the Chicago School and Simmel, that deserve further development, especially those of modernity, sociation and political engagement. From a rather fragmentary and minor British tradition we can also draw on concerns with social inequality and a structural–contextual approach to place. Of course, early urban sociology had grave defects. Among these were an almost total ignorance of political economy, both of the wider logic of the system of capitalist production and the role of the state. The next chapter considers how recent scholarship, much of it developed by human geographers, has attended to that lacuna.

# 3 Cities and Uneven Economic Development

Though best seen as an extended inquiry into the relationship between capitalism and modernity, urban sociology has characteristically concentrated on cities as sites of modernity, neglecting the way in which capitalist economic systems structure cities. In this chapter we draw on the work of urban geographers to show how cities need to be placed in the broader context of the world capitalist system. Such contextualisation, we argue, is important in specifying the relationship between different cities, and between cities and rural areas, so allowing the urban sociologist to avoid the mistake of seeing cities as self-contained objects with clear boundaries – as exemplars of a universal modernity. The significance of examining the economic bases of urban form is that it allows urban specificity to be comprehended, in terms of the particular role which different cities play within the worldwide economic system.

It is, however, not easy to register the importance of the economic context of cities. There is no consensus as to how capitalism operates as an economic system, and in particular how it operates over space, between places, and hence how it affects urban development. This chapter clarifies differing views of the relationship between economic systems and urban development, in order to assess their value in placing cities in their context. It is structured around the way different writers emphasise the temporal or spatial dimensions of urban differentiation and uneven spatial development.

In section 3.1 we consider approaches, largely non-Marxist, which adopt a *temporal* focus, where cities are related to particular stages of historical development, but are rarely analysed in terms of their spatial relation to each other. The principal axiom is that cities evolve in line with broader economic development. This evolutionary perspective is typical of the early urban economists, such as Alfred Weber, Jane Jacobs,

34

Peter Hall and others. The problem with such accounts is that they tend to assume that there is only one type of urban development, which all cities from whatever culture follow, and hence they ignore the diversity and specificity of cities.

This leads to the work of urban geographers who have concentrated their research on the analysis of urban differentiation. Section 3.2 examines Marxist theories of uneven development whose focus is a *spatial* one, where cities are seen as occupying specific places within a worldwide capitalist economic system. Within this broad perspective we evaluate four rather different ways in which such differentiation is explained. The first version is the 'New International Division of Labour Theory', which can be seen as the most important contemporary application of Wallerstein's 'World Systems Theory'. One of the problems with world systems theory is its ahistorical analysis, its inattention to the significance of social conflict on uneven development, and its tendency to ignore dynamic and changing forms of uneven development. Then we consider another Marxist account, that associated with the early work of the David Harvey, which is explicitly concerned with the historical specificity of differing processes (or 'circuits') of capital accumulation, and with the significance of social struggle. In Section 3.2.3 we contrast Harvey's account with that offered by Doreen Massey, which places greater importance on industrial restructuring and has produced a well-documented account of contemporary urban change in Britain and other advanced industrial countries. Both Harvey and Massey incline towards a certain economic reductionism. Finally, in Section 3.2.4 we examine the accounts derived from the 'Regulation School' which has become increasingly influential in urban studies.

## 3.1 Evolutionary theories of cities

In the work of Simmel and the Chicago School cities represented the new and the modern, epitomes of the emergent economic and social order produced by industrial capitalism. Implicitly they drew upon an evolutionary model of economic change. The city of Chicago, in particular, was taken as representative of the modern industrial city, and attempts to apply the concentric-ring model (developed by Burgess and modified by others) to other industrial cities were legion. Within this frame of thought the city was seen as the product of the elaborate division of labour characteristic of modern industrial society. Cities owed their economic role to their pivotal place in this new industrial order as centres of commerce, sites of production, and bases for the most specialised economic activities. In this line of reasoning the city was the most advanced manifestation of an evolutionary process of economic change, 'the workshops of civilisation' in Park's words (see Harvey 1973, p. 195)

Evolutionary approaches to urban development argued that the industrial city was the culmination of a long evolutionary process, stretching back to the earliest historical periods. Lampard (1965) distinguished two urban epochs in human history. These were, first, 'primordial urbanisation' where settlements first emerged in the years between 15 000 BC and 4000 BC, as a collective form of organisation additional to the usual migratory agricultural activities. The importance of the second period of 'definitive urbanisation', which began in Mesopotomia after 4000 BC, was that cities developed as fixed sites, in which 'by means of its capacity to generate, store, and utilise social saving, the definitive city artefact is capable of transplanting itself out of its native uterine environments' (Lampard 1965: p. 523). This period of 'definitive urbanisation' is itself split into two epochs, before and after 1700 AD. In the first of these, cities were centres for a hinterland and existed in a stable hierarchy, in which hamlets formed a hinterland for villages, villages for towns, towns for cities, and cities for capital cities. Urban expansion was limited since cities were essentially parasitic on a limited agricultural economy. After 1700, the industrial city emerged as a dynamic force, able to increase in size because of the ability of economic production based in cities to sever their dependency on agriculture.

The industrial city was hence seen as the locus of the new industrial society and as ushering in a new period in history when urban growth could continue at a vastly expanded level. Yet since the 1930s the industrial societies which cities were seen to embody have themselves been transformed by deindustrialisation – manufacturing industries in many urban heartlands have collapsed; service industries have arisen and industrial production has developed in new, rural, areas, appearing to cut the apparently close connection between cities and industry on which the evolutionary ideas were based.

Attempts to apply evolutionary lines of thinking have persisted into the present day and have taken a new turn as industrial economies have changed. A good example is the work of Peter Hall who has developed the evolutionary model of the city to encompass deindustrialisation as well as industrialisation (see Hall and Hay, 1980; Hall, 1988). Hall begins by arguing that the urban system has been massively transformed in recent decades. Drawing upon American evidence he argues that four linked processes have undermined the centrality of the large, industrial urban conurbation which characterised earlier periods of industrial capitalism. These are:

1. suburbanisation, where urban growth takes place in suburban rather than central urban areas;
2. de-urbanisation, where the urban population reduces relative to the population of rural and non-urban areas;
3. the contraction of the largest cities;
4. the rise of new regions and the decline of old.

Hall explains this transformation by distinguishing six evolutionary stages through which cities go as industrial economies change and decline. His emphasis is upon the way in which, as regions industrialise, cities develop in size and concentration. After a period of time, however, any industrial area begins to stagnate as innovation occurs elsewhere. Hence cities begin to decline. Because this process of industrial growth and fall is inevitable, all cities pass through the same six-stage cycle.

The six stages Hall specifies are divided into two groups. The first three stages occur during industrialisation, the last three when deindustrialisation begins to take effect in any given region:

1. The stage of 'centralisation during loss' happens during early industrialisation. People migrate from the country to the city, leading to a growing urban population, but the overall population in any region is in net decline as more people leave the region overall.
2. As industrialisation continues, the overall proportion of people living in cities within regions increases.
3. 'Relative centralisation' occurs when the city stretches over its boundaries and begins to develop suburbs. Nevertheless the proportion of urban dwellers continues to grow. This is the type of city which was the focus of the Chicago School studies, where there were large and dense urban populations and suburbs had begun to emerge.

Hall's argument, however, is that urban evolution has now continued beyond this, and a process of urban decline marks a new stage from that studied by the Chicago writers:

4. Suburbs begin to grow faster than the urban core, so that 'relative decentralisation' occurs as people move to the outer reaches of cities.
5. Starting about 1900 in the largest European cities (but generally much more recently) 'absolute decentralisation' occurs as people begin to move out of the inner city as it becomes increasingly specialised around office and commercial functions.
6. The entire city begins to decline as people begin to move out to the rural areas as deindustrialisation proceeds.

This process of 'counter-urbanisation' has been much debated since the 1960s (Fielding, 1982). The period of industrial urban expansion, which earlier writers had expected to continue unabated, gives way, in Hall's view, to a situation of urban decline. ✗

Hall is wary about applying his evolutionary model. It is derived from research in the USA chronicling the decline of large cities from the 1960s. In Western Europe there are different patterns, and 'the different countries' urban systems . . . display marked differences from one another' (Hall, 1988, p. 116). In Britain and Germany the largest cities were declining in population by the 1970s as Hall would have expected. However in France, Italy and the Benelux countries they were not.

Although many cities are seeing significant population loss, there are a number of difficulties with an evolutionary model such as Hall's. First, there is a problem with the way that Hall, in common with other writers referring to the phenomenon of 'counter-urbanisation', characterises the decline of cities in the current period. There is no doubt that in many parts of the developed world population and employment is moving from central urban locations, but whether this should be seen as testifying to the decline of cities rather than their further expansion into new areas is a moot point. If fixed boundaries are drawn round a city at any one point in time, it is always possible that when the population within these boundaries decreases this may be interpreted as urban decline. In reality, however, the city may be expanding outside these boundaries and increasing in significance. Scott, for instances, emphasises the continuing urbanisation process in capitalist societies (Scott, 1988a, p. 63). ✗

Second, there is a problem about generalising from Hall's study of urban trends in twentieth-century Western Europe. It could be argued that contemporary cities are becoming increasingly differentiated according to their role in the world economy, which makes it unhelpful to generalise about a single evolutionary path for all. Five prominent urban types stand out – Third World cities, global cities, declining industrial cities, new industrial districts, and socialist cities – all of which have a different character.

*Third-world cities* are themselves heterogeneous, but tend to possess a number of distinctive features. They are 'over-urbanised' (Timberlake, 1987). This means that they tend to be extremely large relative to the population of the particular country – a result of the fact that inward capitalist investment often focuses upon these capital city sites, a phenomenon described as 'urban bias'. They also tend to be 'dualistic', with major divisions between the formal and informal economy, between city and country, and between social groups. This dualistic format is related, in many cases, to the colonial legacy of 'urban apartheid' (Abu-Lughod, 1980; King, 1990), where colonial rulers lived in separate parts of the city and were subject to a different jurisdiction from that applying to native dwellers.

*'Global cities'* (or world cities) are ones which increasingly depend on international financial services and are linked to the circulation and realisation of wealth. They are frequently the location of corporate headquarters of major multinational enterprises and are the sites of what Massey (1988) refers to as 'control functions', whence the control and management of corporate enterprise is directed. London, New York, Frankfurt and Tokyo are examples of this type of city. They tend to be large, centralised (with a distinct urban core specialising in international financial services), and contain both an élite group of workers and lower-paid servicing workers (Kasarda, 1988).

*Older industrial cities*, now in precipitate decline following the collapse of urban manufacturing, constitute the third type. Britain has many of the most dramatic examples – Glasgow, Liverpool (a trading rather than industrial city) and Bradford being especially prominent. Other noted examples have been found in the North-east and mid-West of America (Detroit, Buffalo, Cleveland), and in Germany (Essen, Duisberg). These cities are characterised by decay and dereliction, high levels of unemployment, poor housing conditions and so forth.

*'New industrial districts'* have recently been given a great deal of attention. These are distinctively *new* urban developments (colonial cities, global cities, and older industrial cities being adaptations of older urban forms), which are not organised around an urban core with a suburban hinterland, but are more decentralised and cover a larger area. Here much development takes place round neighbourhood centres, and around the

major transport networks, in the form of out-of-town shopping malls, employment centres and suburban housing. Examples include the Los Angeles area of the USA, and parts of the Home Counties in South-east England.

Cities in socialist countries have also experienced dynamics very different from those in the capitalist world. They have tended to grow more slowly than their capitalist counterparts. Many socialist regimes have been explicitly anti-urban (Forbes and Thrift, 1987). The immediate post-revolutionary period tended to freeze, and in some cases reduce, urban population growth. These cities have been subject to greater planning and zoning.

The foregoing typology is not exhaustive. Many urban centres fall into several of these categories. The point is that it is impossible to see one form of city as archetypal of the current economic and social order in the way in which Chicago was taken as an exemplar of industrial capitalism in the early twentieth-century. It is not true that all cities experience the same logic of development, but rather that some cities obtain distinct roles in the world economy, and once established they become differentiated from other cities occupying different roles within the same environment.

At the heart of the analysis is the fact that cities exist within a wider world system. The dynamics of this world system affect the way that cities develop and decline. A recognition of this belies a linear historical view of urban differentiation – where different urban forms are reflections of the specific period which any given city has reached in an evolutionary urban cycle – implying instead that spatial dynamics of the world system profoundly shape urban form. It is to a greater consideration of these processes that we now turn.

## 3.2   Competing theories of uneven development

We have shown that evolutionary views fail to recognise the specificity of cities and the distinct roles they perform in a wider world economy. Let us consider in greater detail how these differences are sustained by spatial processes of uneven development. Various theories address this issue. Many are of Marxist provenance, emerging from the revived intellectual reputation of Marxist analysis in the social sciences in the 1970s. The effect was to focus attention on the specifically capitalist mechanisms operating to create the geography of economic life. Thus, rather than

beginning from the nature of industrialism, as did much orthodox eco- ✳
nomic sociology and geography in the post-war period, the central
concerns were ones of capitalist accumulation, competition, exploitation
and restructuring. When applied to the area of urban studies this constituted a more rigorous and detailed approach to the economic bases of
urban systems.

Theories of uneven development, however, are bedevilled by a number of problems. Since these problems recur many times in the following
pages it is worth listing them briefly:

1. Spatial analyses of uneven development may be *ahistorical,* failing fully
   to deal with its historically specific forms.
2. These theories may present *static* approaches, where the explanatory
   weight of the theory is geared to explaining how uneven development between places is sustained. It then becomes difficult to explain
   why some places are able to change their economic standing, possibly
   against the odds, the theory being insufficiently attuned to specificity.
3. Theories may be unable to register the significance of human agency
   in affecting processes of uneven development, particularly in the form
   of social conflict.
4. Such theories may be over-determinist, trying to explain more about
   the character of places or cities than can usefully be derived from the
   process of uneven development itself.

### 3.2.1   *The new international division of labour thesis*

One of the earliest and most original of the new accounts of the contemporary spatial division of labour was presented by Frobel, Heinrichs and
Kreye in their *New International Division of Labour,* (NIDL) first published
in German in 1977. Their concern was with the growing internationalisation of *production* since 1945 and its effects on the world economic
system. Their main point was that manufacturing production processes
which had once been undertaken in core countries in Western Europe
were increasingly located in the Third World, which as peripheral countries within the world economy had previously concentrated on agricultural produce and raw materials for export to the advanced countries.
Whereas in the 1950s Western Europe imported scarcely any manufactured goods, by 1975 much of the production in certain industrial sectors,
like textiles and electrical goods, was carried out overseas, financed and
controlled by metropolitan companies.

The development of the world economy has increasingly created conditions . . . in which the survival of more and more companies can only be assured through the relocation of production to new industrial sites, where labour-power is cheap to buy, abundant and well-disciplined; in short, through the transnational reorganisation of production (Frobel *et al.*, 1980, p. 15).

This process seemed to mark a new phase in the relationships between core and periphery which Wallerstein (1974) had observed. The prime reason for the emergence of the NIDL according to Frobel *et al.*, was the change in the labour process as levels of skill involved in manufacturing production were reduced sharply. In such circumstances, a vast pool of unemployed or underemployed unskilled labour could be exploited on a world scale. The terms of employment of unskilled labour in Third World countries were especially favourable to capital: wages are much lower, working conditions poorer, trade unions weaker, labour forces easier to discipline, etc., than in the West. The improvement in methods of communication and transport made it possible to exploit these new reserves of labour. Other factors such as tax concessions to multinationals, absence of pollution control, and the absence of health and safety legislation enhance the attractiveness of these locations. Also, certain other conditions have to be fulfilled to make overseas sites acceptable: transport costs which depend on the size and weight of the product; the political stability of overseas political regimes; property law; the corruptibility of officials, etc. (see Frobel *et al.*, 1980, pp. 145–7, for a list). But, where such conditions are met, it becomes profitable to transfer machinery to sites outside Europe to take advantage of favourable labour conditions.

The ramifications of this new international division of labour were thought very considerable, both for metropolitan and peripheral countries. One was the changing industrial structure in metropolitan countries, especially the decline of manufacturing employment. 'Deindustrialisation', as the process was first known, had implications also for levels and types of occupational opportunity, with fewer skilled and unskilled manufacturing jobs available at home.

The NIDL thesis was intellectually of enormous importance. It brought to scholarly attention a new form of internationalisation of the capitalist economy, explained recent changes in patterns of employment and indicated how multinational and transnational corporations could exploit spatial differences in labour markets in conjunction with a new technical division of labour within particular industrial sectors. It offered a relatively simple explanation of the phenomenon of deindustrialisation. Derived in part from the neo-Marxist world-systems-theory of Wallerstein it did not depend on any particularly sophisticated economic theory. As Frobel *et al.* express their premises:

> The determining force, the prime mover, behind capitalist development is therefore the valorisation and accumulation process of capital, and not, for example, any alleged tendency towards the extension and deepening of the wage labour/capital relation or the 'unfolding' of the productive forces (Frobel *et al.*, 1980, p. 25).

From that point of view the dynamic was mostly one of profit-seeking and minimising labour costs in deskilled production processes.

What is of particular concern to us is the implication of the NIDL for urban systems. The NIDL thesis can be used, in some ways, to explain the differentiation of cities in different parts of the world. Rather than see cities inevitably decline as an evolutionary concomitant of deindustrialisation, as Hall suggests, the NIDL thesis is able to explain the differential fate of cities in various parts of the globe. At one level, the prime position of Western capital cities could be explained by their coordinating role in the new international division of labour. At another level the growth of large cities, such as Mexico City, in the periphery could also be explained by the role they played as sites for the new decentralised production.

Other important work has focused upon the impacts of NIDL on Western cities and urban systems. The collection of essays by Smith and Feagin, *The Capitalist City*, (1987), perhaps offers the best access to work in this vein. In some old manufacturing towns, such as Buffalo, New York, USA, the removal of production to peripheral locations has led to the collapse of employment (Perry, 1987). In Buffalo employment in manufacturing fell from 200 000 in the 1950s to 100 000 by the early 1980s. In other, often neighbouring, cities, economic expansion – particularly in the service sector – has followed the consolidation of new controlling activities in the NIDL.

It is perhaps because the NIDL thesis is so closely specified in terms of *manufacturing* that it has been applied most often by US and British scholars, for it is in the USA and UK that deindustrialisation has been most severe as old manufacturing towns have been affected detrimentally. There the very force of a description of a changing local economic situation and its obvious impact upon employment opportunities, living standards and social relations is sufficient to demonstrate the effects of corporate restructuring in a global economy. However, since many countries have not deindustrialised, and since most formal economic activity is in the service sector in all Western societies, the overall impact of economic transformations on cities is not fully grasped.

Frobel *et al.* were heavily criticised, partly by people unsympathetic to world system theory (see Gottdiener and Komninos, 1989, *passim*; Hill, 1987; Cohen, 1987). Cohen advanced a comprehensive critique of the general proposition of the NIDL thesis, seeing it as conceptually weak, historically inadequate and empirically exaggerated. Conceptually, Cohen argued that the thesis was excessively economistic, derived from the logic of capital accumulation at the expense of social struggles and that there was too much emphasis on labour costs as against technological innova-tion. Historically, he claimed, there was nothing very new about the international division of labour, for there had been many phases in the past – mercantilism and imperialism among them. Finally, Cohen argued that the numbers concerned were not so enormous. In 1980 only about 4 million workers were employed by multinational companies in all the New Industrial Countries, World Export Zones and world factories. That figure compared with around 40 million in the West and was much the same as the amount of migration to the oil-producing countries in the mid-1970s. Indeed, Cohen was concerned to understand these move-ments in the context of labour migration more generally. There were also empirical objections. It became clear that only some industrial sectors would be fit for restructuring in accordance with the NIDL thesis and counter-tendencies were discovered even within industrial sectors appar-ently meeting the preconditions identified in the thesis (Cho, 1985; Scott, 1988b).

There are three main problems with the NIDL thesis as a tool to analyse urban change. First, it is economistic, since it is incapable of systematically analysing anything other than economic change. As a result it gave few insights into changes internal to any particular city, and can only indicate the broad views of a city's general prosperity. It thus says little about process such as suburbanisation, social segregation or housing provision.

Second, it ignores human agency; in particular there was an assump-tion that jobs, not people, were mobile, and hence that deskilled work would be moved to peripheral locations. This simplistic assumption precludes the possibility that unskilled labour may migrate to existing urban centres, or to growing urban areas in developed countries. The migration of Hispanic workers to south-west USA, for instance, has been of major significance in the development of the Californian economy, pointing to the variety of possible strategies which firms can use to find suitable labour for jobs. The decisions of particular firms are not structural necessities, but are partly choices in the light of a number of alternatives.

Finally, it has problems explaining why some cities were able to carve out particular places for themselves in the NIDL and others were not. In other words it is insufficiently attuned to the way in which urban actors can create a role for a particular place in the NIDL. Why are some manufacturing cities better able than others to readjust to the NIDL and change the basis of their local economies? Lancaster, in the UK, for instance, deindustrialised much earlier and faster than would be expected given its economic base in the 1950s (Murgatroyd and Urry, 1985). The role of corporate actors and local political forces in affecting any city's economic position, even given the broad economic changes sketched out by the NIDL thesis, is largely ignored. While persuasive descriptions of local economic change could be offered the roles of the state and politics were always included as historically contingent responses. The theoretical link between the activities of the capitalist corporation and the political apparatuses of national or local state was absent. Explicitly considered links occurred usually only if the local state had fiscal problems because major employers were closing down their operations. This would encourage them to offer incentives to private firms either to persuade them to stay or to attract new inward investment. Similarly, at the level of local popular resistance, although urban social movements, community groups, etc., were perceived as organising opposition (e.g. Fainstein, 1987), there was no *theoretical* basis for appreciating their significance. These limits were indeed partly recognised by Smith and Tardanico (1987) in their attempts to improve the understanding of the reproduction of labour power within this school of thought. Failings in this respect are partly the result of exaggerating the mobility of capital. The NIDL thesis would lead one to expect much higher levels of geographical mobility among firms than actually occurs, partly, as the 'Californian School' considered below would contend, because they underestimate the importance of economic networks and the benefits of agglomeration.

### 3.2.2 David Harvey, the second circuit of capital and urbanisation

In the 1970s David Harvey attempted an ambitious theoretical approach to the analysis of uneven development, derived from a new appreciation of Marx's economic theory and its implications for urban growth. In many ways it offered a powerful contrast to the NIDL thesis, since it tried to build a theory which is historically sensitive, aware of urban specificity, and deliberately emphasising the importance of social conflict for urban development.                                                                      ✗

Harvey's starting-point was to develop Marx's own analysis of capital accumulation and draw out the implications for the urban structure. This primarily involved an examination of landed property and its role in capital accumulation, a subject about which Marx said relatively little. In Harvey's early work (1973) he specified the distinctive nature of land as a commodity in capitalist society: while it is something which can be bought and sold – like any other commodity – it has a number of peculiarities. The most important of these are that it is spatially fixed, since land cannot be transported: it is necessary to human life, since we all need to live somewhere: it allows assets and improvements to be stored; and it is relatively permanent, since improvements to land (e.g. buildings) tend to survive considerable periods of time, longer than the time it takes for clothes to wear out or food to be eaten, for instance!

Much of Harvey's work can be seen as an exploration of the implications of the specific character of capital investment in land rather than in other areas. He emphasised that such investment is both highly significant for the functioning of the capitalist economy – since a great deal of capital is usually tied up in the built environment – and also that such investment leaves a relatively enduring physical legacy. The resulting built form can help to aid capital accumulation, if it is a profitable avenue for investment, but can also be a barrier to it, when its enduring qualities render it outdated and anachronistic in a relatively short period of time. Much of Harvey's work can be seen as an elaboration of this idea of the double-edged nature of property for capital accumulation.

Harvey, in later work (1977, 1982) developed his analysis of the precise role of land for capital accumulation by examining the three 'circuits' of capital. The primary circuit – the production of commodities within manufacturing – is the one to which Marx gives greatest attention. Harvey emphasised how the accumulation of profit by the exploitation of labour within capitalist enterprises runs into severe contradictions, most notably when goods are overproduced without adequate money in the economy to purchase them. As a result of this, profits may fall and capital lie idle. It is this crisis of 'overaccumulation' that causes capital to be switched into the 'second circuit' – where capital is fixed in the built environment. Money is moved from the primary circuit to the secondary

– so long as a supportive framework for this transition exists, as when a state encourages such investment. The tertiary circuit of capital involves scientific knowledge and expenditures to reproduce labour power. Expenditure in this circuit is often the result of social struggle rather than being a direct opportunity for capital to find new avenues for accumulation.

Harvey's analysis illuminated urban processes in two ways. First, it conceptualised the significance of investment in the built environment in relation to other economic processes, suggesting links between urban restructuring and economic restructuring. Harvey's principal example attributed the growth of suburbs in America after the Second World War to the switching of capital out of the primary circuit, where crises of overaccumulation were emerging. The changing structure of the capitalist city was thus related to broader trends in the capitalist economy. The property boom of the early 1970s in USA and Britain, which saw the development of office blocks in many urban centres, owed much to similar pressures.

The built environment however, is not, simply a means of resolving crises in capital accumulation: it can, in turn, cause further crises. As capital is invested in the built environment and hence the economy is more generally 'cooled down', new opportunities for capital accumulation in the primary circuit open up again: capital moves back into this circuit, capital of the secondary circuit is devalued and it becomes a less attractive avenue for investment. Once constructed, the existing built environment is no longer as 'efficient' as new building and may prove a barrier to effective capital accumulation, so causing capital investment to move to newer and more advanced sites. One result is that the built environment concerned is abandoned or downgraded such that capital moves elsewhere to restore profitability.

Harvey's model of the urban process under capitalism is hence the very opposite of the evolutionary view we discussed above. For Harvey, investment in the urban form offers a temporary solution to crises in capitalism, but then in turn it becomes a problem which needs to be addressed by switching capital investment elsewhere. Cities – and other spatial units – hence grow and decline in an almost cyclical way. Yet Harvey is also attuned to the social and political struggles that can attempt to 'fix' the role of a particular city, against particular economic forces. Struggles by social groups threatened by the removal of capital can prevent capital flight and ensure the survival of an urban infrastructure. The miners' strike in Britain in 1984/85 is an example of a failed attempt to fix investment to particular traditional coal-mining areas. In other cases 'growth coalitions' may succeed in attracting investment. Ultimately, it is a matter of political struggle as to the way that the tendencies within capitalism to make *and* break places work out in practice. This point is taken up in Chapter 7, where we examine urban politics.

Harvey also helped to draw attention to the social and political role of one group within the bourgeoisie – landlords – who had a particular stake within any one place. Capitalists owning land are committed to their investment in a specific place. They often play a crucial role in defending local economies and engage in civic 'boosterism' to encourage the economic prosperity of their place, which will enhance property prices and the value of their land. This theme has been developed extensively by American writers such as Gottdiener (1985) and Logan and Molotch (1987) who identify the central role of landed interests in affecting urban fortunes (see Chapter 7).

The strengths of Harvey's account are several. First, it is possible to use his ideas to explore the *variety* of urban processes in the contemporary world. Whilst his discussion of the tendencies of capital to move between circuits very usefully explores the bases of switches of investment in the built environment, he is also cognisant of the role of political struggle. Thus, he is able to show how social and political forces in a particular city may act to modify, or even thwart, attempts by capitalists to disinvest. His stress on the way in which the built environment is at different times a help and a hindrance for capital accumulation, and thus how dramatic changes can occur to the same city within relatively short time-spans, makes sense of dramatic episodes of contemporary urban change. His theory of uneven development allows historical specificity and recognises the role of human agency.

Harvey's analysis is not without problems, however. The major one is that his work is empirically largely unsubstantiated for little research has actually used Harvey's insights to shed light on processes of urban change. The main exception to this concerns studies of suburbanisation and gentrification, which we examine in the next chapter. Harvey's own case studies, such as that of Paris in the nineteenth-century, seem to lapse all too quickly into detailed historical accounts.

One reason why Harvey's work remains weakly developed empirically emanates from some underlying theoretical weaknesses in his approach. His arguments can be seen as circular. Decisions to invest in the built environment can be seen as resulting from a crisis in the primary circuit which causes a shift of capital to the secondary circuit. How do we know that there is a crisis in the primary circuit? Because capital is being switched into the secondary circuit. In other words, it can be difficult to distinguish the evidence for the causes of urban change from evidence about urban changes themselves. Harvey's theory can be used to explain anything that happens. His more recent work, possibly aware of such a problem, has therefore become more concerned with analysing the dynamics of capitalist economies, and in the 1980s he turned to 'Regulation School' Marxism, discussed below in section 3.2.4.

More specifically, it is possible to question Harvey's rather static conception of the built environment. In his view once the built environment has been produced it is relatively unchangeable, and hence can be a drag on capital accumulation in the future. There are clear examples of this: elaborate motorway systems, for instance, may appear to offer solutions both to overaccumulation problems and to the general economic problems associated with traffic congestion in one year, but shortly afterwards they pose more problems as they attract more traffic than they are designed for. Yet other forms of built environment are arguably more flexible and are less of a constraint once built. Residential and office buildings for instance can be used by different people in varying ways, and the extent to which a given built environment is a constraint to future users would appear to be an empirical matter (see also Saunders, 1986, pp. 253ff).

Third, one of the attractions of Harvey's view is his insistence on the role of social and political struggle in shaping urban processes. This has been developed, in different ways, by other writers, such as Manuel Castells (1983) and American writers on 'growth coalitions' and the like (Logan and Molotch, 1987; see Chapter 7). The problem with Harvey's account however, is, a certain reductionism to social class relations which diverts attention from the significance of other social groups and actors. This is in sharp contrast with Castells who emphasises that urban struggles are rarely based purely on class lines, but are organised around such issues as gender, ethnicity or neighbourhood. This is not to say that Harvey (1985a and b) fails to recognise the complexity of class relations, for he refers to intra-class conflicts, divisions within the capitalist class and the way in which 'regional class alliances' can form as members of the working class and bourgeoisie ally together to defend their stake in particular area. However, he still says nothing about the social significance of groups other than classes.

Finally, there is also a certain tension in Harvey's work between his emphasis upon the dynamics of capital accumulation and his stress on social conflict as forces behind urban development. Ultimately, he sees struggle as caused by the contradictory nature of the relation between classes. Hence, his references to the significance of social conflict for urban development do not, in the end, make serious concession to the argument that social groups, by their own efforts, have important historical effects. Although he tries to resist the implications of his position (see e.g. Harvey, 1982, p. 450), in the final instance his position is economically determinist.

### 3.2.3   *Industrial restructuring and class struggle*

The relationship between social conflict and capitalist restructuring lies at the heart of a third account of uneven development, pioneered by Doreen Massey. Sometimes called the 'restructuring' approach (see Bagguley *et al.*, 1990), it led to a large amount of empirical research, particularly in the UK, concerning the relationship between economic restructuring, urban and regional change, and political conflict.

Massey's approach differs from those discussed above in being concerned less with the abstract logic of capital accumulation, and more with how the strategies adopted by enterprises to survive and prosper in the world capitalist economy affect patterns of spatial inequality. She examines the ways in which organisations restructure in response to changes in their economic environment and the spatial consequences. Whilst the other theories operate at a macro-level, Massey's work occupies a middle ground, providing conceptual guidance as to how specific places are affected by differing types of restructuring.

In her earlier work with Richard Meegan (Massey and Meegan, 1979; 1982), it was argued that firms in different sectors of the economy responded to international economic pressures by adopting different strategies. The most important of these were rationalisation (the closure of specific units of production and centralisation of production in other sites), intensification (making employees work harder), and investment and technical change (involving capital investment and better productivity). These strategies make for uneven development, for some areas lose employment as production is rationalised away from them, whilst others gain employment because they are subject to fresh investment. Spatial differentiation is also linked to the way in which firms deal with resistance to their restructuring strategies. One repeatedly used strategy is to shed skilled workers in one location and replace them, when necessary, with unskilled people somewhere else. Thus, workplaces in the inner cities, often employing union-organised skilled workers might be closed down and the production process, with perhaps new technology, shifted to, or expanded in, other areas where new, unskilled, often inexperienced, and often female, labour will be engaged. There are plenty of examples of this. In Britain rural regions like East Anglia and North Wales have been fastest growing in terms of manufacturing employment in the past twenty years. Again, car production in the USA has been moved out of Detroit and Chicago to sites further south where labour is more docile. For Massey, labour becomes locally (or perhaps more correctly, regionally) specialised as workers with specific skills congregate together.

In her best-known work, *Spatial Divisions of Labour*, Massey developed and systematised this argument by showing how, as firms restructured, they tended to specialise activities in those areas where the cheapest and most pliable labour force could be found. Research and development work, along with the administrative functions of Head Office, was located in those areas where professional and managerial workers were plentiful and near the corridors of power. As a result, she argued, Britain could increasingly be seen as a country divided between a prosperous South-east, where the 'control functions' of large organisations were concentrated, and the depressed peripheral regions, where employment tended to be concentrated in branch plants and largely involved unskilled workers. This polarisation marked a new spatial division of labour, and was a major change from the older patterns, where differing parts of Britain had semi-autonomous regional economies, typically based on a specific product (textiles in North-west England, shipbuilding in North-east England, and so on), and in which skilled, unskilled, and managerial workers were employed in smaller, less spatially disaggregated firms.

The logic of Massey's account is that capital has come to use spatial differentiation in the competitive search for profit, as it invests in those areas where it can draw upon a suitable labour force. Spatial advantage is most readily obtained by discriminating among available labour forces. This acknowledges that capital is nowadays highly mobile, and certainly more mobile than labour, thus implying that many constraints on industrial location which pertained in earlier epochs have been overcome.

Unlike the NIDL theorists and David Harvey, Massey avoids a purely economistic account, and finds a way of exploring how the social character of specific places impacts on processes of restructuring. The social qualities of labour are significant in repelling or attracting capital and hence, Massey argues, it is important to consider how local work cultures are formed and how they facilitate types of militancy or passivity. In the UK, for instance, industrial employment in the Home Counties expanded in the 1980s partly because firms chose to locate to areas without trade-union traditions where workers might be more compliant. Trade-union membership has become much more dispersed recently, indicating the demise of densely unionised towns and regions. As their population have declined, some of the larger industrial cities have lost some bases for labour militancy.

Massey's work avoids many of the problems we have identified in other research. Her account is historically sensitive, and she is not committed to a static view of uneven development where the fortunes of places are fixed into core or peripheral status from the beginning of world capitalism. Most importantly of all, she is explicitly concerned to elaborate on the way that social conflict and local forms of agency impact on forms of economic restructuring and uneven development. It was in developing this insight that research focused in the 1980s, as attention turned to detailed consideration of the way that economic restructuring was both affected by, and in turn impacted upon, local social relations and local cultures. The promise was to find tighter connections between economic restructuring and social and cultural changes within particular places (see Cooke, 1989a; Bagguley *et al.*, 1990). The principal way in which Massey has been taken up in UK studies has been through a series of 'locality studies' including a programme of research into the Changing Urban and Regional System (CURS) (e.g. Cooke, 1986; Cooke, 1989b). This research programme attempted to explore in greater detail both how the social complexion of various places affected forms of economic restructuring, and also how restructuring impacted on these 'localities'. This research strategy entailed detailed localised inquiry, taking the distinctive features of different places seriously and trying to describe and explain differentiation. The promise of such an approach is a better understanding of social and economic activity in its material context, connecting together general forces and specific outcomes.

Massey's framework offered a sophisticated attempt to theorise urban differentiation as the interplay between the restructuring strategies of firms and the social and cultural characteristics of particular local areas. It appeared to resolve many of the weaknesses of other research, and in particular it laid a path from theoretical formalism to a detailed research programme. This programme expanded on Massey's ideas in a number of ways. Important among these was the successful application of her analysis, which was based primarily on restructuring in manufacturing, to the restructuring of 'service' employment, for instance in the health services.

Bagguley *et al.* (1990) and Pinch (1989) were able to show that even in the British health service, not organised on a profit-making basis, many of the restructuring strategies discussed by Massey, and others, were in operation, causing serious job loss. Even though it had been traditionally supposed that service industries were much less spatially mobile than manufacturing firms since they had to be situated closer to their market, they were shown to be subject to very similar process of the spatial separation of functions as those analysed by Massey (see e.g. Marshall *et al.*, 1988).

Despite this success, Massey's impressive research agenda came increasingly under attack in the later 1980s. One theoretical problem was how the 'local' was to be conceptualised. When firms invested in a place were they investing in a neighbourhood, a locality, or a region? The usual response was to develop the idea of locality, seen as a local labour market area (e.g. Cooke, 1989b, see the discussion in Duncan and Savage, 1989). If the principal relevant characteristic for location decisions is the nature of available labour, then that might seem a sensible demarcation. However, labour markets are very heterogeneous and usually have little meaning for people within them, though the life chances of substantial proportions of the population are affected by employment opportunities available. Furthermore, local labour markets are segmented and divided, with professional workers, for instance, usually being able to travel much further to work than a labourer. Local labour markets are also of limited cultural importance to people, who might be more likely to identify with specific neighbourhoods or towns.

The issue of whether localities were meaningful entities, whether their boundaries could be drawn, was one basis of dispute about locality studies. Several critics thought that the implication of the studies was to return to bad habits of empiricist and descriptive geography that looked at places as if they were unique entities whose characteristics were not explained in proper national and international context (Smith, 1986). Others thought that there was a tendency to reify space, to suggest that particular spaces – localities – had causal powers of their own (Duncan and Savage, 1989). Accounts that conceptualised such localities as actors in their own right, by referring to their 'proactive' properties (e.g. Cooke, 1989a) gave grounds for such criticism. To some extent the debate about whether 'localities' exist now appears unimportant but the controversy nonetheless threw into the question the project of relating industrial restructuring to broader social patterns and urban development. For, once it is accepted that localities are not coherent entities, then it has to be acknowledged that firms do not invest in entire local social systems by locating within the boundaries of a place, but only in specific parts of it, drawing on particular workers, and so may have only a tangential, and possibly unimportant, impact on that place. Since the CURS research tended to focus on 'easier' places, where labour markets were small and self-contained, the probability was increased that the local consequences of employment decisions would be greater than in large conurbations. The seven CURS case studies were of Cheltenham, Lancaster, Thanet (encompassing both Ramsgate and Margate), Kirkby in Outer Mersey-side, Teesside, Swindon and South West Birmingham (including Bournville and Longbridge). None was a large metropolitan labour market with a great diversity of employment and long-distance commuting.

The same problem of making labour markets the units of analysis resurfaced when researchers attempted to explain patterns of gender relations within this framework. Even in smaller local labour markets, it proved difficult to tie processes of economic restructuring to social change. It was often assumed that women were 'cheap' or 'docile' labour, but rarely was sustained effort put into examining the social processes which caused women to be cheap or docile. Bowlby *et al.* (1989) argued that the research took the subordinate position of women in the family to be unproblematic and 'given', and did not subject the construction of patriarchal social relations to critical inquiry. Work was often mistakenly deemed coterminous with paid employment, and household work – in the form of domestic labour – was not satisfactorily integrated into analyses of economic restructuring (though see Warde, 1988).

It also proved difficult to relate local political mobilisation to processes of economic restructuring in any simple way. Massey (1991) has recently insisted on the way in which 'locality research' was designed to throw light on the way that political organisation might best be developed locally. Yet many of the local studies concerned ended up by asserting the autonomy of local political processes from economic determinants. In the case of Lancaster, for instance, battles over town planning fought in the mid-1980s were not dominated by conflicts between capital and labour, but instead involved a great number of social groups. Amongst the most active were different elements of 'service class' (managers and profession-als) which had not been studied by those examining restructuring in any detail. Elsewhere Urry (1990b) emphasised the role of professional inter-ests within local councils in creating local policy: the connections with economic restructuring were now highly tenuous. Increasingly the most interesting research arising from the CURS programme pointed to the social indeterminacy of economic restructuring.

So far, restructuring theory has offered a series of major insights into processes of economic restructuring, but was limited in its attempts to explain social and cultural processes.

### 3.2.4   *Regulation Marxism and the California School*

The final approach to uneven development and urban differentiation which we consider is associated with the Regulation School, in particular through its impact on neo-Marxist geographers such as Allen Scott, Michael Storper, Richard Walker, and the more recent work of David Harvey. As with work inspired by Massey, one of the main attractions of this theoretical current is its ability to support a wide-ranging research programme. Also in common with Massey this approach is historically sensitive and attuned to urban specificity.

Regulation School theory is descended from French structural Marxism of the 1970s (see Jessop, 1990, for an overview). Its principal figures, Aglietta, Lipietz, Boyer, and others, have employed a distinctive set of theoretically generated concepts – regime of accumulation, mode of regulation, Fordism – to explore relationships between capital, labour and the state. The main starting-point for these writers is the argument that nation-states play a crucial role in regulating capital accumulation, and they see the differing ways in which capitalism is regulated as historically specific 'regimes of accumulation'. Much of their work is thus an historically grounded attempt to consider the implications of the contemporary shift from one 'regime of accumulation' – Fordism, to another 'regime of accumulation', neo-Fordism, or post-Fordism.

The Italian Marxist, Gramsci, apparently coined the phrase 'Fordism' to characterise the mass-production methods pioneered by Henry Ford in the inter-war years of the twentieth-century, and some of their effects on social and family life in Italy. The concept re-entered contemporary social and economic thought through the writings of the Regulation School who referred to a complete era in capitalist development as Fordist. Their argument is that Fordism was the dominant mode of industrial organisation in the mid-twentieth-century and that it constituted a distinctive 'regime of accumulation'. The regime of accumulation is based on a specific 'mode of regulation' (whence the name of the School), where regulation refers to things like the forms of the state, the nature of intervention, welfare arrangements, legal forms, and so forth. In addition, for the Regulation School, phases of capitalist development are defined both by the mode of production and consumption. The Fordist era was characterised by mass production and mass consumption. However, they

argued that in the 1980s this regime was gradually giving way to a neo-
or post-Fordist one, with less demand for mass-produced goods and in
which competitive pressures required much more flexible methods of
production.

The concept of post-Fordism, like many other concepts prefixed by
the delimiter 'post', is primarily constructed as a negative ideal-type,
identifying characteristics that were not present in a preceding, and better
understood, institutional setting. The model of Fordism is relatively well-
established, and many commentators would think of Fordist arrangements as characterising the leading manufacturing firms from the 1930s
through to the 1970s. The Fordist firm is one characterised by scientific
management, economies of scale, mass production, and technical control.
Post-Fordist production arrangements are associated with the declining
size of production units, small batch production, customised products,
flexible working practices, greater worker discretion and more responsible autonomy.

Critics of regulation theory see it as bearing many of the alleged defects
of its structuralist predecessors: functionalist, economistic, reductionist,
excessively abstract, ignoring individual action and underemphasising
social struggles. Nevertheless, the technical vocabulary of the Regulation
School is frequently slipped into discussions of new flexible forms of
production, though often in a highly eclectic way (e.g. *Society & Space*,
1988). Quite often the concepts are invoked without regard to the
theoretical scheme from which they were derived. Nonetheless the
notions of Fordism, post-Fordism and flexibility have been widely taken
up to analyse new patterns of spatial inequality. David Harvey's book, *The
Condition of Postmodernity* (1989) is an important example.

In *The Condition of Postmodernity* Harvey dissects the demise of the
post-war settlement. His account is based on the proposition that:

> the contrasts between present political–economic practices and those
> of the post-war boom period are sufficiently strong to make the
> hypothesis of a shift from Fordism to what might be called a 'flexible'
> regime of accumulation a telling way to characterise recent history
> (Harvey, 1989, p. 124).

Fordism was the regime of accumulation that supported the 'long boom'
after 1945 and was epitomised by the operations of the Ford motor
company which produced cheap automobiles using assembly-line techniques while paying their (generally very bored) workers comparatively

high wages. 'What was special about Ford (and what ultimately separates Fordism from Taylorism) was his vision, his explicit recognition that mass production meant mass consumption, a new system of the reproduction of labour power, a new politics of labour control and management, a new aesthetics and psychology, in short, a new kind of rationalised, modernist, and populist democratic society' (Harvey, 1989, pp. 125–6). For Harvey, consistently with other exponents of Regulation Theory, observes: 'Post-war Fordism has to be seen, therefore, less as a mere system of mass production and more as a total way of life' (ibid, p. 135). The post-war settlement generally worked well, productivity rose, wealth increased, and the gains were in part redistributed through the mechanism of the welfare state and social democratic political policies – a particular mode of regulation. Not everyone was satisfied or contented: there were many workers on poor wages, poverty was not eliminated even in the core countries; immigrants into Europe, of whom there were many, were particularly disprivileged, and the effects on the Third World were far from positive. Nor was it a permanent solution: it began to show signs of difficulty in the mid-1960s, and the early 1970s, which saw not only the end of a stable international financial system, but also oil-price rises and inflation; and the beginning of a fresh recession effectively ended an era. For Harvey, 1973 was the turning-point, a change that he sees associated with the emergence of post-modernism as an aesthetic (see Chapter 6).

Harvey interprets this in terms of a transition to a regime of flexible accumulation. He observes changes in the labour market with a growing disparity between core and peripheral workers; changes in industrial organisation, especially the emergence of subcontracting, but also of homeworking, sweat-shops, and the use of women's domestic labour. Small-batch production entails a move away from the economies of scale that Fordism offered. New products – particularly responding to quickly changing fashions – require constant innovation from capital. This also has cultural consequences:

> The relatively stable aesthetic of Fordist modernism has given way to all the ferment, instability and fleeting qualities of a post-modernist aesthetic that celebrates difference, ephemerality, spectacle, fashion, and the commodification of cultural forms (Harvey, 1989, p. 156).

Employment in service industries increased. The dialectic between mono-polisation and competition in capitalist economy works out in a new way, with tighter organisation achieved through access to, and control over, information and a complete rejigging of the financial system since the mid-1970s. This is a result partly of new information technology and its rapid transmission, partly of new opportunities for capital gains and partly of powers beyond the control of nation-states. Moreover, Harvey discerns changes in attitudes and norms, seeing the emergence of a 'rampant individualism' associated with entrepreneurialism.

Harvey explains the shift in terms of his older stress on the logic of over-accumulation, but sees the 1970s as a particular configuration of conditions. He develops a distinctive analysis in terms of 'time–space compression'. In the world of new information technology the circulation-time of capital is reduced. Effectively the size of the globe shrinks as it becomes possible to trade stocks and shares throughout 24 hours – when the London Exchange is closed either New York or Tokyo will be open, and *vice versa*. The capacity of firms to use different spaces for different purposes is another aspect of time–space compression. Economically we live in a smaller world.

Harvey uses his analysis to explain the rise of what he terms 'the condition of post-modernity'. We consider his arguments on this score in Chapter 6, but suffice it to say that Harvey does not, in this book, consider in detail the urban transformations brought about by the new form of flexible accumulation. Whilst Harvey might have strengthened his analysis of the contemporary transformation of capitalism, he has not applied his framework to uneven development and urban change in any detail.

It is in this field that the geographers of the 'California School' have made greater strides. They might be seen as attempting to prove a theoretical account of the dramatic development of the Californian urban conglomerations of Los Angeles and (to a lesser extent) San Francisco. Los Angeles is perhaps the most discussed city of the late-twentieth-century world (Davis, 1990; Soja, 1989; Jameson, 1984, etc): for the School, Los Angeles is to the 1980s and 1990s what Chicago was to the early twentieth-century, a particularly stark example of the urbanising processes which are to be found throughout much of the world economy. They see the rise of the Californian economy as tied to the decline of the old industrial regions of the north-east of the USA (the 'Rust Belt') and the fact that new industries, such as electronics and defence, are located in California, while contracting ones, like shipbuilding, are in the Rust Belt. They concentrate on the experience of recently growing industrial sectors and argue that establishments in these sectors are tending to cluster in 'new industrial districts'. They provide evidence for a variety of sectors

– for example, motion pictures (Christopherson and Storper, 1986) animated pictures (Scott, 1988b) printed-circuit fabrication (Scott, 1988b) – where factories tend to cluster together in the same district of a large metropolitan area. The reason for this is to obtain economies of scope rather than the economies of scale that were the objective of Fordist mass production.

Although the Californians deploy Marxist concepts (particularly of regulation theory), the core of their current position is a theory of the firm associated with the economist, Oliver Williamson, (for a summary see Williamson, 1990) who has developed the theory of 'transaction cost analysis'. Very simply their theory distinguishes those situations under which firms find it best to internalise contributory activities (such as marketing, or research, or various production functions), and those where it is best to externalise them, by using subcontractors or buying services on the market. Scott (1988b) pursues the spatial implications of this contrast, observing that when firms externalise their activities they tend to congregate close to the other firms involved in their production network, leading to agglomeration economies and the emergence of New Industrial Districts. Alternatively, if activities are internalised, firms may be able to separate functions spatially onto different sites. Massey's account of the spatial separation of production functions will apply only to such cases.

These writers largely accept the empirical trends identified as flexible accumulation in Piore and Sabel's (1984) analysis of the Third Italy, and argue that they testify to the rise of new industries, based on external linkages. Firms tend to be smaller and to subcontract activities, leading to vertical disintegration. The development of new products encourages the concentration of small firms that can share expert knowledge, for which purposes social networks, often based on face-to-face interaction, are ideal. New industrial districts tend to contain firms in advanced innovative sectors, attracting and retaining workers with appropriate knowledge and expertise. In some versions strong priority is accorded to technological developments (e.g. Storper and Walker, 1989) where the development of new products is deemed conducive to external links between firms as, for instance, new companies cluster round the innovating enterprise.

 Much of the work of the California School is directly purely towards explaining industrial location and tends to avoid any wider discussion of its effects on urban development. An exception to this is Scott's (1988a) *Metropolis: From the Division of Labour to Urban Form*. Having outlined the process whereby firms reorganise, compelled by the benefits of vertical disintegration, he makes a series of claims about the way in which the concentration of workers' residences near to the new 'neo-Marshallian' industrial districts in which they work has effects on social segregation, ethnic differentiation and community formation.

Beginning from the premise of the spatial separation of home and workplace in capitalist economies, Scott (1988a pp. 217–30) argues that the employment relation is a key determinant of residential location. He uses data to show that although there are other cross-cutting bases of residential segregation, occupation is primary, universal and constant in large cities of the advanced capitalist societies. Blue-collar and white-collar workers live in different zones of the city. The reasons for this are several: blue-collar workers who travel shorter distances to work will concentrate around workplaces; state practices of zoning segregate social groups; and there are group preferences as regards housing that are mediated by cost. However, Scott goes beyond these factors to try to make out a case that:

> neighbourhoods are the privileged locales within which social repro-
> duction of the determinate forms of life engendered in the capitalist
> city goes on . . . Here, I use the term *reproduction* in its double sense to
> mean both generational replacement and the maintenance of stable
> subjective/ideological accommodations with workaday life (Scott,
> 1988a, p. 223).

The significance of this is threefold. First, neighbourhoods are sites of educating and socialising children, and families tend to choose them on the basis of their educational facilities with a view to ensuring that children get an education appropriate to their anticipated class position. Parents try to prevent their children becoming downwardly mobile and choose schools accordingly. Second, neighbourhoods signify social pres-tige and status, and social groups differentiate themselves by adopting particular behavioural and cultural traits that are reinforced and sanc-tioned in local communities. Third, neighbourhoods are places where inter-family social networks develop. Sometimes in poor neighbour-hoods a network is protection against the insecurities of employment, in others it constitutes the source of information by which new jobs are found. On this third basis the concentration of ethnic groups can also be explained, Scott claims, because they tend to have access only to limited niches in the labour market: 'ethnicity in the American metropolis is thus pre-eminently a contingent outcome of local labor market pressures and needs' (Scott, 1988a, p. 226). Ultimately industrial location gives rise to neighbourhoods composed of people who work in the industries, and the social homogeneity of these neighbourhoods becomes self-reinforcing over time.

Scott's account is not entirely convincing simply because firm re-organisation and labour market are insufficient as basic mechanisms to generate the complex range of social effects. The Californians, unlike Harvey and certainly Massey, say very little about social conflict and its impact on economic restructuring and social change. Their analysis is conducted at the level of economic theory and even at that level it is probably too narrow. The Californians take little notice of trends in the service industries and their role in employment, since they see ser-vices as largely dependent on manufacturing production (see Sayer and Walker, 1992). If urbanisation is connected only to industrialisation, as it is by Scott, then we have a limited grasp on the impact of most economic activity.

One final problem with the Californian account, and another sense in which it may be seen as unduly economistic, is that it almost entirely ignores the state. Here again this may be the result of focusing attention on one country, the USA, where the federal government in particular is relatively non-interventionist in regional planning. Nevertheless the state does many things short of direct intervention that set the framework for business activity. This criticism is developed by Feagin and Smith (1987) and Gottdiener (1989).

## 3.3   Conclusion

In the past decade, theories of uneven development have become increas-ingly sophisticated and aware of the problems raised at the beginning of Section 3.2. Accounts have grown more sensitive historically and have identified explicitly how different places may be affected in diverse ways by uneven development. It has been demonstrated that urban develop-ment is not some evolutionary process through which all cities pass. Rather these new theories have demonstrated the instability of urban fortunes and the reasons why cities rise and fall, fall and rise. Causes include the dynamics of the world capitalist economy which allow the relocation of industry across the globe; the cycles of investment and disinvestment in the built environment; forms of corporate restructuring; and the dynamics of product innovation. As a result, particular cities cannot be deemed emblematic of a form of social organisation, in the way that the city of Chicago stood for industrial capitalism. Instead we should recognise the inherent impermanence of the economic foundations of cities and the multiple roles of cities in a world capitalist economy.

Jointly, these theories succeeded in analysing the economic foundations of urban change and identifying a series of forces which derive specifically from mechanisms of the capitalist organisation of production. As such they have proved an important corrective to the previous neglect by urban sociology of such matters. Individually, each seems to have identified some characteristic recent strategies and processes of the global economy. Their disagreements stem partly from concentrating on different nations and different industrial sectors, though there are more fundamental theoretical sources of dispute too.

Theories of uneven development have been far less successful at explaining the sources of intra-urban change and social change within cities. Once they move away from delineating the economic position of particular places, and begin to refer to the impact of uneven development on their urban structure, social order and cultural patterns, they begin to falter. Although Harvey sought to capture the importance of social conflict for urban development, Massey sought to show how economic restructuring is related to local social and political change and Scott sought to try to demonstrate how neighbourhoods are produced by industrial location, their solutions are at best partial.

Theories of uneven development need to be supplemented by a much fuller analysis of the social, cultural and political processes which shape, and are themselves shaped by, cities. Much might be gained by uniting some aspects of classical urban sociology with the enhanced understanding of capitalist spatial development. Subsequent chapters examine material inequality, sociation, the cultural specificity of place and the nature of political conflict in the contemporary city, all themes that have featured prominently in urban sociology. Typically though they were explored through analysis of the nature of modernity, rather than of capitalism. What is required is better specification of the relationship between capitalist dynamics and the social conditions of modernity. A principal connection is through the analysis of the inequalities constantly generated by the mechanisms of accumulation which are reproduced, modulated or transformed in the course of the mundane practices of daily life captured by analyses of the experience of modernity.

# 4    Inequality and Social Organisation in the City

Social inequality is inherent within capitalist societies. In this chapter we will examine how capitalist inequalities based on social class relate to other inequalities – notably those based on patriarchal gender relations – and how these inequalities affect urban form, and how they are themselves shaped by urban processes. Traditional approaches to urban inequality were primarily interested in segregation, the spatial expression of inequality. This chapter begins, in section 4.1, by briefly considering this research, documenting entrenched patterns of segregation as exemplified by studies of Britain and North America. In section 4.2 we consider the extent to which urban inequality arises from unequal access to housing, focusing upon the work of neo-Weberians such as John Rex and Robert Moore, and, more recently, Peter Saunders. We show that processes of economic production and restructuring, whilst not determining patterns of segregation, nonetheless exercise a more powerful mediating role than these accounts would imply.

General analyses of segregation have increasingly given way to analyses of specific urban developments, notably suburbanisation and gentrification. This has arisen from speculation about the cultural ramifications of social concentration. The suburb, the ghetto and the gentrified enclave are all expressions, through segregation, of inequality. In such areas, groups visibly display some distinctive cultural characteristics in their daily activities which constitute the reproduction of social identity and, to a variable degree, social solidarity.

The interplay of inequality, group identity and organisation is the subject matter of the later sections of the chapter (and is further developed in parts of Chapter 5). In section 4.3 we show how the social character of particular urban areas – suburbs and gentrified inner cities – emerge out of structured inequality and appear as a type of subcultural expressiveness.

Drawing upon both Marxist and Weberian views, we show that suburbanisation and gentrification cannot be explained purely in terms of economic production, but nevertheless are both closely related to class and gender divisions. We show how the creation of these new social zones in cities bring about new cultures, and are themselves partly the product of cultural change.

In section 4.4 we move on to consider whether some of the trends we have discussed indicate that cities are becoming more polarised. In order to address this question we examine the role that analysis of households is coming to have in urban studies – in some respects a return to the British tradition of urban research based on Le Play's trilogy of 'Place, Work and Folk'. We look in detail at one study of a specific local environment in the context of arguments about increasing social polarisation occurring between households.

## 4.1　Urban space and segregation

Segregation of urban space occurs because land is limited. In capitalist cities land is privately owned, each parcel of land having a different value depending upon its size, its location and its current and potential uses. Property in land has many uses: some of it will be devoted to industrial purposes (increasingly those of service industries); some will be residential; and some will be devoted to urban infrastructure like roads and parks that are publicly owned and accessible to anyone. Much land is already built upon, and built-form contains historic residues and new opportunities, which affect its value.

In these propertied spaces different kinds of human activity are sited. What happens on any given site is partly a result of a history of struggle, competition, planning and regulation. It is also partly the result of the ways in which people currently use the space. As we pointed out in Chapter 3, usage of the urban fabric is partially constrained by the original purposes for which it was designed, but it may also be adapted to new purposes, as is instanced by the innovative uses in most large cities of old factories and warehouses (for housing, museums, offices, and so forth). The resulting patterns on the ground are complex; there is much flux; hence the difficulties of explaining the spatial distribution of activities.

More important for urban sociology than segregation of land use is the segregation of social groups. Social inequality is expressed spatially. It is rare indeed to find millionaires living alongside unskilled labourers. Thus in 1981, in London 59 per cent of people living in the City of London were in households where the head of the house was in social classes 1 and 2, the upper and middle classes, whereas, nearby in Tower Hamlets, only 9 per cent of the population lived in such households. But segregation is not simply in terms of class. Patterns of ethnic segregation are marked: in Britain, 43 per cent of Afro-Caribbeans, 23 per cent of Asians, but only 6 per cent of all whites live in the inner-city zones of London, Birmingham and Manchester (Smith, 1989, p. 34). One can also detect a spatial separation of family types: nuclear families tend to live in suburban areas, whilst single people tend to live in more central urban areas. As a result, the analysis of the segregation of cities tells us much about the nature of social inequality, about how different forms of inequality are related, and trends in urban segregation can be read as evidence of social changes.

Early interest in examining segregation took the form of detailed studies of individual cities: Booth's study of London in the 1880s classified every street according to its social grading. One of the most publicised achievements of the Chicago School was their attempt to systematise a general model of segregation in the modern city. In this concentric-ring model (see Chapter 2) Burgess identified a number of typical zones which tended to radiate from the centre of the city. These included the Central Business District in the middle, surrounded by a 'zone of transition' – an area which was being 'invaded' by light industry and commerce, but into which the most marginal groups of city dwellers were also forced. This area contained ghettos, and what Burgess described as a 'black band'. Outside this was a working-class ring and, on the urban periphery, middle-class suburbs.

This model was largely based on impressionistic research, and hence since the 1920s there were attempts to gain precision by quantifying the incidence of households with different social characteristics in defined small areas within cities. Beginning with that of Burgess, a variety of techniques for measurement and mapping were developed: land-use modelling, social-area analysis, factorial analysis – all with some affinity to human ecology approaches. This provided a basic, positivist, description of social differentiation within cities (a useful summary of these techniques can be found in Ley, 1983, pp. 60–84).

As a result of these exercises, a variety of models of segregation were advanced, each of which hypothesises a typical pattern for the distribution of major urban activities. The Chicago School model (a) (see Figure 4.1) identified zones, radiating out from the centre of cities, each with its own

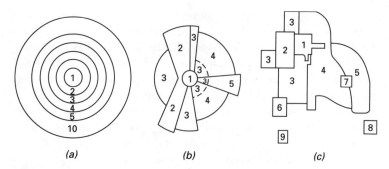

District

1 Central Business District
2 Wholesale Light Manufacturing
3 Low-class Residential
4 Medium-class Residential
5 High-class Residential

6 Heavy Manufacturing
7 Outlying Business District
8 Residential Suburb
9 Industrial Suburb
10 Commuters' Zone

**Figure 4.1**   *Models of urban land use: (a) Burgess' concentric zone model; (b) Hoyt's sectoral model; (c) Harris and Ullman's multiple nuclei model.*
*Source*: C. D. Harris and E. Ullman, 'The Nature of Cities', *Annals, American Academy of Political and Social Science*, 242 (1945): 7–17, fig. 5.

specialised activities. Another model (b) suggests a sectoral pattern, with concentrations of activities in wedge-shaped corridors emanating from the middle. The third model (c) accepts that there are concentrations of activities in particular spatial areas, but that there is no regular pattern, with clusters of specialised activity spread around the city. According to Herbert and Johnston (1978, p. 20), testing the two main competing models – Burgess's concentric rings and Hoyt's (1939) sectors – indicated that:

> the geography of socio-economic status (i.e. social class) was largely sectoral; that of family status was largely zonal (with young families in the outer suburbs and the apartment renters close to the city centre), whereas that for ethnic status indicated significant clusters in both zones and sectors.

Generally, research showed that ethnic segregation is more pronounced than class segregation (Badcock, 1984, p. 205). American cities (the principal focus of studies of segregation) appear highly segregated largely because of the separation of black people from white, though patterns also reflect the very diverse ethnic origins of urban dwellers in America. In general European cities are less segregated: ethnic minorities live in very high concentrations in micro-areas of cities but because they are relatively few in numbers they make less of an impact on overall patterns. Hence one should be wary of assuming that the patterns of segregation identified by American urban sociologists apply to Europe. Segregation in European cities is more likely to be along class lines, though religious affiliation is also sometimes important. But while we can see patterns, it is rare to find class-homogeneous social areas. Such homogeneity is greater in recently built housing, since any new residential development will tend to attract people in similar material circumstances (Young and Willmott, 1975, p. 193). Also, the bigger a settlement, the higher the degree of segregation that is likely. However, there are still differences in patterns between places of similar size. Degrees of segregation, either by socio-economic status or ethnicity, have not reduced during the twentieth-century. Evidence on American cities, for instance, showed a level of segregation in the 1970s similar to that in the 1920s, implying that ethnic inequalities were undiminished (see Ley, 1983, pp. 62–7 for a summary; for more recent US data based on the 1980 Census, see White, 1987).

The original Chicago interest in spatial analysis of urban life continued to flourish in the USA until the 1970s, and in many ways it remains a starting-point for geographical studies of the city (e.g. Ley, 1983). Subsequently, though, British and American geographers and sociologists lost interest in segregation. One reason for this among geographers was the reaction of the discipline to positivist and statistical techniques which came out of the growing influence of Marxism in the late 1970s, which had little use for that kind of empirical data, and an increasing recognition that statistical description was often wanting in providing explanations of social process or giving the feel for the texture of everyday life (see Ley, 1983, for an attempt at the latter). In particular analyses of changes in urban segregation became more preoccupied with cultural processes which could not be examined by statistical methods (see section 4.3).

Nonetheless, mapping social segregation in cities remains an important descriptive exercise. Older methods of estimating levels of social segregation have appeared in recent accounts (e.g. Byrne, 1989, on urban inequalities; Morris, 1987, on the impact of unemployment; Rose 1988, on women and gentrification; Smith 1989, on race). At the point when interest shifts from merely describing segregation and the focus becomes the explanation of other processes then the methods of segregation analysis may again become useful.

## 4.2   Labour markets and housing markets

Patterns of urban segregation do not themselves reveal their causes. Therefore, from the 1960s onwards theoretical issues surfaced. The crucial topic for discussion became the extent to which housing position could be seen as dependent upon employment position. Some neo-Weberian writers advanced powerful reasons for suggesting that people's housing (in terms of tenure, type and zone) was not simply dependent upon their jobs but was also related to other factors. If this is true, then to see urban segregation, and more generally one's housing position, simply as an expression of social class is mistaken. Instead, it implies that urban inequalities are at least partly autonomous from those of class and hence need to be treated in their own right.

There has always been a practical, reformist interest in housing among urban researchers, as expressed in concern about housing shortages, overcrowding, sanitary facilities, level of rents, ease of access, and so forth. It was only from the 1960s, however, that it began to be a subject of theoretical attention. It was the work of Rex and Moore (1967) on the role of housing in race relations in Birmingham, England, that triggered debate. They were concerned with the way in which access to housing disadvantaged immigrant households, pushing them into inner-city 'zones of transition' where they rented or bought old and often dilapidated houses. The causes included various forms of discrimination, the city council's policies for the allocation of public housing among them. Working explicitly forward from the Chicago School approach, they proposed a 'theoretical model of the city and urban processes as they bear on "the twilight zones" (Rex and Moore, 1967, p. 272) in which the concept of housing classes expressed the unequal benefits of different kind of 'housing situation'. In their words:

> there is a class struggle over the use of houses and . . . this class struggle is the central process of the city as a social unit. In saying this we follow Max Weber who saw [that] class struggle was apt to emerge wherever people in a market situation enjoyed differential access to property and such class struggles might therefore arise not merely around the use of the means of industrial production, but around the control of domestic property (Rex and Moore, 1967, pp. 273–4).

They admit that housing depends 'in part' upon income and thus labour market position but add 'it is also the case that men in the same labour situation may come to have differential degrees of access to housing and it is this which immediately determines the class conflicts of the city as distinct from those of the workplace' (ibid, p. 274). Rex and Moore thus chart out one of the most important differences between Marxist and Weberian positions. In terms of their notion of housing classes they assert: 'there will be . . . as many potential housing classes in the city as there are kinds of access to the use of housing' (ibid, p. 274). 'Kinds of access' include both housing condition and household composition (see Table 4.1 for their typology). New immigrants found it very difficult, Rex and Moore argued, to get as high as (3*a*) in this hierarchy of housing type, being largely restricted to the lowest levels.

The concept of housing classes was subsequently abandoned. It was thought by Saunders to be ultimately unhelpful, because it meant that people were allocated to two, parallel, social classes: one on the basis of their employment situation, another based on their housing situation (Saunders, 1984; 1986; 1990). As a result the concept of social class became far too elastic, trying to explain too much. In the end, Saunders argued, it is more useful to restrict the concept of social class to relations based on production and employment, and to recognise that divisions in housing situation are separate from – but no less real than – social class ones. The study of social stratification needs to examine both the divisions of social class and those arising out of consumption processes, which he terms 'consumption sector cleavages'.

**Table 4.1**   *Types of housing situation*

1. that of the outright owner of a whole house;
2. that of the owner of a mortgaged whole house;
3. that of the council tenant –
   (*a*) in a house with a long life;
   (*b*) in a house awaiting demolition;
4. that of the tenant of a whole house owned by a private landlord;
5. that of the owner of a house bought with short-term loans who is compelled to let rooms in order to meet his repayment obligations;
6. that of the tenant of rooms in a lodging-house.

*Source*: J. Rex and R. Moore, *Race, Community and Conflict* (Harmondsworth: Penguin, 1967) p. 274.

The concept of housing classes also, mistakenly according to Marshall (1990, p. 144), stimulated concern with urban managers – the gatekeepers who allowed people access to housing – whether in the housing department that allocated council houses, the planning department that zoned cities to decide what uses could be made of particular areas, or mortgage companies who made decisions about lending on properties. For a while it was asserted that people in these positions were making relatively autonomous decisions that resulted in the differential distribution of different types of resident. Though this notion too was subsequently dropped, since it seemed that these decisions were determined by other institutions and structures of power, the sense in which housing distribution was mediated, in particular by state decision-making procedures, was important. One of the key contributions of Weberian scholarship was to insist constantly on the importance of the role of power and the state.

One outcome of this Weberian concern was that increasing attention was paid to understanding what difference housing tenure made to people's life chances, a particularly interesting issue in the UK where there was a dramatic shift from private renting to owner-occupation and council-tenancy after the Second World War. Another outcome was that much more attention was paid to the buying and selling of domestic property – in other words, to housing markets. Much of the most sophisticated work in recent years in this field has been trying to show explicitly the connection, mentioned by Rex and Moore, between labour-market position and outcomes in the housing market.

The crucial issue in the discussion is the extent to which housing position is dependent on employment. At first glance it seems obvious that one's housing is critically dependent on one's income from employment. Only those people with regular, secure incomes can purchase houses on a mortgage. Furthermore the higher one's income, the larger the mortgage one can obtain, and hence the better the house it is possible to buy. It would seem, in this case, that differences in housing are effectively caused by differences in employment.

This argument, however, is too simple. Saunders advances a number of reasons why housing position is not dependent simply on employment. First, he argues that it is usually possible to achieve capital gains from housing, since the price of housing tends to rise, and it is therefore possible to sell a house for more money than was used to buy it. This capital sum can be used to purchase new housing and, since this money is in no way affected by one's employment, it serves to cause all owner-occupiers, regardless of their employment situation, to make money and move into better housing as they grow older. Second, he argues that inheritance is becoming increasingly important, and it is possible for people to acquire owner-occupied housing from windfalls rather than from their employment. The proportion of people who gain from inheritance will increase as the proportion of owner-occupiers in the population grows. Third, there is a major difference between one's employment position and one's housing position. We are usually employed as individuals, but we live in households, which often contain more than one person. Hence a couple with two small incomes may be able to pool their financial resources to afford the same type of house as one person on a larger income (see Randolph, 1991).

One indication of the fact that employment does not determine housing is the fact that people of all social classes may live in owner-occupation, and hence it cannot be seen anymore as a 'middle class' tenure (see Table 4.2). Instead Saunders suggests that people living in similar sorts of housing and in similar residential areas may come from a variety of employment backgrounds. A relatively well-off suburban area might contain, for instance, a five-person household with a man in a managerial job who is the sole earner; a two-person working-class household where both partners work in routine manual or non-manual work; a young student who has bought a house because her grandfather left her a large cash sum in his will; and a retired couple who bought the house a long time ago when its price was low, and whose mortgage is now paid off.

A further implication is that people move into particular housing types and areas to maximise their housing position. Suburban housing tends to increase its price more than inner-city housing, and hence people trying to maximise the money they can make from housing may move to these areas. Although they may have different employment backgrounds they become united by their common housing position.

A considerable empirical debate has opened up as to whether Saunders is correct in these arguments. The empirical research is complex, but generally is critical of Saunders's claims, at least in their strongest formulation. In order to sustain his case it is important for Saunders to show that all people who own their houses are able to make equivalent capital gains. If middle-class owner-occupiers are able to make more capital gains than working-class ones, then the strength of his case collapses, since the gains one makes from housing are still critically related to one's employment position.

This indeed was disputed by David Thorns (1982) who argued that

72

**Table 4.2** *Accommodation type and tenure of households: by socio-economic group of head of household,[1] 1986 (Great Britain)*

| | Professional | Employers and managers | Intermediate and junior non-manual | Skilled manual and own account non-professional | Semi-skilled manual and personal service | Unskilled manual | All heads of households |
|---|---|---|---|---|---|---|---|
| *Tenure of households (percentages)* | | | | | | | |
| Owner-occupied | | | | | | | |
| Owned outright | 23 | 30 | 30 | 23 | 20 | 19 | 25 |
| Owned with mortgage | 67 | 53 | 38 | 40 | 19 | 10 | 38 |
| Total owner-occupiers | 90 | 83 | 68 | 63 | 39 | 29 | 63 |
| Rented | | | | | | | |
| Local authority/new town | 3 | 8 | 20 | 29 | 47 | 59 | 27 |
| Unfurnished private[2] | 2 | 4 | 8 | 6 | 10 | 10 | 7 |
| Furnished private | 2 | 1 | 3 | 1 | 2 | 2 | 2 |
| Rented with job or business | 4 | 4 | 1 | 1 | 3 | – | 2 |
| Total rented | 10 | 17 | 32 | 37 | 61 | 71 | 37 |
| Total households in sample[3] (= 100%) (numbers) | 541 | 1800 | 2101 | 3041 | 1723 | 554 | 9760 |

[1] Excludes households headed by members of the armed forces, full time students, and those who have never worked.
[2] Includes those renting from a housing association.
[3] Excludes those living in caravans or houseboats, and cases where tenure is not known.
*Source: Social Trends,* 19, © Crown copyright 1989.

since house prices tended to increase faster in expanding, more middle-class, parts of Britain such as the South-east, it was the middle classes who benefited most. However Thorns's arguments are not entirely convincing. There are some working-class areas where house prices have increased very quickly against his expectation. Munro and Maclennan (1987) show that Glasgow is such a place. Also, over time house-price increases, first registered in the South-east, do tend to trickle down to the rest of the country (Hamnett, 1989), so that the more working-class areas do eventually tend to see house-prices rise in the same way as in middle-class areas. Third, as Hamnett (1989) shows, because house-prices vary systematically by region, and because owner-occupation is the dominant tenure for all social groups except unskilled workers, there can be no doubt that many working-class owner-occupiers in the South-east, and other regions, have shared in house-price gains.

There are, however, some more powerful arguments against Saunders's claims. First, although there are many working-class owner-occupiers, entry into owner-occupation is powerfully affected by one's employment situation, and it is much easier for middle-class individuals to become owner-occupiers than for working class individuals. Savage *et al.* (1991) carried out a survey of the housing destinations of the children of council tenants in Surrey, England. Around 85 per cent of children in middle-class jobs had moved into owner-occupation, but only 42 per cent of those children who were unskilled workers had done so. Second, Saunders's own survey of the housing histories of a sample of owner-occupiers in Burnley, Derby and Slough showed that because middle-class people have, by and large, been in owner-occupation longer than working-class people, they have accrued more money from the housing market with which to improve their housing position. This is because they were more likely to buy their houses when they were extremely cheap, and have therefore gained more as their house prices have increased. Saunders's figures suggest that the average professional or managerial household has gained £30 523 in capital gains, compared with only £6734 for the average working-class household (Saunders, 1990, p. 171). Third, inheritance of housing is becoming more significant, but it is predominantly middle-class people who benefit because the generation currently dying, and leaving their houses to kin, tend to have been owner-occupiers a long time. Since working-class households only moved into owner-occupation on a large scale since 1960 they are, on average, younger and usually still alive. Finally, middle-class employees are often entitled to occupation-related benefits – mortgage subsidies and so forth – and hence are often able to have their housing costs paid by their employers (see the discussion of these points in Savage *et al.*, 1992, ch. 5).

Finally, it should be emphasised that Saunders's concern with housing tenure is arguably very narrow. Rex and Moore's work on housing classes, and the earlier literature on social segregation had not seen tenure as the only important indication of housing quality. In Britain tenure is subject to very important regional differences, with parts of the North of England and Scotland having very high proportions of council housing, concentrated in the inner cities and the outlying estates of big cities. It is less stigmatised in areas of mainly council housing (around half of all households on Tyneside and in Strathclyde live in council property), and where owner-occupation predominates parts of the stock, usually of small Victorian terraces, are in poor repair and have limited amenities. It is thus inappropriate to assume that the causal agent involved is the tenure of the housing: rather the process is one of the people who are poor taking council tenancies. As Table 4.3 shows, there is a strong material basis to occupancy, but still the very poorest sections of British society most often live in privately rented housing, the least preferred of all forms.

**Table 4.3**    *Distribution of tenure by household income, 1983*

| Income quartile | Local authority tenants | Privately rented | | Owner-occupiers | |
|---|---|---|---|---|---|
| | | Unfurnished tenants | Furnished tenants | Purchasing | All |
| Lowest | 44.3 | 47.2 | 41.2 | 2.3 | 12.2 |
| Second | 30.6 | 25.9 | 29.6 | 15.0 | 21.4 |
| Third | 17.0 | 15.6 | 21.6 | 34.3 | 29.8 |
| Highest | 8.1 | 11.3 | 7.5 | 48.4 | 36.6 |

*Source*: adapted from G. Bentham, 'Socio-Tenurial Polarization in the UK 1953–83: The Income Evidence', *Urban Studies*, 23(2) (1986), table 2, p. 160.

It would therefore appear that whilst there are real differences in people's housing position, these are related to social divisions arising out of employment. For this reason it seems most useful to argue that housing divisions and employment divisions often overlap and reinforce each other. In this respect, rather than encouraging sterile debates about whether housing is more important than class or *vice versa*, it seems more useful to consider how housing and employment processes work together to generate urban inequalities.

Perhaps the best theoretical formulation of this argument is Badcock's book, *Unfairly Structured Cities*. Badcock conceives the city as a mechanism which redistributes real income between social groups. He argues that the demand for housing is primarily the result of the structure of employment, position in the labour market is the principal determinant of household financial resources which is, in turn, the main factor constraining access to housing. City institutions – the transport system, educational provision, public amenities, etc. – act as a secondary mechanism in the distribution of resources. Living in a 'good area' means easy access to a supply of high-quality facilities and services which are unevenly spread geographically. He argues that the urban land and housing markets operate to reinforce and compound the inequalities initially arising from the labour market. Local and central states intervene sometimes to moderate the tendency for privileges to concentrate through redistributive policies in favour of the initially disadvantaged. Moreover, groups of people, unprepared to accept the existing allocation of benefits, organise to improve their own circumstances – though then the more powerful the group the more likely it is to succeed. The ultimate outcome of these mechanisms determines important dimensions of the quality of life.

## 4.3 The production of social space: suburbanisation and gentrification

We have maintained that processes of social segregation in the city should not be seen as operating independently from those in the sphere of employment, but that they combine together to produce distinct forms of urban inequality. This section will elaborate this argument by considering how two important recent developments in urban segregation, suburbanisation and gentrification, are linked to wider forms of social inequality. Our point is that particular built forms, with their associated social tones, cannot be seen as caused by economic production processes alone (as Harvey would suggest), but are linked to the operation of wider social inequalities, especially those based on class, gender and ethnicity.

Furthermore, we also want to show through these two cases that the urban form is not simply the effect of the housing preferences of preconstituted social groups. Although structural inequalities are not themselves affected by urban residential patterns, the wider formation of people into social groups is very strongly affected by the existence of a suitable habitat. Hence the production of specific types of urban environment is itself a vital factor in the formation of groups with shared cultural values and outlooks. The rise of suburbia went hand in hand with the hegemony of the middle-class nuclear family; and the more recent development of gentrification is a new form of cultural expression of those middle classes seeking to find alternatives to the nuclear family.

## 4.3.1   *Suburbanisation*

Most residential areas, especially those of the working class, lay in close proximity to places of work during the nineteenth-century. In the absence of quick means of private or public transport people's place of work was likely to be within walking distance of home. This 'employment linkage' was broken with the onset of suburbanisation, a process which occurred from the later nineteenth century in Britain and the USA. In some countries, but not all, new means of transport coincided with the building of new houses on the outer edges of cities, much as the Chicago School concentric ring model described. First trams and railways, then the automobile, made relatively longer journeys to work possible.

Suburbanisation, the decentralisation of population from the cities, happened in class waves. First the bourgeoisie, then sections of the middle classes and eventually the working class, began to live away from the city centre. The rate of growth of suburbs varied from decade to decade and from country to country. The USA has the most extensive suburban development, and mass suburbanisation occurred after the Second World War. The effect has been a shift in land-use from relatively concentrated cities to sprawling metropolitan regions. Such spreading of housing has often been opposed by planners, city authorities worried about losing revenue, conservation interests, and so on, but without much overall success. The UK is something of an exception, partly because of its prevalent anti-urban sentiment, having maintained comparatively compact cities, with London still bounded by its Green Belt designed precisely to preclude urban sprawl.

The development of large tracts of land as new suburbs, the typical form of new private housing development in the USA and Australia, has the effect of creating new settlements that initially attract a fairly homogeneous population – nuclear families with children, each with similar financial means, are typical new residents. This probably was one basis of the notion that the suburban location produces particular styles of life. Such uniformity usually declines as the housing ages and is sold as requirements change.

Not all housing on the peripheries of cities can be seen as suburban. In Britain, Swenarton and Taylor (1985) identified the tendency for the new inter-war suburban areas to be owner-occupied. But policy changed thereafter, many council estates being built on the periphery of large cities, as in Glasgow, Liverpool and London. Initially these had a fairly wide mix of social classes – indeed the early estates were deliberately designed for the lower middle class and respectable working class – though like all British public-sector housing, they have increasingly become the homes of the least skilled manual workers, the unemployed and the retired. Shifts in industrial location (since manufacturing industry has also decentralised from central urban locations) significantly expanded employment in suburban workplaces from the 1960s onwards in Britain. In the USA that process began earlier, from the turn of century when, as Gordon (1984) argued, it was seen as one way of dealing with heightening class struggle in industrial cities.

Descriptions of the process of suburbanisation are fairly well agreed but explanations are contested. There are disputes between neoclassical economists, Marxists and feminists, among others. The orthodox accounts tend to assume that the growth of suburbs represents the meeting of supply and demand for a particular type of housing and residential environment. More specifically it is held that land is cheaper and more plentiful on the fringes of cities and that people prefer to live in reasonably priced, spacious houses with gardens providing they can conveniently get to work. However, such an explanation, if not tautologous, begs many questions about why the suburban solution arises when it does and why there had been the earlier preference for living in the city centre.

This is the starting-point of recent Marxist accounts (Walker, 1981). Distinctive to these is the idea of the second circuit of capital and the building of urban infrastructure as a way to solve problems of over-accumulation (see the discussion in section 3.2). The building of the suburbs allowed capital to be invested in the built environment, so resolving the problem of over-accumulation. This explains the precise period when suburbanisation developed on a mass scale, in the period immediately after the Second World War, since this was a period of economic growth, when the tendency for over-accumulation reached particular heights, and a period when the state provided specific inducements for suburban building. The Marxist account also stressed that suburbs tended to be class-exclusive and, in the USA, were influential in class formation, both increasing the solidarity of the middle classes and creating fragmentation within the working class. As Walker put it: 'The suburbs are not middle class because the middle class lives there; the middle class lives there because the suburbs could be made middle class (Walker, 1981, p. 397).

Weberian accounts, while accepting many of the economic factors just described (though not subscribing to their theoretical premises) usually emphasise more the market for housing. Suburbs were originally built largely for owner-occupation, single family houses, detached in Australia and USA, more likely semi-detached in the UK. They developed a particular image – as containing the nuclear households of the middle classes, often with a particular life-style (see e.g. Fox, 1985, for strong claims about the homogeneity of the American suburbs in the 1950s as middle-class and privatised). To the extent that such a portrayal is true – and there are strong arguments advanced by Gans that we can no more talk of a suburban way of life than we can of an urban one – it is more a function of the way in which houses are financed, built and initially populated. New housing estates tend to be occupied by people in similar income brackets who are at similar life-cycle stages. But it is doubtful whether the explanatory factor is the suburb itself.

Feminist accounts offer yet another explanatory perspective on the suburbs. Davidoff and Hall (1983) document the coincidence in Birmingham, England, of moves by bourgeois households to suburban location and the intensification of domestic life for women in the Victorian era. Wives became household managers, directing servants, but lost any public or business roles they previously occupied. For the middle classes in both the UK and the USA, the disappearance of the domestic servant which began around the time of the First World War altered some of the constraints on suburban living. This partly reflected the unpopularity of the job, partly the growth of average wages which made servants comparatively more expensive to their employers. Thus, whereas many middle-class women had been effectively domestic managers, overseeing the work of sometimes quite a number of servants who tended to do the most labour-intensive, dirty and monotonous jobs, they became housewives, working alone to complete the many tasks that comprise housework. The position of women living in the suburbs was perhaps even less envious than those in more dense urban areas since there were fewer services available. One response to this new situation was the adoption of new domestic technology; the purchase of mass-produced consumer durables increased sharply in the inter-war years, with advertisements typically showing the suburban housewife as the user of such machines. The advertising clichés, of housewives, nuclear families and assorted industrial products are legendary (see Glucksmann, 1990).

There is considerable disagreement among feminists about the nature of technical change within housework (cf. Davidoff 1976; Cowan, 1983; and Luxton, 1980 and 1986). Cowan's book, *More Work for Mother* (1983), examines the changing content and technological context of domestic labour in the USA. It shows how housework alters over time, and differs between groups (richer and poorer) at the same period, but why it never reduces in quantity. One might have thought that with more services available for purchase and new domestic technology it would become less onerous. However, it continues to be said that a woman's work is never done; and there is little perceptible difference in women's response to their labours. The reasons are many, but one is that some new technologies create extra tasks; this was the case with the automobile in inter-war years in America where increased suburban living meant that housewives then had to travel to shops and ferry children around — a new set of jobs. Other technologies encourage standards of living to rise: new laundering techniques, a more readily available water supply and washing machines, not to mention more clothes, also make more work for mother.

While Cowan's account in part supports some of the functionalist–Marxist arguments about the role of suburbanisation in creating demand for manufactured white goods, it also challenges Marxist accounts in that it points to the implications of the process for gender inequalities too. The isolated suburban housewife, looking after small children, has one of the least enviable working conditions of all people, as Oakley (1974) showed.

Suburbanisation, then, emerged from and reinforced social inequality. The building of the suburbs made profits for builders and landowners. It left the poorest sections of the population in the central areas of cities. Residence in a smart middle-class suburb reduced some of the negative consequences of the experience of modernity and, because the housing market effectively excluded the less-affluent, helped to create solidarity among the middle classes. However, quality of life varied from one suburb to another, with the most distant ones in Australia and the USA housing the working classes and providing limited amenities. In addition, suburbanisation reproduced gender inequalities, for location in the sub-urbs restricted job opportunities for married women and further en-trenched the domestic division of labour within the household. It was in the suburbs that the nuclear family reached its mid-twentieth-century prominence. Here the husband went out to work, often in the city centre, whilst the wife stayed at home, carrying out domestic tasks, without help from servants. In the next section we show how challenges to this domestic form is related to a new form of living – gentrification.

## 4.3.2 *Gentrification*

Since the beginning of the 1970s there has been a lot of scholarly debate about gentrification, which in its loosest definition means the movement of middle classes back into city centres. The term was apparently coined by Ruth Glass in the 1950s to refer to changes in the housing stock of London. Gentrification is identifiable as the coincidence of four processes:

1. resettlement and social concentration entailing the displacement of one group of residents with another of higher social status;
2. transformation in the built environment exhibiting some distinctive aesthetic features and the emergence of new local services;
3. the gathering together of persons with a putatively shared culture and life-style, or at least with shared, class-related, consumer preferences;
4. economic reordering of property values, a commercial opportunity for the construction industry, and often an extension of the system of the private ownership of domestic property (Warde, 1991).

All in all it is a process of the middle class replacing the working class; increasing property values; alteration in the built environment and the emergence of a new urban style of life. This process is developing in most of the larger Western cities and, according to some, in the countryside too (Thrift, 1987).

A good example of the process of gentrification is that described by Sharon Zukin's *Loft Living* (1988). She describes change in an area of Manhattan, New York, which shifted from being an area of garment industry sweat-shops, through deindustrialisation, to an area where Bohemian artists took over factory-floor space and turned them into domestic 'lofts'. This was an expression of a certain aesthetic taste for restored industrial premises and was a cheap way of obtaining an inner-city place of residence. This made the area 'interesting' and as it encouraged the opening of art galleries and some specialist shops, the place became relatively habitable and carried some radical chic. This in turn, attracted the attention of property developers who began to see opportunities for profit in further expanding desirable residential accommodation. At that point much wealthier middle-class people began to buy lofts and effectively priced Bohemian artists out of the local housing market. As a result the New York City Council pronounced the area an artists' quarter, actually protecting the artistic community to some extent, in order to retain what had become a tourist attraction. With the social upgrading of the resident population went also the opening of assorted specialist boutiques and service facilities, which completely transformed the area over a period of less than twenty years. It amounted to the revitalisation of an inner-city area and it made vast fortunes for firms in the property and building trades who bought up and converted lofts for upper middle-class use. What this shows, among other things, is the link between capital accumulation and aesthetic taste or life-style and the process whereby social areas in cities change their functions over time. Zukin frames her explanation in concepts derived from Harvey, but gives considerable weight to cultural factors shaping living spaces.

Recent analysis has exposed a variety of popular misapprehensions about the process of gentrification. It has, for instance, disabused us of the notion that it is an unambiguously beneficial process of inner-city revitalisation. For a start, it means displacement for indigenous, poorer groups who usually become more marginalised as they move on to other areas within the city. Improved services and renovated exteriors are only beneficial to part of the population. Nor does it, at least in New York, lead to increasing wealth of the city as a whole. Gentrification was encouraged, particularly by American local governments, because it was thought that it attracted new, high-income residents who through their tax contributions would help to solve the fiscal problems of the cities. However, it was shown that gentrification was not a return of the professional and managerial classes from the suburbs, rather that it merely represented movement within the city boundaries of such people. It was just a concentration of wealthier, better-educated citizens in particular districts; as Smith (1979) put it, it was a return not of people, but of capital, to the city. As such it merely contributes to greater residential segregation.

Explanations of gentrification are controversial. Some writers, especially those influenced by Harvey, emphasised supply-side factors, such as the appropriate investment in the built environment. Others emphasised demand factors, notably the desire of some people to live in the centre of cities. Hamnett's (1984a) review of the literature distinguished six different, plausible accounts:

1. by living in the inner city people trade-off improved accessibility to work and city services against a loss of domestic space available in the suburbs – a consideration related to the disadvantages of commuting;
2. demographic changes – the baby boom and new household patterns – sharply increased the number of households requiring accommodation in the 1970s, the demand for which could not be met through new suburban building. Constraint rather than a preference for city life then accounts for the revitalisation of the inner cities;
3. gentrification is purely a matter of consumer preference, of life-style and consumer choice.
4. occupational change has resulted in the emergence of a new social class for which gentrification is a material and cultural expressions.
5. the housing market has, through restrictions of supply and price, made cheaper inner-city areas the most accessible points at which initially to become an owner-occupier.
6. gentrification has been explained by the logic of 'the rent gap', where financial considerations of ground-rent and accumulation from property determined that real-estate development in certain areas of cities becomes a profitable use of capital.

As Hamnett points out these need not necessarily be seen as mutually exclusive, but all have constituted the central mechanism in different accounts and suggest alternative theoretical orientations.

The 'rent-gap' explanation, developed by Neil Smith and drawing on Harvey's work, offered the most theoretically concise account of why gentrification occurs. It explains why some areas become ripe for gentrification. It is a matter of the financial returns to landowners on their property. As a district deteriorates, the rent obtainable from letting houses falls and the value of the land for new development is minimal. Hence existing landlords let properties deteriorate even further because they will never get returns on investment in maintenance. At a certain point in this cycle of decline, though, it becomes profitable to change the use of the land. Land, and the buildings on it, can be bought up very cheaply and houses attractive to middle-class tenants or owners can be erected at a profit. This account probably applies most forcefully to the USA where some areas of cities tended to become largely derelict before housing was renovated by big property developers. The sociology of 'real estate business' is of major importance in America. Dereliction occurs less frequently in the UK, where gentrification often more resembles an informal social movement as individual purchasers renovate their newly bought Victorian working-class cottages in an approved style: Williams (1986, p. 57) claims to be able to spot gentrification by 'brass door knockers, pastel colours, paper lanterns, bamboo blinds and light, open interiors, now supplemented by iron bars, security screens and alarm system'. However there are intra- and international variations in approved aesthetic styles of gentrification: what is considered worthy of restoration varies between Melbourne, Sydney and Adelaide, for example. There are also international differences in the proportions of restorations of old houses (prominent in Australia and the UK), as against demolition and new construction (more prevalent in USA and Canada). In this sense, then, urban sociologists have identified commercial and production interests lying behind a process which is often thought of as a matter of individual taste. However, rent-gap theory does not, of itself, explain shared taste. Its critics concede that it might identify one precondition of gentrification, but that it offers no purchase on the cultural aspects of the preference for living in the city. In particular, as Zukin emphasises, it ignores the fact that an essential prerequisite for gentrification is also a process whereby a cultural vanguard initially move to an area to give it cultural legitimacy.

Gentrification has normally been thought of as a class phenomenon and it is true that the upgrading of the class composition of an area is a defining feature of the process. However, compared with suburbanisation and the movement of the middle classes to rural locations, it is not a very popular choice of the middle classes. It is the trend of a middle-class minority. Explaining what are the key characteristics of that minority of gentrifiers has proved difficult and despite it being attributed to 'the new middle class' (Jager, 1986; Smith, 1987) it has not been clearly established that it is their employment characteristics that differentiate gentrifiers from the middle classes who live elsewhere. Careful empirical studies of gentrifying areas give support to the hypothesis that it is related more to changing gender relations within middle-class households.

One sociologically important precipitating factor in the growth of gentrification has been the rate of new household formation. Demand for houses increased sharply in the mid-1960s as the children in the baby-boom of the immediate post-war years began to set up their own homes. There was not sufficient new suburban building to meet the demand and anyway suburban housing was often too expensive for young couples; hence, the search for 'improving neighbourhoods' within the city. The effects on Western cities of changing household composition, size and organisation, is much underestimated. In Britain by 1989, over 25 per cent of households contained only one person, and another 34 per cent only two people. In big cities households containing one or two adults make up a very large majority of the total. Large family households are a decreasing proportion of all households and are relatively rare in big cities. They are especially rare in gentrifying areas. To some extent, then, gentrification reflects a change in Western household types.

The most distinctive element of gentrifying households is the extent of female participation in professional and managerial labour markets. The distinctive social attributes of populations of these areas include: female population increasing faster than the male population; an unusually high proportion of young and single women; very high proportions of women in professional and technical occupations; high levels of academic credentials; a high proportion of dual-earner households, but few children; presence of young single professional women: and the postponement of marriage and child-bearing (Smith, 1987; Mills, 1988; Rose, 1988; Beauregard, 1986). Reasons for this include increasing numbers of women in highest income jobs, with associated housing opportunities and constraints; minimising journey-to-work costs for households containing more than one earner; facilitating the substitution of marketed services for domestic ones; diversifying 'ways of carrying out reproductive work', partly because there is 'a concentration of supportive services' and 'a "tolerant" ambience' (Rose, 1988, p. 131). Markusen (1981, p. 32) sees gentrification overall as 'in large part a result of the breakdown of the patriarchal household' and Smith (1987) considers it a result of effective pressure by the women's movement.

The living arrangements of the central city permit women to reorient their behaviour in the housing market to meet domestic and labour-market pressures. Gentrification is thus related to changes in women's career patterns, and has accelerated in parallel with the gradual extension of educational opportunities for women since the 1960s, wider employment prospects for married women in particular, and revised calculations regarding the integration of the activities of income generation and child-rearing. Among single households generally, access to commercial alternatives to services typically provided by women in family households can be readily obtained. The location of dual-earner households in the inner city is a solution to problems of access to work and home and of combining paid and unpaid labour. Thus, for utilitarian reasons, the life-course stage reached and the gender division of labour within households support the demand for inner-city residence.

Besides the use-value of inner-city location there are also cultural reasons for gentrification. The social marginality of first-stage gentrifiers has often been noted (e.g. Zukin, 1988) and it may be that the symbolism of gentrification signals uncertain status. Thus, Warde (1991, p. 230) hypothesised that 'the aesthetics of renovated properties reflect a certain status insecurity arising from the adoption of unconventional household strategies within the middle classes'. 'Unconventional' in this case might refer not just to employed middle-class wives but also to gay households and one-parent, female-headed families living as 'marginal gentrifiers' in the inner cities (see Rose, 1984). The stylish post-modern exuberance of the condominia and the gravitas of restored Victoriana might be seen as alternative sources of identity-value, compensating for imagined status deficits associated with unorthodox household forms.

Other accounts, however, have shown that the well-established middle classes are also present in inner urban locations. In a study of two newly gentrifying enclaves in Hackney, one of the poorest boroughs in inner London, in 1988–9, Butler (1991) showed that the residents typic-ally held cosmopolitan values, with positive images of city-living based on a deep dislike of suburban environments, an attachment to the area in which they were living, and strong political aversions to the Conservative Party and reductions in public expenditure. Leisure activities tended to involve sociability, involving quite extensive usage of the cultural facil-ities of central London. These features distinguished the interviewees, who were predominantly professional and administrative workers, from the average members of their occupational groups; indeed the gentrifiers had higher incomes, longer education and came from higher social classes than the average. If not living alone, they were overwhelmingly (88 per cent) in dual-earner households. They represented, thus, a fraction of the British middle class, distinctive in economic, cultural and political dispositions.

Gentrification, like other forms of segregation, is an expression of inequality and social closure. However, it is governed as much by forms of household organisation as by capitalist logic. The rise of gentrification is also the story of the rise of new forms of middle-class social groups, and thus shows how the formation of particular urban spaces is intimately tied up with the development of social groups themselves.

## 4.4   Changing inequalities? Polarisation and survival strategies

The analysis of gentrification raises a number of broader issues about contemporary processes of urban segregation which we pursue in this section. One of these is the issue of whether gentrification accentuates polarisation within the city or diminishes it. A second is the importance of household relationships for affecting forms of life chances and patterns of segregation.

### 4.4.1   *Social polarisation*

Polarisation has become a very popular metaphor which is used to encompass contemporary changes in patterns of socio-spatial inequality. Saunders, for instance has summarised contemporary social change as 'a stark polarisation of British society which is expressed in a number of forms – the division between north and south, between inner city and suburb, between black and white, between unemployed and employed' Saunders (1986, p. 8). New Right politics in Britain and the USA have, as a matter of policy, sought to increase some social inequalities (see e.g. Hudson and Williams, 1990). Reduced social-security spending, more-limited state intervention and subsidies for other welfare services, and lower tax-levels for the rich, have altered the distribution of income and wealth to the disadvantage of the poor. In addition, as we saw in Chapter 3, industrial restructuring has altered the rewards and content of different jobs, creating many insecure service jobs and making many workers redundant. However, despite the rhetorical appeal of describing this as polarisation in order to express concern, it is unclear whether these inequalities are systematic and cumulative rather than being just another round of reordering the material inequalities that are endemic to capitalist societies.

Gentrification has been seen by Williams and Smith (1986, pp. 219–21) as the 'geographical polarisation of the city' because it accentuates divisions between the new privileged middle-class residents of inner cities and other working-class inhabitants. But it is important to distinguish the essential features of a genuine process of polarisation, as opposed, say, to one of concentration or divergence. The term 'polarisation' derives as metaphor from the language of electrolysis and magnetism where the tendency for materials to be attracted to poles sets up an opposing force-field between those poles. This is a useful metaphor for sociological purposes, for some social processes do have the effect of causing two groups of people to develop internal solidarities which, in turn, generate mutual tensions. A genuine process of polarisation will therefore imply:

(i) social groups moving to two separate poles because of the operation of a single causal mechanism;

(ii) the existence of tension or conflict, between those two social groups, deriving from the same causal mechanism.

Identifying such a mechanism can provide an interesting and parsimonious account of certain types of social structuring and social conflict. However, many of the processes described as polarisation do not have the requisite formal properties.

Gentrification is a process which entails inequalities of power and wealth between the gentrifiers and the displaced population. However, in cases of successful gentrification it is only the gentrifiers who develop solidarities since almost always the displaced are spatially dispersed to other parts of the city. If on the other hand the indigenous residents resist gentrification there is no group of gentrifiers to feel aggrieved. There is thus no basis for a surviving 'force field' of tension. The asymmetrical outcome ought to preclude the use of the term 'polarisation'.

The term is used more helpfully by Chris Hamnett (1984b; see also Bentham, 1986), who has coined the term 'socio-tenurial polarisation'. This refers to the tendency for people with limited material resources to be increasingly concentrated in residualised public-sector housing, often on large estates, either in the inner city (for instance, in Hackney or Newham in London), or in large out-of-town estates (such as Kirkby in Liverpool, or in much of central Scotland). More affluent households increasingly join the ranks of owner-occupiers. At the high point of the British welfare state, from the end of the Second World War to the mid-1960s, council housing was occupied by people of all social classes and was generally considered as providing improvement in the quality of housing. Since 1966, however, at the latest, there has been an increasing tendency for affluent groups to abandon rented housing of all kinds and enter owner-occupation. The inhabitants of council houses are increasingly likely to be the elderly, the unemployed and those reliant on other forms of social security payments. This process might be seen as self-reinforcing – as council housing gains an increasingly residualised status so the incentive for middle-class people to move out becomes greater.

This socio-tenurial polarisation has been seen as helping to produce an 'urban underclass' of people permanently excluded from good housing and secure employment (Pahl, 1988; Dahrendorf, 1987). Lydia Morris refers to the fact that:

> at the two extremes it is possible to identify a process of polarization which extends not simply to household types but also to spatial and social groupings of households, in terms of both access to employment and exchange of mutual aid (Morris, 1987, p. 333).

The idea of the underclass is also taken up in discussions of polarisation taking place in the 'world cities' where major corporate and governmental power is located. Here affluent professional and managerial workers purchase consumer services that are staffed by low-paid, often immigrant, workers. Sassen-Koob identifies polarisation as occurring within leading industrial sectors between 'high-income and low-wage jobs' (Sassen-Koob, 1987, p. 140) and notes that 'economic polarisation patterns seem to be particularly pronounced in major cities such as New York and Los Angeles' (ibid, p. 140), which she attributes to agglomeration economies. She finds evidence of 'polarisation in the consumption structure' because gentrification 'rests in the last analysis, on the availability of a vast supply of low-wage workers' (ibid, p. 141) and she relates all these to increases in the size of the informal economy.

This theme is taken up by a number of American writers. Kasarda (1988) discusses the huge fall in employment located in central urban locations, with the result that many working-class people living in urban centres have been made unemployed. He also points out that of the employment which remains in the centre of large cities, increasing proportions are geared to professionals and managers. In the centre of New York only 22 per cent of employment was in 'white collar services' in 1953, a proportion which increased to 49 per cent by 1984. Unemployment falls particularly hard on the ethnic minorities who also tend to be segregated in inner urban sites. The same picture is painted of Los Angeles by Mike Davis who examines the massive economic, social and cultural disparities between the exclusive white suburbs and the ganglands of the downtown.

This does appear to be a more accurate use of the idea of polarisation. In world cities, economic transformations associated with the global operations of the financial institutions have effects on the resources of urban residents, and, hence, on the relationships between different groups of workers in cities. This is more properly a process of polarisation because the same mechanism, industrial restructuring, creates the occupational places locally for both the middle classes and those employed in menial work and they remain symbiotically connected. Moreover, to the extent that these groups live in close proximity to one another this may be a source of social and political conflict.

One area of major importance in assessing claims about the creation of an underclass is the possible existence of an informal or household economy in large cities. What is crucial here is whether it is possible for those excluded from secure formal employment to rely on informal work and household resources as compensation, or whether, by contrast it is those who are already advantaged in the labour market who stand to benefit most.

## 4.4.2   *Households and their work strategies*

While revenue from property and occupation is the most basic source of inequalities between individuals in capitalist societies, there are other kinds of resources that can be mobilised in pursuit of social survival. Urban sociology has always shown an interest in the contribution of reciprocal relations within communities and, more recently, has investigated the nature of the informal economy which can provide supplementary or alternative resources for those involved in appropriate social networks. The informal economy in some accounts (e.g. Pahl, 1984) refers only to communal economic arrangements – sometimes legal, sometimes not – which are beyond the scope of formal or state regulation. In other accounts (e.g. Harding and Jenkins, 1989) it also includes work done within households. We prefer the first usage, since the familial social relations typically involved in domestic work are significantly different from those of the communal exchange of labour and goods. Both work done at home and that exchanged with friends, neighbours and associates contribute to household standards of living and thus can affect the nature of inequalities. Many authors have seen these processes as particularly critical in the advanced societies in recent years as increased unemployment and cut-backs in welfare provision tend to reduce the resources of the poorer sections of the population.

This concern with the nature of the informal economy and household relations overlaps with the sociology of the family and there are some close connections between literatures on the family in industrial society and those on urbanism, as we suggested in Chapter 2. For instance, in the UK the studies of Willmott and Young in Bethnal Green and Woodford are much quoted as part of our understanding of social relations in neighbourhoods in the city. Community studies have usually taken detailed note of behaviour inside households. One aspect of what we know about mining communities is that they are patriarchal, characterised by disparities of power between husbands and wives (e.g. *inter alia*, Dennis *et al.*, 1956). Another key feature about family sociology is the exploration of levels of contact between members of different households, sometimes with other kin but equally often with neighbours, members of interest groups and associations, etc. Debates about privatisation of the family, the loss of community, the political consequences of owner occupation, etc. hang on these inter-household relationships.

Feminist scholars in particular have insisted, partly in order properly to appreciate gender inequalities in heterosexual relationships and partly to register changing domestic arrangements, that we should work with the concept of household rather than family. Indeed, concentration on households has produced a lot of new insights into change in the city and in everyday life, as well as throwing more light on gender relations.

Let us examine an important empirical study concerning household relations, the different work done by household members, and their relationship to the local economy both formal and informal. Ray Pahl, since the 1960s, has worked on the emerging themes in urban studies – urban behaviour in rural locations (Pahl, 1965), planning issues (Pahl, 1970), urban managerialism and urban inequalities (Pahl, 1975). In the late 1970s, inspired by theses about the informal economy and an emerging 'self-service society', he began research about the changing nature of work in industrial societies and its effects on social class and inequality. The resulting book, *Divisions of Labour*, (Pahl, 1984) is in part a report on a study of life and labour in a period of industrial restructuring in one locality, the Isle of Sheppey, off the Kent coast in England. It is in many ways an archetypal product of urban sociology. It has the mix of objects of study, the interrelationship of an examination of industrial change, in a particular place looked at contextually, referring to household, life-cycle work, class and consumption. It might be seen as a latter-day study of 'place, work and folk'.

In 1981 Pahl and Wallace administered a questionnaire to 730 people inquiring as to how households organise their time and resources in order to 'get by' in a period of economic recession. The central questions concerned what services households consumed and whose labour was used to provide those services. The study began from a contemporary political issue, the extent of the so-called 'black economy' – that is, work done for money but not declared to the Inland Revenue, thus evading taxation. It was imagined that the unemployed (a rapidly expanding category at the time) might be particularly prone to such behaviour, using their 'free time' to work for an undeclared income. Pahl discovered these beliefs to be almost totally unfounded. There was little evidence of a flourishing informal economy, whether black or communal, on the Isle of Sheppey. On this point it might be asked how representative Sheppey might be, for the informal economy is central to economic life in many cities not only in the developing world, but also in Italy and some of the American world cities (Mingione, 1987; Redclift and Mingione, 1985; Sassen-Koob, 1987).

What Pahl discovered instead was an enormous amount of work being done in the domestic mode of provision. Moreover, the more people in a household that were in formal, paid employment, the more work they did at home. It was this that suggested to Pahl that a process of social polarisation was occurring. Households with more than one earner had relatively high incomes but also produced more services for themselves – house improvements, home cooking, etc. As a result their standard of living was substantially higher than those households with little or no paid employment. What Pahl perceived was not so much a post-industrial, but rather a self-service, economy emerging, a trend illustrated by the explosion of expenditure in Britain on do-it-yourself products and domestic machines of all kinds.

Pahl examined the deployment of labour in terms of 'household work strategies': 'how households allocate their collective effort to getting all the work done that they define has, or they feel needs, to be done' (Pahl, 1984, p. 113). Households were conceived as units that 'import' some labour services and 'export' others. Outputs are certain forms of work: employment, aid to associates, paid informal work and domestic labour. Inputs are to be understood in terms of the economic 'sector' by means of which services are obtained by the household, namely, the formal, informal-paid, communal and domestic economies.

Pahl examined in detail which types of household did which tasks. The pattern was partly as expected. Stages of the life-cycle explained some variations – households without small children do not change nappies. Income was also of some importance: people who cannot afford cars are not engaged in car-maintenance tasks. Importantly, Pahl argued that household income was largely the result of the number of earners. Social-class differences mattered little by comparison. Nor was class germane to understanding the distribution of domestic labour. Within the household women did considerably more domestic work than men. The share of work done by a married woman depended largely on whether she had a paid job and her stage of the life-cycle: women do the most unequal proportion of domestic labour when they have young children, precisely at the point when there is most work needing to be done. But overall, for Pahl, one of his principal empirical findings was that the quantities of services provided to different households led to polarisation between work-rich and work-starved households: 'the distribution of work on the island [of Sheppey] is producing a pattern of polarisation' (Pahl, 1984, p. 309). The mechanism invoked is the combination of the growth of paid employment for married women and the way in which the British benefits system discourages the wives of unemployed men from taking paid employment.

One of the problems with Pahl's analysis lies in its methods. Pahl managed to contextualise household strategies to only a limited extent. Using structured interviews in hundreds of households means that only the barest bones of local context can be taken into account in explaining individual behaviour. Household decisions are examined at a distance and conceived as individual choice rather than as collectively constructed. The general absence of an ethnographic strand to the research (with the exception of a close examination of two households, Pahl, 1984, pp. 277–310) reduces the sense in which decisions are seen to be made in a particular context and tends to render each household isolated from its environment.

Nonetheless, Pahl's approach proved powerful in pulling together the concerns of political economy and industrial change with the daily material practices of households. Restructuring alters the economic context in which households make decisions about – or perhaps put into practice – the organisation of subsistence. However, besides some reservations expressed about the concept of household work strategies (e.g. Crow, 1989), Pahl's conclusions about the receding importance of social class for understanding inequality have caused considerable debate.

The central issue arising out of all the recent urban research discussed in this chapter is the extent to which the concept of social class remains of much value. The idea that there is increasing polarisation between a 'middle mass' and 'underclass' questions the extent to which the older social class division between working class and middle class makes much sense. The idea that housing position is an important factor on life chances and cannot be linked to class also contributed to this belief about the inadequacy of class analysis. Perhaps most importantly of all, gender relations are also crucial, and appear to cross-cut class relations – so that there are huge differences, for instance, between the suburban middle-class household of employed husband and dependent housewife on the one hand, and the dual-career households of the cosmopolitan middle classes.

This has led to a more general debate about the virtues of examining inequality in terms of class. This partly reflects a general sociological reassessment of the role of class in late capitalist society. Pahl argues that social class is no longer particularly useful as a practical tool of analysis and advocates, instead, using life-style groupings in the manner of the advertising industry. Analysts of class relations tended to find this wildly exaggerated (see Marshall, 1991; Crompton, 1991), though at least one urbanist (Mullins, 1991) thought he had not gone far enough. One problem with the critique is that it is often unclear whether criticisms are directed at the concept of class in general – so that it might be claimed that the concept never had any use, even in the heyday of industrial capitalism – or that it was at one time useful but has today been made obsolete by social change. As a result it is sometimes also unclear whether the idea of social class is being criticised, or the idea that particular social classes exist (for instance, the working class).

Defenders of class analysis have tried primarily to show the value of class measures in quantitative analysis. In particular Marshall *et al.* (1988) have argued that social class, at least as measured by Goldthorpe's neo-Weberian class schema, is still a powerful correlate of life-chances, cultural values, and political beliefs. Indeed critics of class analysis using quantitative questionnaire evidence have to some extent admitted defeat (Saunders, 1990; and see Chapter 7). However it is unwise to rely too heavily on such evidence, which largely ignores context. Savage *et al.* (1992) argue that it is important to retain the concept of social class as an exploratory tool. However, it is essential to recognise two constraints: that gender relations cannot easily be abstracted from social class and hence that classes are gendered (Savage 1992); and also that class relations are not only structured by the division between capital and labour, but also by cultural and organisational factors. Once this is done, changing forms of social inequality can be explored using the concept of class in the present period as in earlier historical periods.

## 4.5 Conclusion

This chapter has examined recent literature on social inequality in cities, much of which has been inspired by Weberian theorising about how cities act as a distributor of benefits. Urban sociology has for a long time considered such matters in terms of segregation and one of the main spatial patterns, on the ground, has been the segregation of different categories of people in different areas of the city. The wing of the Chicago School using ecological analysis had long realised and described the extent of such segregation but had done little to explain the process. The more ethnographic wing of the School had been relatively little interested in inequality as such, being more concerned to give accounts of subcultural differences among groups rather than dwell on material inequalities. Both Marxist and Weberian scholars in the past two decades have been prominent in bringing such matters onto the agenda for urban studies. In addition feminists have highlighted the gendered aspects of such inequalities. The result has been more theoretically informed analyses of social inequalities and their spatial representations in processes like gentrification, suburbanisation and ghettoisation. These processes remind us that patterns of segregation are dynamic and that urban development continuously reorders the sociospatial mosaic of residential inequality. We are thus sceptical whether there are any universal patterns of inequalities within cities, for the vast socio–structural difference between a World City and the Isle of Sheppey suggests that overall generalisation is likely to be inadequate.

Heuristically, it seems beneficial to see the generation of material inequalities in terms of capitalist-market mechanisms for the distribution of rewards, regulated and coordinated through state policies for land-use, employment and welfare. Accounts of inequalities within cities have begun to make some progress in linking economic production to patterns of segregation. Emphasis on the role of capital in property development and its effect on urban form and the development of theories of the housing market, which consider both house construction and patterns of purchase and rent, have improved our understanding of processes within cities. But as yet, the theoretical connections to the more general theories of uneven development remain relatively weak. The ways in which cross-cutting social divisions of class, gender and ethnicity mediate the logic of capital accumulation are complex. The determinants of everyday life of subcultural groups, which emerge on the basis of material inequalities, remain obscure.

We still know insufficient about the texture and experience of the daily life of different groups of people in the city. Information about the distribution of inequality remains greater than our knowledge of the varied experiences of urban living. The need for repeated ethnographic studies that can tease out *changes* in everyday life remains. It is one of our main arguments that it is necessary to appreciate the dialectical relations between the mechanisms of capitalist production and the experience of modernity. The growing focus on the household is useful in this regard for it is, simultaneously, a unit of material resources, a site of work, a locus of the reproduction of labour power and a hub of everyday life. Survival strategies that encompass cooperation with other households as well as competition through impersonal market channels entail a complex embedding of households in their external environments. The patterns of sociation – reciprocity, conviviality, solidarity, competition and conflict – that routinely arise in and between neighbourhoods and subcultural groups remain critical to the experience of city life. Such matters have in the past been addressed in terms of urban culture, divorced from questions of inequality. However, social inequality remains a foundation of the experience of everyday life in cities and the recently renewed intellectual interest in urban culture should not be allowed to diminish its importance.

# 5 Perspectives on Urban Culture

The early urban sociologists, especially those associated with the Chicago School, were intent on probing the forms of social interaction found in cities. Borrowing the concept of sociation from Simmel they examined the informal social relations which existed in different parts of the city and which underpinned everyday life for various social groups and the processes of social organisation and disorganisation which they saw as typical of modern urban experience.

They bequeathed an interest in urban culture. But this legacy has proved a difficult one for later urban sociologists to utilise. Empirical studies suggested that urban cultures could rarely be distinguished from rural cultures. Conceptually, Manuel Castells (1977) dismissed the study of urban culture as ideological, as being incapable of rigorous theoretical definition. Other writers in the early 1980s denied that it was possible to discern a distinct urban culture (Saunders, 1981; Smith, 1980). Yet in the past decade there has been a major revival in cultural studies, particularly amongst those interested in debates on modernity and post-modernity. There have also been a growing number of studies examining the experience of urban living, in all its ramifications (e.g. Castells, 1983; Wilson, 1991; Jukes, 1990; Harvey, 1985b). The study of urban culture has returned to the agenda.

There are two contrasting approaches to the study of urban culture. The first attempts a generic definition of some sort, where writers discern some common threads which apply to all cities. This project is usually concerned with delimiting an urban way of life. A second approach abandons the quest for a single form of urban culture and suggests that every city has its own specific culture, its own meaning. Here, the task of the writer is not to come up with statements about an urban way of life which holds, in some form, for all cities, but to identify the processes

96

which give different meanings to cities. This chapter considers the value of generic definitions of urban culture. The next considers how we might think in terms of specific urban cultures.

There were two alternative classic attempts to establish a generic definition of urban culture. The first of these was developed by Louis Wirth in 'Urbanism as a Way of Life' (1938), which sought to generalise from the studies of his colleagues in Chicago. We will argue that this was largely concerned to distinguish between cities and rural settlements, thereby defining urban culture spatially. The second, and prior, approach was that of Simmel, who defined the nature of modern urban culture temporally, in relation to older social forms. Whilst Wirth contrasts the city with the countryside, Simmel contrasts the modern urban dweller with rural and small-town residents of an earlier epoch.

We begin by discussing Wirth's arguments, indicating some of the problems with his account which subsequent discussion has bought to light. We then contrast Simmel's account of metropolitan culture, taking pains to show how it differs from Wirth's. Simmel's work has recently experienced a major revival, leading to new lines of research on urban culture which we review. Nonetheless, we conclude that generic definitions of urban culture are bound to fail because they cannot deal with the variety of urban meanings tied up with cities.

## 5.1   Louis Wirth and the 'urban way of life'

Louis Wirth's 'Urbanism as a Way of Life', published in 1938, was one of the most influential sociological articles ever written. In it he laid down a research agenda for examining how cities produced forms of social interaction different from those of rural settlements, and hence how urban and rural ways of life could be distinguished.

Wirth (and Redfield, who also helped to develop an interest in urban and rural cultures) wrote at a time when the pre-eminence of Chicago was threatened by other American departments championing a more scientific brand of sociology. The Chicago School itself in the 1930s also reformulated traditional themes within a positivist framework, more congenial to the intellectual climate. Thus Wirth attempted to analyse urban culture by distinguishing three 'independent variables' – size, density and heterogeneity – which could be seen as causal factors for urban cultural life. In order to tighten up the study of urban culture, it became more important to compare it with another, 'dependent' variable, in this case rural culture. In one important respect Wirth succeeded beyond measure, setting up an empirically testable hypothesis, which has sustained intense debate ever since.

Wirth's basic argument was that city life was characterised by isolation and social disorganisation, and that this was due to the fact that all cities were large, dense, and heterogeneous. In his own words:

> Large numbers count for individual variability, the relative absence of intimate personal acquaintanceship, the segmentalization of human relations which are largely anonymous, superficial and transitory, and associated characteristics. Density involves diversification and speciali-zation, the coincidence of close physical contract and distant social relations, glaring contrasts, a complex pattern of segregation, the predominance of formal social control, and accentuated friction, among other phenomena. Heterogeneity tends to break down rigid social structures and to produce mobility, instability, and insecurity, and the affiliation of the individuals with a variety of intersecting and tangential social groups with a high rate of membership turnover. The pecuniary nexus tends to displace personal relations, and institutions tend to cater to mass rather than individual requirements. The indi-vidual thus becomes effective only as he acts through organized groups (Wirth, 1938, p. 1).

All three traits mentioned by Wirth were seen as being characteristic of urban rather than rural life: only cities had large numbers, dense and heterogeneous social relations. Hence a distinct urban way of life could be distinguished. Wirth thus implied that there was some connection be-tween type of settlement and psychic life, that certain sorts of personal-ities, psychological traits, and attitudes to life, were associated with being in the city. Strong social identities were eroded by urban life. In making this argument Wirth drew upon earlier sociological writers who had distinguished communities from more fragmented social relations. Most famously, Toennies's distinction between *Gemeinschaft* and *Gesellschaft* (usually translated as community and association) has often been inter-preted in the same way – that different kinds of place, rural as opposed to urban, determine different kinds of social relationship. *Gemeinschaft* is often thought of as being 'community', where relationships between people were intimate and personalised. In small, rural communities, people formed close, intense and overlapping ties which bound them together into a coherent cultural whole. In modern societies, based on *Gesellschaft*, social relations of association predominate, people inter-relating impersonally and instrumentally. In this situation actors encounter more other people than in a *Gemeinschaftlich* society, but they deal with them for specific purposes only, forfeiting the density of contacts which characterise *Gemeinschaft* (for further elaboration see Lee and Newby, 1982, ch. 3). From this reading of Toennies comes a whole genre of work that considers urban culture as the experience of anonymity, loneliness, isolation, and fleeting relationships. The implicit contrast is with the security and warmth of the rural community.

## 5.1.1   The critics of Wirth

From this contrast emerged a series of debates in the 1950s and 1960s about the transformation of the American personality, the decline of community, the entrenchment of mass, individualised, society, and the existence of an urban–rural continuum. All these debates were organised around Wirth's belief that as urbanism spread, so primary social relationships would weaken and decline. They were hence predominantly concerned with the idea of disorganisation, with the decline of secure and pervasive social bonds in an urbanised society. This was a continuation of the way in which the Chicago School presented cities as, essentially, disorganised and disorderly. But the other emphasis of Chicago writers – on the informal social bonding in urban areas – was neglected. The maelstroms of invasion and succession, of weak traditional ties, of competition between groups, etc., were seen to cause particular urban problems, a view that probably continues to have some sway over policy-makers.

The considered response, over fifty years, to Wirth's arguments and the debates they generated, has been to reject the idea of there being 'an urban way of life', largely because of the persistence of segregated, collective life in even the largest cities. More specifically the objections are threefold:

1.  it misspecified the determining character of space;
2.  empirical inquiries found communities in the city and conflict in the countryside;
3.  the diversity of group cultures challenged the idea that there was one dominant way of life.

Let us consider these points in turn.

## (i)    *Spatial determinism*

There can be no doubt that there are many lonely, isolated people living in cities. What is in doubt is whether they tend to predominate there, and even if they do, whether cities themselves can be held responsible. One of the most important post-war writers on this issue is the American, Herbert Gans. He claimed that:

> Wirth conceived the urban population as consisting of heterogeneous individuals, torn from past social systems, unable to develop new ones, and therefore prey to social anarchy in the city . . . [This] ignores the fact that this [inner city] population consists of relatively homogeneous groups, with social and cultural moorings that shield it fairly effectively from the suggested consequences of number, density and heterogeneity. This applies even more to the residents of the outer city, who constitute a majority of the total city population (Gans, 1968b, p. 99).

Gans admitted that there were some sections of the population in cities who were rootless, transient and anonymous, but he doubted their typicality, and also whether this loneliness was produced by cities. The recent study by Dear and Wolch entitled *Landscapes of Despair* (1987) is a case in point. They studied the deinstitutionalisation of former mental hospital patients consequent upon the introduction of community care in North America in the 1980s. Still in need of help and support, expatients tended to congregate where there were day-care facilities, available housing and branches of state agencies with some responsibility for their well-being. These areas tended to be in central urban locations, and a self-reinforcing process ensued whereby facilities were located near those in need and, in turn, those in need gravitated towards the facilities. This effect, however, arose not from city life itself, and not because of the three variables of size, heterogeneity, and density discussed by Wirth, but because of the type of people, the type of policy, and the type of facilities which exist in any given area.

Nor is it self-evident that the marginalised, isolated and lonely live in the inner cities. In some areas marginalised groups can be found living in other types of places, such as council estates situated on the outer rim of cities, or New Towns, well away from the centre of the urban milieu itself. Meegan (1990) has examined the way in which the most marginal groups of Liverpool's population are found in the outer council estates in Speke and Kirby. In a similar way, the movement of poor working-class residents away from the centre of Glasgow to the outer Clydeside council estates saw people move from an environment rich in cultural facilities and resources to a new environment with very few amenities (Savage, 1990). This was partly due to the fact that the Labour Council which commissioned the building of new council estates was dominated by a temperance lobby which did not want public houses to be built on these outer estates. In other words, Wirth's stress on the effects of size, density and heterogeneity alone is misplaced; insofar as there is urban isolation it is linked to the types of social groups who typically – but not inevitably – live in central urban sites, the processes which cause them to concentrate there, and the types of urban policy which affect their resources and environment.

Gans also questioned whether the supposed isolation, individuation and autonomy of city life accurately described more than a small proportion of people. He pointed out that the inner cities also contained groups of people of common ethnic origin and cosmopolitan types, such as gentrifiers. Studies of the moral order of the slum have usually suggested that all the necessary properties of a predictable subcultural way of life (norms, values, ties, rituals, reciprocities, etc.) are present, though these are substantively different from those of a dominant culture. The city was not a place of incipient anarchy. Let us develop this point in more detail.

## (ii) *The urban–rural typology*

A second source of discontent with the urban way of life model was the fact that sociological investigations threw up endless counter-examples to the supposedly anonymous and anomic pattern of urban life and to the integrated community of the countryside. Sociologists and anthropologists who carried out research on parts of large cities found neighbourliness, tradition, moral order and even strong ties of 'community' in inner city areas like Bethnal Green in East London or Boston's West End. 'Urban villagers' – people living in cities, identifying with their particular neighbourhood and having close ties with their neighbours – abounded.

Young and Willmott (1962) did a survey of the Borough of Bethnal Green in inner London and a series of in-depth interviews there between 1953 and 1955. Bethnal Green was a poor, inner-city area which might have been expected to exhibit features of the urban way of life and the atrophying of family relations. On the contrary, Young and Willmott 'were surprised to discover that the wider family, far from having disappeared, was still very much alive in the middle of London' (Young and Willmott, 1962, p. 12). The frequency of kinship contact of people in Bethnal Green, with brothers and sisters, aunts and uncles, and particularly with parents, was prodigious. As regards married people with a parent still alive, 'More than two out of every three people . . . have their parents living within two or three miles' (ibid, p. 36). About 30 per cent of those married women lived in the same street as their parents. Moreover 55 per cent of married women with a mother alive had seen her within the last 24 hours. The centrality of the mother–daughter link and the extent of mutual aid was probably the most notable feature of all. However, the picture, generally, was of intense kinship contact which in turn fostered dense social networks throughout the community. Young and Willmott remarked that:

> far from the family excluding ties to outsiders, it acts as an important means of promoting them. When a person has relatives in the borough, as most people do, each of these relatives is a go-between with other people in the district. His brother's friends are acquaintances, if not his friends; his grandmother's neighbours so well-known as almost to be his own. The kindred are . . . a bridge between the individual and the community (ibid, p. 104).

Thus was discovered a set of strong extended kin and neighbourhood ties in the very centre of the city, completely confounding any generalisation that social bonds had evaporated. Bethnal Green was like a village, where long residence and dense social networks had produced 'a sense of community, that is a feeling of solidarity between people who occupy the common territory' (ibid, p. 113). When they compared a new London County Council housing estate built at Greenleigh, 20 miles east on a green field site, Young and Willmott found far more isolated and privatised ways of life.

Subsequent criticism has contested the sense of community said by Young and Willmott to exist in terms of the difference between public and private accounts of social life. Cornwell (1984) argued that East Enders' public accounts tend to give a rosy impression of the past, whereas private accounts, collected using oral life-history techniques, tell of jealousies, competition, conflict and violence as well. While realising the popular attractions of a garden and some control over the fabric of a house, effectively unattainable in Bethnal Green but a feature of Greenleigh, she still found people who had moved back into its very low-grade housing because they missed the companionship or preferred the social connections of the inner city.

Gans in another celebrated study also described as an urban village the

West End of Boston – a mixed area, with many nationalities, but predominantly Italian; not quite a slum, though often thought of as such. It was ugly, noisy, had poor facilities, and bad housing, but nevertheless was convivial and socially highly organised, mostly through peer groups and through kin. Gans examined a whole range of local institutions of everyday life – family, associations, caretakers, political bosses, etc. – and argued that ethnic groups do very similar things in different countries, and that this is because of class location rather than specific ethnicity. Accordingly he isolated the features of what he called lower-class subculture, which included a central role for women who usually had working-class aspirations, while a significant proportion of the men were drifters and seekers of exciting action. Nevertheless, Gans showed, this inner-city area exhibited tight social bonds and strong institutional forms.

While such studies showed that parts of cities exhibited characteristics of 'community', inquiries in rural areas challenged romantic views of social life in the countryside. Studies initially indicated that although in villages people knew their neighbours and met many of them regularly, life there was neither harmonious nor necessarily highly integrated. Lewis's re-study of the Mexican village that had been Redfield's model for his influential ideal type of 'the folk society' was often cited because it showed high levels of real and latent conflict (Redfield, 1947; Lewis, 1951). The post-war British community studies similarly showed conflict and resentment emanating from inequalities of class, status and participation (Frankenberg, 1957; Littlejohn, 1963; Williams, 1963). Subsequent studies, like Newby (1977) on East Anglian farmworkers, relied not at all on models of rural life or community. Observed deferential behaviour by farm labourers was shown to be situationally specific action, their concerns and practices being in most part similar to those of other working-class occupations. Moreover, by the 1970s, the proportion of the population of rural areas employed in agriculture had diminished to such an extent that villages were inhabited by urban 'off-comers' who bought second homes for holidays or commuted daily to the city. This caused appreciable social divisions, pushing the poorly paid rural labourers into enclaves, within or beyond the village, which Newby termed 'encapsulated communities', that separated them geographically and socially, partly for purely financial reasons. The irony of this process is that the in-migrants themselves destroyed whatever 'community' they had imagined would support a better quality of life in the country.

Of course, Britain is a very highly urbanised society. In states with much greater land mass, and/or where agricultural production remains a

significant source of employment, rural settlements may be less fragmented. Thus Dempsey's (1990) study of Smalltown, Australia, a town-
ship and hinterland containing fewer than 4000 people, 250 kilometres
from Melbourne and 110 kilometres from 'the nearest town of any size'
(Dempsey, 1990, p. 23), showed a strong sense of belonging, an attachment to the place and a high degree of social cohesion. Class inequalities
exist between farmers, in-migrant professionals often employed state
welfare agencies, local working-class households and some marginalised
people. There are considerable and visible differences of power between
men and women. Yet high levels of social interaction, a strongly held
view that life in Smalltown is clearly superior to that in a city, and the
exigencies of getting along in a small and isolated place, produces a way
of life that does have strong elements of *Gemeinschaft*. However, the
conditions for the existence of such settlements are such that they face
constant pressure from external forces that have, over time, reduced their
number.

Despite its widespread use, the concept of 'community' has often
proved to be troublesome because of its vagueness. Hillery (1955), for
example, in a much-quoted observation distinguished ninety-five different senses of the term used in sociological literature. More usefully, Bell
and Newby (1976) distinguished between three analytically different
connotations of the concept:

1. it is used as a purely topographical expression, to describe a finite,
   bounded areas, such as a village, a tract of land within a city, a housing
   estate, or whatever.
2. it has a sociological expression, characterised by the degree of interconnection of local people and their social institutions, implying some
   level of mutual social involvement or integration, a phenomenon
   conceptualised by Stacey (1969) as a local social system.
3. community describes a particular kind of human association, a type of
   social relationship, which has no logical connection with' places or
   local social systems. This kind of relationship Bell and Newby usefully
   prefer to call communion, indicating warmth of feelings, personal ties
   and belongingness. However, this is not necessarily secured by geographical proximity: modern city-dwellers may obtain this sense of
   communion through churches, clubs, social movements, gangs, and
   the like. They entail face-to-face interaction, but may be obtained
   through more or less formally organised meetings. In sum, there is
   only a contingent link between area, local social system and the

hallowed sense of communion. There no doubt are geographical areas with relatively complete local social systems that generate a sense of communion. There are also places where people hate their co-residents. It is a mistake to imagine that settlement type produces specific qualities of social relationship.

Research into communities became bogged down in a series of intractable problems of a conceptual and methodological character. These problems finally undermined the use of the term as it was recognised that its use was ideological, that is to say, that it reflects widespread cultural assumptions and biases, rather than reality. The idea of community itself is much revered, regret being widely expressed about the loss of intimate, face-to-face relationships of small rural villages. A myth of an idyllic rural way of life has had pronounced effects on British society at least for 200 years. The myth has been dissected many times in informative ways (see Williams, 1973; Newby, 1979) and has been shown to have important consequences for the declining profitability of British industry (Wiener, 1981). The attraction of the countryside in the British imagination has been a conception of the special kind of social relationships imagined present in the rural village. This has very often missed the oppressive and restrictive character of life in small, preindustrial communities. Ethnographic studies of rural areas have begun to pick out conflictual rather than cooperative social relations (see Gasson *et al.*, 1988, for a survey). In the urban planning literature, nostalgia for an imagined lost community has obscured the way in which architects of new urban settlements have conceived the restoration of the relationships of 'community' principally in terms of more effective social control of subordinate social groups (see Bell and Newby, 1976).

By the 1970s the community studies were denounced as scientifically flawed, though they were appreciated as interesting ethnographic accounts – they were, and still are, fascinating and absorbing reading, describing the minutiae of everyday life, mostly of the working class, as seen voyeuristically by social scientists. Their failings were that they were non-cumulative, since it was difficult to compare them systematically, as they were written by different people in varying wavs. They made no contribution to theory, often preferring to stick close to their empirical investigation. Also they gave unsatisfactory explanations because they were concerned only with processes internal to the community.

The result of this long line of inquiry was therefore to dismiss the idea that the countryside was full of communities, whilst cities were not. It proved, however, remarkably difficult to research communities in such a way that Wirth's expectations could be rigorously tested. Since strong social ties, based upon subcultural affiliation, existed in the city, the evidence for the urban–rural contrast was found unconvincing.

### (iii)   *The proliferation of subcultures*

Wirth's view that there was an urban culture always sat somewhat uncomfortably with the Chicago School's recognition of the existence of varied practical cultures in the Western city. If the practices of the Gold Coast and those of the slum were so very different, as charted by Zorbaugh (1929), then in what sense was it possible to maintain that there was some generalised 'urban' culture? The objection was that responses to the opportunities of urban life largely depend upon the social group to which someone belongs – defined in terms of life-cycle stage, generation, class and ethnic group (see Gans, 1968b). The implication of this position is that the 'urban' ceases to be a first-order cause of particular social practices, and is replaced by central sociological variables (demographic and socio-economic) as the way to explain differential experience within the city.

Sociologists have recently shown relatively little interest in the varied everyday life of different subcultural groups. Yet that was one of the most interesting features of the classics of both the first and second generations of the Chicago School. Such work has recently been left to scholars in the fields of cultural studies and urban anthropology (and to some extent human geography) who have taken over as the principal investigators of the urban experience.

Some of the best work is, as we have argued it always was, straight-forwardly ethnographic, describing and analysing patterns of daily life in quite specific contexts. Ethnographic methods (which community studies also usually deploy) rely on the researcher observing and participating in the social situations being studied. This allows the identification of rules and norms governing social interactions that would be completely invis-ible to people with only a casual or passing awareness. What might seem disorder to the outsider is understood as structure and regulation to the involved ethnographer. It is, however, difficult to summarise such work because the persuasiveness of such accounts relies on the cumulative effect of detailed description of events, situations and interactions. (For an overview of the history of such studies see Hannerz, 1980; and for the tradition of community studies see Bell and Newby, 1974).

Substantively, such studies lead away from issues of urban personality or urban culture towards the identification of a variety of different modes and patterns of everyday life. For example, Ken Pryce's *Endless Pressure* (1979), is a study of social groups and life-styles within West Indian circles in St Paul's, a small area of Bristol. Distinguishing initially between categories of people with an 'expressive-disreputable orientation' and those with a 'stable law-abiding orientation', he goes on to identify several groups within each. Within the first category he isolates hustlers, regulars and teenyboppers, each with distinct patterns of sociation and ways of surviving materially and socially. The interplay between these groups, their concerns and objectives, their loyalties and their conflicts, their ways of using public space, etc., make sense of a network of people living on the boundaries of legality and social acceptability. For the types involved in that network are looked at with suspicion by the majority of respectable West Indians in and around St Paul's. The life-styles of this second category are also differentiated. Pryce identifies differences between 'proletarian respectables', 'saints' (adherents of the Pentecostalist church whose members formed a separate and exclusive social network) and 'mainliners' ('the most law-abiding, the least militant and the most conformist element of the black community': Pryce, 1979, p. 219). A principal difference between the first and third groups was their political reactions to white racism. The overall impression is of an everyday social world where networks of people pursue distinctive styles of living partly in accommodation with, partly in ignorance of, others in the vicinity. What it shows is that urban life is heterogeneous – but not thereby anomic, impersonal, unconstrained or unpatterned. There are many forms of moral order maintained by people in different social networks.

Ethnographic methods, like all others, have certain limits and partialities. One of the great contributions of the community studies is that they show precisely how to understand the alien cultures of our neighbours. The impression of normative coherence that urban ethnographies often transmit may arise partly from the selection of a group of people to study – a West Indian locality, railway workers, drug addicts, a street corner gang, etc. – where the group is defined by its shared culture and norms. The opposite impression, of the city being enormously diverse, is created because we continually pass people in the street whom we do not know, and whose cultures we are not party to, and thus understanding them is very difficult. Then the city gives the impression of being an enormously fragmented place.

The sheer variety of subcultures to be found in any city makes it impossible to identify some dominant type of urban social relations.

There are certainly strong forces making for competition, individuation and personal difference; but there are counter-tendencies in shared interests, sociability, friendship and kinship, membership of organisations, etc., that induce cooperation and communality. What studies of urban villagers, of Bethnal Green, of ethnic groups, etc., have constantly shown is that heterogeneity is in part an illusion, behind which integrated, homogeneous groups are involved in high levels of interaction. This also weighed heavily against Wirth's theoretical synthesis.

One of the most detailed studies of social interaction in the city was carried out by Claud Fischer (1982) in Southern California. Fischer's argument runs directly counter to that of Wirth. He argues that urban living allows the proliferation of social ties and identities, since people can choose a variety of bases on which to identify. Urbanism allows such subcultures to proliferate since a critical mass for the formation of a distinct culture is often only possible in a city of a certain size. Thus only when the number of potential members of a given group rises above a threshold can they form a collectivity. Furthermore, once it is known that a subculture exists in a certain city, selective migration takes place as people choose to move to that area in order to join. Subsequently, conflict or interaction with other social groups may reinforce a sense of shared identity.

Fischer discusses the emergence of homosexual subcultures in urban areas in precisely these terms. In some urban areas, such as San Francisco, selective migration of gay men to the city over a long period led first to them becoming a large group able to sustain their own social and cultural life. Other gay men, often moving from more repressive rural areas and small towns, were encouraged to migrate, reinforcing the gay subculture. Frequent conflicts with homophobic public authorities have served to strengthen the subculture.

## 5.1.2   *Reappraisal of Wirth*

Thus Wirth's arguments were found wanting. This three-pronged critique of the notion of an urban way of life made a considerable contribution towards better understanding the city. Many defects of Wirth's synthesis were identified and laid aside; for example, notions of the urban personality, the urban–rural distinction, the uniformity of the urban temperament, the idea that cities *per se* had effects, and the belief that communal and community networks had atrophied. Nonetheless, whilst Wirth's arguments cannot be sustained in their entirety, they contain important insights into the nature of life in modern cities. In three important areas it can be argued that the critics have overstated their case.

First, the ethnographic and community studies demonstrating the persistence of social bonds tended to look for coherence and interconnections. This is partly because it is easier to carry out research in communal settings than on specific private households. Persuasiveness in anthropological work has typically come from giving a coherent and understandable picture of some network of social interaction. The analysis of such interaction systems need not exclude conflict; the best anthropology has a lot to say about dispute, negotiation and conflict, as was apparent in community studies. However, such research has focused on particular groups of people in contexts where there are high levels of interaction and some recognisable moral order. The method itself tends to enhance the impression of coherence. This has been appreciated by modern anthropology and current best-practice guards against such misrepresentation. Nevertheless many of the key empirical studies in the debate from the 1950s to the 1970s upon which the critique was based probably overemphasised the coherence of social groups. The fact that urban communities were discovered in cities may partly reflect the methods used by researchers.

Second, the contextual aspects of human interaction, the sense in which configurations of co-presence are an important part of the construction of distinctive group subcultures, got lost in the most thoroughly aspatial theoretical critiques of Wirth (e.g. Saunders, 1985). Although settlement type does not directly generate particular types of social relations, the frequency, density and context of personal contact does have effects on sociation. In Bethnal Green and in Smalltown widespread face-to-face interaction was one precondition of communal practice and a sense of belonging. Repeated interaction encourages more intense interpersonal sentiments, whether of belonging or antagonism. Often the specific features of the local environment – its lay-out, the memories it invokes, the public spaces that it contains – frame a distinctive context that supports particular forms of interaction. Distances, boundaries and configurations between sites for association restrict some and enable other types of joint and collective behaviour. That spatial arrangements do not determine the quality of social interaction does not entail that they be ignored altogether, a point that recent research on space and place has increasingly appreciated.

Third, the critique tended to reinforce the sense that sociation should be explored as an antinomy: *Gemeinschaft* or *Gesellschaft*; rural or urban;

cooperative or competitive; communal or anonymous. In fact, these characteristics usually exist together; more of some and less of others in particular groups or situations, for sure, but the texture of life in late capitalism is a mixture. We learn both competition and cooperation for both are required in a society with a division of labour and private ownership, an insight from Durkheim of which Wirth was fully aware. These antinomies are not alternatives; almost everyone has both in their social repertoires for use in different circumstances. Nor are they spatially determined. Rather, they are supported or undermined by particular types of social interaction situation and material contexts. These last are more appropriate objects of study.

Urban sociology after 1945 tended to generalise unacceptably from Wirth's model of an urban way of life without necessarily doing the kind of research that would corroborate or refute its key tenets (see Fischer, 1975). In addition, statistical approaches to segregation failed to depict sociation satisfactorily. Demographic and material characteristics as identified through census-type variables are insufficient to understand everyday life. Groups in similar socio-economic circumstances may have quite distinct life-styles. Ley (1983) quotes a comparative study of two affluent social areas in Vancouver. Both were among the richest 10 per cent of neighbourhoods by socio-economic status, but exhibited enormous differences in terms of settledness, background, respectability, leisure activities and friendship patterns. Residential distribution generates different social milieux. Case studies, those with a historical component as well as ethnographies, which often take a territorial area as a convenient unit for studying social relationships in context, are essential to understanding the diversity of urban living.

## 5.2   Simmel and metropolitan culture

Wirth failed to sustain the idea of a generic urban culture differentiated from rural culture. But an alternative approach is possible, thinking in terms not of its spatial differentiation from a rural way of life, but of its temporal distinctiveness from older, traditional cultures. This is the line which Simmel developed.

Thirty-five years before Wirth published 'Urbanism as a Way of Life', Georg Simmel had produced another classic essay on urban culture, 'The Metropolis and Mental Life'. It is common to see these two essays as part of the same tradition, with Wirth elaborating and systematising some of

Simmel's ideas (e.g. Saunders, 1986; Smith, 1980). However, Wirth misunderstood Simmel's essay in important respects, for his project was rather different. Simmel was primarily concerned to establish that urban culture was the culture of modernity.

In 'The Metropolis and Mental Life' Simmel rehearsed many of the themes which crop up in Wirth's later essay: the metropolis as the site for the lonely, isolated individual, shorn of strong social bonds: 'the relationships and affairs of the typical metropolitan usually are so varied and complex that without the strictest punctuality the whole structure would break down into an inextricable chaos' (Simmel, 1950, p. 412). More specifically, Simmel argued that there are four distinctive, but interrelated, cultural forms which are characteristically found in urban settings. These are:

1. 'intellectuality', where the urban dweller 'reacts with his [*sic*] head instead of his heart' (Simmel, 1950, p. 410).
2. urban dwellers are 'calculative' (ibid, p. 412) – instrumentally weighing up the advantages and disadvantages of each action.
3. people are blasé.
4. urban dwellers retreat behind a protective screen of reserve, rarely showing emotion or expressing themselves directly to others.

These traits all seem consistent with Wirth's account. There, however, similarity stops. Unlike Wirth, Simmel did not claim that cities *per se* caused these cultural forms. Although Simmel has frequently been interpreted as positing a causal link between cities and cultural life, so that the mere fact of population density itself produces the effects he discusses, this claim is dubious. The belief that Simmel was showing how size of settlement affected cultural life – a view similar to that of Wirth – is often justified by evoking Simmel's interest in the sociology of numbers, and the way in which the formal properties of quantities affect patterns of social interaction (Mellor, 1977, p. 184; Saunders, 1986, p. 89). Yet although Simmel did write extensively about this issue in his earlier work, by the time he wrote 'The Metropolis and Mental Life' he had abandoned his rather formalistic treatment and rarely mentioned the significance of size alone, and was careful to qualify any statements relating to it: hence his observation that 'it is not only the immediate size of the area and the number of persons which . . . has made the metropolis the locale of freedom' (Simmel, 1950, pp. 418–19). Rather, Simmel's concern had become the relationship between quantitative and qualitative relationships. In this context, he emphasised the sociological significance of money whose 'quality consists exclusively in its quantity' (Simmel, 1978, p. 259). Numbers only became sociologically significant because they were premised on a money economy, and it was this which Simmel regarded as most important.

Hence Simmel did not, in this paper, seek to establish any clear causal links between cities *per se* and these cultural traits, and he was certainly not interested in contrasting the city-dweller with the rural-dweller. What is striking, on a careful reading of Simmel's paper, is that his point of contrast was generally not between cities and rural areas, but between contemporary cities and towns in earlier historical periods. Indeed, the usual contrast is with the 'small town', especially in antiquity (e.g. Simmel, 1950, p. 417). Simmel rarely compared the city-dweller with the rural-dweller directly, and on the few occasions that he did, it is unclear whether he was referring to the rural-dweller in earlier historical periods or the contemporary era. Generally Simmel was not arguing for a distinction between urban and rural cultures, because he believed emphatically that in the modern world the metropolis's influence spreads throughout the whole society, including its rural hinterland:

> the horizon of the city expands in a manner comparable to the way in which wealth develops . . . As soon as a certain limit has been passed, the sphere of the intellectual predominance of the city over its hinterland grow(s) as in geometrical progression. . . . For it is the decisive nature of the metropolis that its inner life overflows by waves into a far-flung national or international area (Simmel, 1950, p. 419).

Simmel also did not explain the specified cultural traits in terms of the causal effects of cities *per se*, but it is the role of the city as centre of the 'money economy' that he developed at greatest length, and is consistent with the overall tenor of his mature social theory (see Frisby, 1985, especially pp. 77ff). Since the money economy is most highly developed in cities, so too are the cultural traits. The decisive evidence for this argument is that Simmel himself thought the *Philosophy of Money* his most important work, noting at the end of 'The Metropolis and Mental Life' that 'argument and elaboration of its major cultural–historical ideas are contained in my *Philosophy of Money*' (Simmel, 1950, p. 424). His book analysed many of the same cultural traits discussed in the shorter essay, and he was happy to explain them in terms of the dominance of the money economy. He thus spent two pages discussing the blasé attitude without mentioning cities once (Simmel, 1978, pp. 256–7). He argued that money is by its very nature instrumental, a pure means to something else. Hence the dominance of the money economy in modern societies explains the associated calculative attitudes. From time to time in *The Philosophy of Money* Simmel referred to cities, but always merely to illustrate the effects of the money economy. His observation that 'our whole life also becomes affected by its remoteness from nature, a situation that is reinforced by the money economy and the urban life that is dependent upon it' (Simmel, 1978, p. 478) is typical.

In short, Simmel's arguments cannot be used to justify the idea that an urban way of life stands in contrast to a rural way of life. Simmel's main stress, like that of Toennies, was an historical one, in which modern societies, based on the dominance of the money economy, exhibited very different cultural traits from traditional societies. Cities were interesting because they exhibited these new emergent features most clearly, not because cities themselves possessed some generic causal power.

Simmel's contribution to the analysis of urban culture was thus rather different from that suggested by many of his interpreters. As his most perceptive advocate, David Frisby, has hinted, the importance of Simmel's work lies in his arguments that the nature of modernity makes it virtually impossible to pinpoint any coherent way of life at all. Frisby has argued that Simmel should best be understood as a sociologist attempting to develop an account of 'modernity' – 'the modes of experiencing what is "new" in "modern" society' (Frisby, 1985, p. 1). In this context Simmel's constant refrain is the fragmentation and diversity of modern life. As Simmel stated:

> the essence of modernity as such is psychologism, the experience and interpretation of the world in terms of the reactions of our inner life and indeed as an inner world, the dissolution of fixed contents in the fluid element of the soul, from which all that is substantive is filtered and whose forms are merely forms of motion (quoted in Frisby, 1985, p. 46).

For Simmel, modern life saw a rupture of inner, spiritual life and feelings from outward behaviour – in Simmel's terms 'the separation of the subjective from objective life'. In order to protect ourselves from the potential instability and chaos, given the diversity of stimuli which bombards the senses in the course of everyday life, we are all forced to retreat into an inner, intellectual, world which acts as a filter on our experience.

This account is not without problems, for he appears to have used an empiricist theory of experience, in which the outside world is able to affect our senses of their own accord (see Smith, 1980). Even if we adopt a weaker version of Simmel's thesis, that we need to control our perceptions intellectually in order to maintain identity and personality, it is clear that the implication of Simmel's argument is still to deny that we can specify a distinct way of life at all. The very concept of 'way of life' suggests a fusion between thought and practice, social position and individual action, which he regards as absent in the modern world. If we recognise that our activities are context-specific (i.e. we behave in different ways in different settings) and that each person may interpret or intellectualise the same actions in a different way, then it becomes very difficult to accept a notion of 'a way of life' – implying as it does a certain coherence to people's activities, and a fusion of culture and practice.

Simmel's real significance is that he problematised the very idea of urban culture, if by this is meant a single and unified urban way of life, based upon axes such as urban alienation or loneliness. Ironically, one of the most powerful critiques of Wirth can be found in Simmel's own, earlier account, which offers a more sophisticated notion of contemporary culture. There are four major differences between Simmel and Wirth:

1.  Wirth made what had been a largely historical claim, about traditional communities turning into modern societies, into a spatial one about the difference between cities and villages;
2.  relatedly, he made the study of urban culture part of a comparative project with rural cultures, in an unprecedented way;
3.  he claimed that the three defining characteristics of the city were causal forces behind urban cultures, whereas Simmel made no such claim;
4.  he used a concept of culture as a 'way of life', which diverged from Simmel's more aesthetic and fragmentary definition.

In all these ways Wirth's innovations proved unhelpful.


## 5.3   The culture of modernity

Recently, urban culture has again become a focus for study, mainly by writers from outside the terrain of urban sociology. Many are associated with literature and literary criticism, some with the visual arts. In this section we will consider whether Simmel's account of urban culture as the culture of modernity can be rehabilitated. We maintain that whilst Simmel's work is indeed the correct starting-point for the analysis of contemporary urban cultures, recent writers have been unable to advance on Simmel's rather general, and at times nebulous, statements. Simmel's framework is not particularly helpful in exploring an important part of the experience of modernity concerning the differentiation of urban experience and urban meaning.

We develop this argument by considering the merits of recent writing which draws upon Simmelian themes in four main areas, namely: the visual, modernist aesthetics, sexual identity and the nature of street life.

## 5.3.1   The visual

On the first point, several have developed Simmel's arguments that the 'eye', or the visual, gains particular prominence in modern urban culture. Simmel saw the urban as characterised by the dominance of the visual sense over all others. Clark (1985) echoes this stress on the dominance of the visual when arguing that the rise of French Impressionist painting in the mid-nineteenth-century was associated with the development of the modern urban form. The painting of Impressionists such as Manet, Monet, Dégas and Seurat did not 'fix' images to known social referents. Instead they marked the proliferation of visual signs and symbols which the new urban spaces had brought forth (see also Hannoosh, 1984; Reff, 1984). In contrast, earlier painting – for instance, British eighteenth-century landscape painting – was organised through literary forms. For Pugh, 'the discourse of the "landscape" and the "rural" was first negotiated through verbal modes of representation . . . the verbal interpellates the visual' (Pugh, 1990, p. 3).

John Urry (1990a), in examining the construction of the tourist 'gaze', also stressed the visual. The construction of particular vistas, the development of viewing points, and so forth, can be seen as a major element used to draw people to particular sites. In a similar way post-modern architecture of the 1970s and 1980s is designed to elaborate and enhance the visual imagery used in architecture (Harvey, 1989; Connor, 1989); grand ornamentation contrasts with the functional, plain style favoured by modernists. We return to this point in section 6.3.

The most critical analysis of the development of the visual sense in modern urban cultures comes from feminist writers who relate it to the voyeuristic male gaze (e.g. Pollock, 1988). It is only men who are able to cast their wandering eye freely around the urban landscape. Furthermore, it is often female bodies which are the target of such gazes. The dominance of the visual is hence linked to male power and women are largely excluded from the culture of the gaze.

## 5.3.2   *Modernist aesthetics*

A second recent issue in the analysis of the city and modernity idea has been the connecting of Modernism – as a cultural movement affecting literature, the visual arts, and music in the first part of this century – with the urban experience. Modernism seems, in many ways, to be an artistic elaboration of many of the themes which Simmel developed in 'The Metropolis and Mental Life'. The most celebrated modernist works – for instance Proust's *In Rememberance of Things Past*, T.S. Eliot's *The Wasteland*, and James Joyce's *Ulysses* – all developed a form of 'high aesthetic self-consciousness and non-representationalism in which art turns from realism and humanistic representation towards style, technique, and spatial form in pursuit of a deeper penetration of life' (Bradbury and McFarlane, 1976, p. 25). This is linked to the 'intellectualisation' of life in response to psychic overload emphasised by Simmel (Sharpe and Wallock, 1984).

Bradbury (1976, p. 97) observed 'Modernist art has had special relations with the modern city, and in its role both as cultural museum and novel environment' (Bradbury, 1976, p. 97). In part this simply reflects the growth of a Bohemian artistic culture in the metropolises of Paris, London, Vienna and New York as young *avant-garde* artists moved into the big cities. At another level, however, it reflected the way in which modernism was a reflection upon the urban experience as such. These new immigrants to the city saw it as strange and wonderful, in contrast to their often rural or small-town upbringing, and hence it became the source of artistic inspiration (Williams, 1989, p. 45). Urban sights and sounds became the topic of modernist work:

> in the early part of this century, for painters like Chagall, Stella, Marin and Severini, being modern meant coming to terms artistically, with the juxtaposition of urban sights and sounds, the compression of history and modern technology on a single street (Sharpe and Wallock, 1984, p. 11).

According to Berman (1983), cities such as St Petersburg offered remarkable scope for modernist work since the contrast between old and new, tradition and modernity, could be most directly observed in street life. The Nevsky Prospect, for instance, a modern consumer street in a city still dominated by a feudal social order, was a frequent source of inspiration for the Russian modernists.

Associating the modernist sensibility with urban experience has however led to disagreement over one vital matter. It remains unclear whether the links apply to modernist art, narrowly defined, in a small number of 'great' metropolitan cities in a small time-span between, say, 1890 and 1930, or whether there is a more general association between urbanism and particular forms of cultural production. Berman (1983) argued that the experience of 'modernity' is a generic feature of all social life in the nineteenth and twentieth-centuries, and continues to see the urban experience as the wellspring of creative art. Perry Anderson (1984), however, claims that Berman's arguments do not apply after the 1920s, since modernist art was effectively a commentary on the slow transition from an aristocratic landed order to an advanced industrial capitalist order, and so, with the triumph of capitalism after 1930, modernism lost its distinctiveness.

Feminists have also been critical of claims about the universality of the experience of modernity. Pollock (1988) and Wolff (1987) argue that writers such as Simmel, Benjamin and Berman do not recognise that the experience of modernity as they define it is primarily a male one. Indeed, the same process whereby men moved into the public sphere, enjoying the excitement and insecurity which that involved, depended on a parallel process by which women were confined to the domestic, private sphere. Yet, as Pollock (1988) shows, there were female modernist painters, using similar sorts of experimental techniques as those practised by men. However, unlike men, their chosen subjects were frequently domestic and familial. If female artists are given proper recognition, then artistic modernism cannot simply be seen as a commentary on urban change.

Thus, while there is clear evidence for a specific association between particular cities and particular cultural movements, it is altogether more difficult to claim a generic association between cities and cultural life. Particular types of modernist culture may have had close ties to Vienna, New York and Paris, but not to Rome, Birmingham or Copenhagen. Some forms of modernist art, often that by women, seemed relatively oblivious to the urban milieu.

## 5.3.3  Sexual identity

Similar issues, both also pertinent to modernism, arise in the other two elaborations of Simmel. The third development concerns the relationship between sexuality and modern urban cultures. Simmel, as we have seen, saw the intellectualisation of life as a typical feature of modern urban culture. The process of developing a sexual identity, interrogating intellectually the nature of this identity, and forming specific subcultures based upon it exemplify his view. Recent research has pointed to the way in which the urban milieu has a prominent role as a site in which subversive and non-conforming forms of sexuality may take root. One example of this is the siting of gay and lesbian cultures in large urban areas, such as San Francisco and New York (Castells, 1983; Fischer, 1982, ch. 18). Feminist writers (e.g. Benstock, 1986), have also noted the greater potential for women to find alternative, less patriarchal ways of living in urban contexts. This is also an aspect of gentrification (see Chapter 4).

Wilson (1991) argues that urban living threatens patriarchal, familial ways of life characteristic of smaller towns and rural areas. She sees the disorder and potential subversion inherent in the culture of modernity as threatening to men, but as enhancing options for women. 'The city offers women freedom. After all, the city normalises the carnivalesque aspects of life' (Wilson, 1991, p. 7). Their power challenged, men find ways of clamping down on the licence and 'freedom' of urban living – through such devices as planning. As a result, urban culture is a complex interplay between male and female principles: 'urban life is actually based on this perpetual struggle between rigid, routinised order, and pleasurable anarchy, the male–female dichotomy' (Wilson, 1991, pp. 7–8).

Wilson's view, however, is romantic. One might object that the heightened significance of fashion and appearance in urban environments increases the pressures for rigid sexual identities to develop. Similarly it is not self-evident that unconventional forms of sexuality can only find a haven in the city: there is a long tradition of retreating to rural environments where the public gaze is thought less intense – for instance, in Utopian communities (Taylor, 1980). Furthermore, despite Wilson's claims concerning the possible development of subversive forms of sexuality in cities, they are also the sites for sexual activities which reinforce and sustain patriarchal sexuality – most notably, prostitution. Interestingly in this regard, Simmel attributed the concentration of prostitution to the dominance of the money economy typical of modernity (Simmel, 1978, pp. 376ff). As with the case of artistic modernism, it seems unwise to generalise: some cities such as New York and San Francisco may be homes for gay subcultures, but other metropolises may not. Single women may be able to create their own alternative culture in some inner cities, London for example, but not in all.

## 5.3.4    *The nature of street life*

The final development of Simmel is by Marshall Berman who examined the way in which encounters on the street are linked to the culture of modernity. Working within a largely unacknowledged Marxist elaboration of Simmel's framework, Berman explored the double-edged nature of modern life by arguing that people's freedom to develop and change goes hand in hand with the insecurity caused by the resulting lack of certainty. Hence:

> to be modern, is to experience personal and social life as a maelstrom, to find one's world in perpetual disintegration and renewal, trouble and anguish, ambiguity and contradiction . . . to be a modernist is . . . to grasp and confront the world that modernisation makes, and strive to make it our own (Berman, 1984, p. 115).

Berman sees the street as a microcosm for modern life and the battle for public space as at the heart of the modernist quest: 'I've come to see the street and the demonstration as primary symbols of modern life' (Berman, 1984, p. 123).

Berman connects the role of the street to wider concerns by arguing that street encounters are unpredictable and unknowable. We are never sure whom we will meet, or with what consequences. At one level this gives us unparalleled potential – to meet the love of our life, a potential employer, an old friend – but at another level it is deeply worrying – we may be robbed, attacked, or slighted. This general insecurity reinforces the role of the visual in urban cultures – as we scan passers-by in order to assess their risk or value to us. This in turn lead us to highlight the visual imagery we wish to emphasise to others, hence the significance of fashion and style. Sexual codes are written into these forms of display.

Such contributions deepen Simmel's analysis of how the 'psychic overload' of modern urban life is related to the culture of modernity. However, it is by no means clear that tensions which Berman sees as characteristic of the street are unique to it. Given the relative instability of family, household and personal relationships in contemporary societies it might very well be argued that household life is composed of the very same blend of promise and danger as the street. Feminists might argue that the street fails to possess any excitement at all given its status as male territory, where women are under constant threat. His view might also be said to adopt a male perspective by locating both promise and danger in encounters with strangers. Women might object that they are more usually endangered by men known to them, often fathers or lovers, since the majority of sexual violence takes place within the family. Equally there seems no reason why one cannot see promise or excitement in relations with people one knows very well. Furthermore, to take only one well-known aspect of street life – its potential dangers – recent studies in criminology, echoing the Chicago School, have shown that there are highly localised differences in the incidence of crime within large cities. Not all streets are the same. Berman recognises this implicitly, since he plays particular attention to some types, such as the central-urban shopping street. It is better to recognise the specificity of street cultures, rather than to generalise about the street *per se*. Finally, we spend only a relatively small part of our time – even if we live in cities – walking around them. In short, the stress on the 'sociology of the street', cannot bear the theoretical weight placed on it by Berman or Jukes (1990).

## 5.4   Conclusion

Urban sociology has learned much from its various attempts to depict the key attributes of a culture of the city. An elaborate understanding of sociation – neighbouring, kinship, friendship and association – has emerged from the concern with the quality of life and social relationships in cities. We can also appreciate the proliferation of subcultures in contemporary society, the contexts of their development and the structured social divisions transposed through them. Moreover, the attention devoted to urban culture recently has expanded further the interdisciplinary contributions to urban studies as the techniques of literary criticism and art history have been brought to bear.

Nevertheless, attempts to develop an understanding of the generic meaning of living in cities have had only limited success. This is because relatively little can be said in general terms about the meaning of urban life in the contemporary world. It seems that a good deal of what has been valuable in explorations of urban culture could more appropriately be grasped as illumination of the experience of modernity. The culture of modernity, which in Simmel's time found its clearest expression in urban life, is now virtually universal throughout developed countries. The problems, dilemmas and potentials of modernity are of the utmost importance,. but they cannot be consigned to the category of urban culture. Cultural differences emerge between and within cities. Different cities and different quarters support alternative, and sometimes competing, patterns of cultural existence. To some extent it is unique combinations of attributes that make places recognisably different the one from the other. It may be better, then, to explore how cities take on their own specific meanings and how these are communicated and interpreted, rather than to refer to urban culture as a whole. This does not imply that we should be content with merely describing the particular cultures of individual cities. Rather, a more analytic approach recommends itself, considering how cities can be seen as individual texts, and how these texts are constructed and read. This is the subject of the next chapter.

# 6  Modernity, Post-modernity and Urban Culture

The critique of the idea of a generic urban culture is often seen as exhausting all interest in urban culture. But this does not follow. In most forms of cultural analysis it is the diversity of possible meanings in any given cultural form that inspires inquiry. We do not stop interpreting novels if we conclude that they have different meanings! In a like manner, a framework is required to show how and why cities develop particular meanings, and how these are constructed, interpreted and sustained.

One approach is to think of the city as a text, in the same way that a novel, or a film might be a text. This text has certain authors, is constructed in a particular way by various procedures and techniques, has a series of meanings embedded within it and is subject to forms of reading. Conceiving the urban as text in this way may help in understanding how cities gain their specific meanings. However, the merits of textual analysis are disputed. In some forms it is closely associated with 'post-structuralism', which posits that texts have their own meanings which cannot be reduced to their authors or their origins, and hence, in the famous words of Derrida, 'there is nothing outside the text'. Within this approach texts may be taken out of their context, and textual analysis becomes a way of reading 'clever' interpretations into a given piece of work. As a result it becomes inappropriate to establish a 'right' or 'wrong' reading of a text. Thus cultural analysis becomes descriptive, and, in the end relativist (Jameson, 1991, pp. 186–8). However, analysis need not involve 'decontextualising' texts, but rather can be about the way that they are constructed, or given 'preferred' meanings, and how different audiences can read different meanings into the same one. The technique we follow has parallels to that adopted by Stuart Hall. For him meanings are 'encoded' and 'decoded'. Encoding is the process by which meanings are placed in the text by its creators, in a coded and hence indirect form, whilst decoding occurs as readers retrieve its meanings – possibly in a way not intended by the original authors.

This chapter circumvents theoretical debates about textual analysis. Instead three strategies for understanding the construction of urban cultural difference are examined. We begin by considering the most conventional, what we term the *architectural approach*, where the diversity of urban meanings is attributed to their differing architectural forms. Analysis of urban culture as the product of an architectural text, however, lays too much emphasis upon the meanings placed on cities by their developers and founders, and anyway, interpretations of the built forms are subject to considerable ambiguity. The way in which people interpret the urban form on the basis of their own experience is missed.

In section 6.2 we examine alternative attempts to explain urban meaning, inspired by Henri Lefebvre, in which space is seen as socially constructed. Emphasis is laid upon the way that places are given meanings through social and cultural processes largely independent of the actual built form of the city. This is to recognise the fluidity of urban meaning, and the way in which places are culturally re-evaluated. However, it tends to describe, rather than explain, somewhat abstract cultural images of place, and fails to relate urban meaning to individual experience.

Section 6.3 considers a third approach, that associated with the Marxist cultural critic, Walter Benjamin. Widely discussed within literary criticism, he has largely been ignored within urban sociology. We briefly outline some of his ideas and explain their relevance to the study of urban culture. He addressed urban meaning as an interface between personal memories and experiences, and the historical construction of dominant meanings and values. The city, for Benjamin, was a site where cultural contradictions could best be revealed and dominant cultures criticised.

We finish the chapter by surveying the debate about post-modernity and urban culture. We examine the different, often contradictory understandings of post-modernity, our main claim being that no clear break from modernity is established. Instead, using Benjamin, we suggest that debating post-modernity is a contemporary way of thinking about our modernity.

## 6.1   Architecture and urban meaning

One commonsensical way of identifying what distinguishes cities from each other is to note their differing buildings and architectures. Urban meaning might, perhaps, be seen as the product of architectural forms and styles. This is a conventional approach to the study of the city as text, stretching back at least as far as Lewis Mumford in the 1930s. He took the built form as a document testifying to the cultural values of its creators, being more concerned with the meanings loaded into its production than its contemporary interpretation. Mumford, though an American, was heavily influenced by the British tradition of Geddes and Branford and he saw the urban form as the embodiment of social values embedded in architectural styles and forms. 'The city, as one finds it in history', he wrote, 'is the point of maximum concentration for the power and culture of community . . . the city is a form and symbol of an integrated social relationship . . . the city is also a work of art . . . mind takes form in the city and in turn urban form conditions mind' (Mumford, 1938, pp. 3, 5). In a history of the urban form since antiquity, he indicated how, in each period, it reflected the social and cultural values of the day. Thus, for example, Mumford attributed the development of the avenue in the baroque city of the sixteenth-century to the growing militarisation of society and the consequent need for troop mobility. In the twentieth-century, he maintained, the forces constructing cities were becoming steadily more impersonal and oppressive, and hence the task

> of the coming city . . . is to put the highest concerns of man at the centre of his activities: to unite the scattered fragments of the human personality, turning artificially dismembered men – bureacurats, specialists, 'experts', depersonalised agents – into complete human beings (Mumford, 1961, p. 652).

Mumford's account was an attempt to 'read' the cultural values lying behind the construction of the urban form in different historical epochs. His was a humanistic account, with the main focus on how people have become divorced from their 'natural' impulses through the development of impersonal social arrangements, as manifested by the modern urban structure. For this reason his work was revered by many urban reformers in the mid-twentieth-century. His attempt to relate the built environment to the social values and order of the day has been regularly repeated, and is a commonplace of architectural history. Mark Girouard's recent *The English Country Town*, for instance, relates the urban structure of different towns to the effects of different cultural styles: 'Georgian towns are based on an ideal of consensus . . . a Victorian town was a battlefield' (Girouard, 1990, p. 190). The approach surfaces in more recent urban sociology. Richard Sennett (1990), for instance, argued that the modern separation of public affairs from private matters has led to the decline of the city where different buildings had a distinct moral function. Today, the erosion of a public, moral sphere has led to an urban fabric where the only public spaces are those orchestrating consumption and tourism. In such a fashion, the architectural form of the modern city represents a certain set of cultural values.

Reading the urban built form as symptomatic of a wider set of social values is, however, deeply problematic. One of the difficulties lies in the idea of the 'hermeneutic circle' (Eagleton, 1983; Thompson, 1984; Longhurst, 1989). A given text only makes sense by placing it in its wider cultural context. Since knowledge of this wider context can only be acquired through examining different texts, a firm starting-point for inquiry seems difficult. Thus the social values underlying given cultural artefacts – such as architecture – can never be clearly established.

Architectural history in the past two decades has become less inclined to analyse architecture as symptomatic of its age and instead to consider it as produced by specific social groups, often in conflict. A good illustration is in an essay of David Harvey on the basilica of *Sacré Coeur* in Paris (Harvey, 1985c). He begins his account by emphasising the diversity of people coming to the church, with their resulting multiple understandings of the monument. Harvey aims to restore meaning to *Sacré Coeur* by embarking on a historical account of its construction in the aftermath of the Paris Commune, when the Catholic Church saw it as a symbol of the defeat of the revolutionary communards and the restoration of clerical authority. Noting the controversies about the building between left- and right-wing political forces until the First World War and after, he concluded that *Sacré Coeur* had a political, conservative, meaning relating to the circumstances of its building; 'The building hides its secrets in sepulchral silence. Only the living, cognisant of this history . . . can truly disinter the mysteries that lie entombed there' (Harvey, 1985c, p. 249).

Harvey's account demonstrates that the built form cannot be read simply as the product of an age. Rather it is the product of specific social groups struggling for cultural hegemony and social and political power. The built environment is an arena of contestation. Consequently architectural forms of the same period, far from expressing the common values of the age may diverge and conflict. A number of meanings may be discovered in different buildings throughout a city.

The approach represented in Harvey's paper has flourished. Rather than facile attempts to relate towns to the *Weltanschauung* of an entire historical epoch, the built environment is related to social conflicts, with the urban form the product of dominant social groups. In Olsen's formulation, 'we can regard cities as complex but legible documents that can tell us something about the values and aspirations of their rulers, designers, builders, owners and inhabitants' (Olsen, 1983, p. 264). Here, whilst Mumford's attempt to read the city as a text is retained, it is related to specific groups, not to society as a whole. This permits a more nuanced account recognising the conflicting meanings which social groups try to place on the city.

Carl Schorske argued in similar vein about Vienna in the nineteenth-century. For Schorske, the creation of the *Ringstrasse* was a visual expression of the values of a social class. Until the mid-nineteenth-century Vienna had mostly baroque architecture, symbolising the dominance of the monarchy and aristocracy. The *Ringstrasse*, a large thoroughfare surrounding the inner city and containing a number of monumental buildings, epitomised new Vienna. It represented the triumph of the liberal middle classes over the old dynastic regime. It encircled, and almost cut off, old Vienna, its new buildings testifying to the hegemony of the emergent constitutional regime. Four new buildings, 'represent as in a wind rose liberalism's value system: parliamentary government in the *Reichsrat* building, municipal autonomy in the *Rathaus*, the higher learning in the University, and dramatic art in the *Burgtheater*' (Schorske, 1961, p. 36). Domestic architecture for the middle classes, by contrast, continued to ape traditional aristocratic forms of taste: 'the conception of the middle class that emerges from these housing designs reflects the slow pace of Austrian capitalist development and the social archaism which consequently marked some of the most vigorous artistic spokesman of the middle class' (Schorske, 1961, pp. 48–9).

Schorske's reading of Vienna's urban form as an expression of class relations has been repeated many times in other cities and countries. In the British case, R.J. Morris argued that 'as part of the process of seeking, consolidating and defending power, the middle class, especially their ideological, political and social leaders undertook the creation of the concept of town as a discreet, self-aware integrated social and constitutional entity' (Morris, 1983, p. 298). This involved, amongst other things, the elaboration of a distinctive architecture pretending to urban grandeur.

One of the important developments in these same Victorian cities was that of a strong separation between public buildings and private buildings, and, more generally, between public and private spaces. Daunton (1983) argued that Victorian cities saw a growing demarcation between public spaces increasingly regarded as a sort of 'waste' space, and ones with specific uses (domestic, or recreational, or business oriented). The latter, regulated by bye-laws, became increasingly the focus of social life. There have been a number of attempts to relate this development to social conflict. Sennett (1977, 1990), following in Mumford's footsteps, preferred a much more traditional approach, arguing that the growth of a distinct private sphere entails the decline of 'public man', with a consequent loss of human potential. Other writers, influenced by Habermas's writings on the 'bourgeois public sphere,' have identified the social class bases for these distinctions. Habermas (1989) maintained that in early capitalism the emerging middle classes created a distinct set of public sites where debate and interaction could take place. As capitalism developed, however the 'bourgeois public sphere' began to be eroded, and the physical form of cities changed accordingly.

More recently, feminist writers have elicited the gendered implications of the distinction between public and private spaces. Davidoff and Hall (1983) documented the way in which the public sphere was identified as male and the private sphere as female, especially for the middle classes. New urban space was related to the consolidation of new forms of male domination, based on the very physical outline of the city: 'by the 1850s, Birmingham, a town of over a quarter of a million inhabitants, had suburban promotion well underway. The heart of this development was the home, centred on the services of a dependant woman' (Davidoff and Hall, 1983, p. 344).

This example indicates the difficulty of reading one specific meaning into any urban landscape, one compounded by the ambivalence of architectural forms themselves. Olsen attempted to theorise the link between classes and form by comparing the social construction of Vienna, Paris and London in the nineteenth-century (Olsen, 1983, 1986). Unlike his predecessors, Olsen recognised the autonomy of the aesthetic dimension in the urban form. He treated architecture as language, drawing upon the post-modernist architects, Jencks and Venturi. The problem is that having declared architecture a language, it is dubious strictly to assign languages to particular social groups, especially in view of post-structuralist arguments that language is not reducible to some exterior reality. Olsen is consequently forced to concede that messages revealed by buildings are many:

> what can a city, in its capacity as work of art, accomplish? . . . it can tell a story, or many stories. It can establish a mood. It can surprise and delight by unexpected juxtaposition of forms, textures, colours, and movements. It can soothe and reassure by repetition of familiar forms,

textures, colours and movements. It can stand for or represent ideas, qualities, institutions (Olsen, 1986, p. 283).

In place of Schorske's reading of Vienna as the product of specific class forces, Olsen emphasised the multiple meanings its architecture contains: 'the *Ringstrasse*, for instance, is "about" monarchy, empire, law, science, music, sculpture, scholarship, order, joy, movement, commerce, war, industry, horticulture, thrift – not necessarily in that order' (Olsen, 1986, p. 285).

Ultimately Olsen retreated from his potential relativism by suggesting that links between architecture and social groups can be established empirically, by indicating some cases where apparently secure connections can be drawn. He pointed, for instance, to 'representational architecture', where buildings are deliberately used to emphasise social standing. This is not a satisfactory resolution of the problem since it can only be applied to particular types of buildings, but does indicate the real difficulty involved in escaping from a crude determinism (in which architecture can be read to reveal specific meanings based on particular social foundations) without becoming entirely relativist.

Architectural analysis has become more sophisticated and attuned to the complexity of the social forces which construct the built environment. Diversity of meanings and values are expressed by the variety of buildings and architectural forms. A city is not simply the product of the world view of an historical period, but rather is a physical testimony to the social conflict and political processes whereby the powerful leave their marks on cities. However, an architectural approach is insufficient to the wider aim of explaining urban meaning. There are a number of reasons for this. First, there is a tendency to privilege the architectural highlights of particular places and their construction. Laudable enough in its own terms, this neglects more mundane and less glamorous sites. Second, it ignores the way that people themselves interpret and understand the meanings of the built form. In Harvey's example of *Sacré Coeur*, the analysis of its origins in the social and political conflicts of the French Third Republic may be historically accurate, whilst being irrelevant to the many thousands of contemporary visitors. As most branches of cultural studies insist, audiences interpret cultural forms. Third, urban meaning is not constructed through architecture alone. Places derive values from other cultural processes, as in the use of urban images in films, literature, the popular press and so forth. For a full understanding these too must be considered. We turn to this task in section 6.2.

## 6.2 The social construction of urban meaning

Another – contrasting – school of thought considers urban meaning to be socially constructed, but not as arising from the architecture of particular places. Its theoretical origins lie with the work of the French neo-Marxist, Henri Lefebvre. His starting-point is that in capitalist society, space is used instrumentally, as a commodity. Space is no longer defined in terms of its geographical and physical attributes, but is increasingly the product of capitalist forces. He proposed that industrial capitalism gives way to what he terms the 'urban revolution'. As the world becomes subordinated to the capitalist global market a counter-movement takes place in which spaces become increasingly differentiated symbolically. As leisure industries spring up, and since capital's mobility means that enterprises can shift, so a battle occurs over the images of places, that they might appear attractive and desirable to others.

Lefebvre is particularly concerned with the relationship between three elements of space: spatial practices, representations of space; and spaces of representation; or as he has also termed them, the experienced, the perceived, and the imagined. He aimed to establish that these are dialectically related, so that the social construction of space involves not just a purely discursive process whereby places are valued differently, but also the alterations in people's actual experiences of places. By examining the social production of space, Lefebvre sought to surmount dichotomies between structure and agency, discourse and practice.

Lefebvre's work, only recently translated into English, remains rather arcane and abstract. His influence, however, is profound. One central feature adopted both by David Harvey and Anthony Giddens is the idea of 'created space'. In Harvey's words, 'created space replaces effective space as the overriding principle of geographical organization' (Harvey, 1988, p. 309). As real geographical differences between places are eroded in a global system, so symbolic differences become more important: 'the signs, symbols and signals that surround us in the urban environment are powerful influences' (Harvey, 1988, p. 310). Giddens echoes Harvey in seeing one of the distinctive elements of contemporary societies as the dominance of created space, one result being a problem of developing a sense of 'ontological security' in a world where even spatial settings cannot be treated as fixed or permanent (Giddens, 1981).

Lefebvre reorientated analysis of the construction of spatial imagery through linking practice with discourse. A point of contrast is Raymond Williams's study, *The Country and the City* which surveyed literary constructions of the city and countryside by English writers as diverse as Oliver Goldsmith, William Wordsworth, Thomas Hardy and T.S. Eliot. He showed that they all tended to present a picture of the countryside as an 'image of the past and the common image of the city as an image of the future . . . the pull of the country is towards old ways, human ways, natural ways. The pull of the idea of the city is towards progress, modernization, development' (Williams, 1973, p. 357). He insisted that the images so constructed were misleading, since the myth of country as rural idyll failed to correspond with the countryside as the actual site of exploitative capitalist relations in agriculture. However, though extremely influential, Williams's emphasis on the cultural construction of places tends to lose Lefebvre's insistence on the dialectic with experience.

Early sociological studies of the symbolisation of places also suggested that symbolic processes defined experience, rather than there being a reciprocal relationship. Anselm Strauss, for instance, explored the use of urban symbols as synecdoches, where one specific symbol would come to stand for the whole city: 'thus the delicate and majestic sweep of the Golden Gate Bridge stands for San Francisco, a brief close up of the French Quarter identified New Orleans, and most commonly of all, a New York skyline from the Battery is the standing equivalent for that city' (Strauss, 1961, p. 9). Given the inevitable diversity of ways of seeing any one place, the symbolisation of cities involves selecting a small number of symbolic representations and marketing them as the city itself. These may be buildings, as in Strauss's examples, or they may be social types, such as the Beefeaters, often used to symbolise the Tower of London, which might typify London itself. Strauss, however, like Williams, retained a strong distinction between images and 'reality', emphasising the frequent disjunctures between them. Thus he discussed the phenomenon of disappointment, where the real experience of seeing a city does not live up to its promise. In the case of New York, 'the imaginative impact of that skyline is sometimes so conclusive, so overwhelming, that to see the city in normal perspective, and in detail, may be anticlimactic' (Strauss, 1961, p. 11).

Gerald Suttles (1984) also provided an account of the way that urban cultures are constructed around a series of symbolic markers. Suttles distinguished three main sources of what he terms 'city images'. First, there are representations of 'community founders', such as Henry Hudson, who helped found New York. Second, there are notable 'entrepreneurial leaders', whose names have come to stand for the city as a whole, such as the Morgans of New York. In both cases they are celebrated not only by the local press, but also by their names being used for prestigious buildings, and by statues and other memorabilia. Suttles probably exaggerated the local notables, however. Although many Victorian cities in Britain also bear the imprint of their founders, it becomes difficult, in an era of corporate capitalism to associate cities with individuals.

The third source identified by Suttles is the use of local artefacts, particularly those which are enshrined in local museums. Suttles refers to what he terms 'museumisation', where

> ageing collective representations . . . become increasingly protected from alteration, sometimes literally by entering a museum or archive, more often by an organized effort at conservation . . . [T]he inventory of artifacts now considered representative may be vastly enlarged to include elements once regarded as quite ordinary and undistinguished (Suttles, 1984, p. 299).

The industrial museum and conservation area thus contribute considerably in defining a city's image.

Despite difference in detail, both Strauss and Suttles suggest that the complexity of modern urban experience needs to be simplified into discrete images and sights in order to gain popular currency. Yet neither elucidate how these images are developed or sustained, nor do they explore popular experiences of place. Shields (1991) has offered the most ambitious remedy. Also indebted to Lefebvre, he developed the notion of 'social spatialisation', 'to designate the ongoing social construction of the spatial at the level of the social imaginary (collective mythologies, presuppositions) as well as interventions in the landscape (for example the built environment)' (Shields, 1991, p. 31). Social spatialisations define particular places as good or bad, sites of danger, work or whatever; for Shields, places are constructed meaningfully through social spatialisation.

Shields developed his position by dissecting the construction of place-myths around a number of sites. He examined, for instance, the way in which the North–South divide in England was culturally constructed and sustained in the British realist films of the 1960s (for instance *Saturday Night, Sunday Morning*), in soap opera, and in newspaper reporting. More generally he claimed that place-myths are constructed in novels, popular publishing, the mass media, advertising literature and the like. The contrast with the architectural approach could not be greater: rather than urban meaning arising as the by-product of built forms, places are discursively defined by broader cultural media, with little reference to their precise physical qualities.

Shields's study illustrates some of the advantages and disadvantages of working in the vein of Lefebvre. The advantages include a sophisticated appreciation of the construction of places in cultural media, an awareness of the reworking and re-evaluation of these images over time, and a powerful rebuttal of architectural determinism. However the organising concept of 'social spatialisation' is ultimately rather slippery. Theoretically it is designed, after Lefebvre, to encompass both representations of place and how people use these images in everyday life. But in practice, the actual experience of urban living is entirely ignored in favour of discussions of the place-myths themselves, with Shields asserting that 'the actual presence or absence of the activity is beside the point . . . the question . . . is about the power of social spatialisation and myths to overrun reality' (Shields, 1991, p. 106). A concept originally designed to overcome the polarity between discourse and practice ends up by giving priority to the former.

Nor can Shields explain types of place-myth. He provides detailed descriptions of the development and reformulation of place-myths over time, but without saying why these social spatialisations are changing, and at whose behest. In this respect his analysis is retrogressive since the architectural writers were much more sensitive to the causal role of social forces.

In sum, Lefebvre's laudable project to find a bridge between experienced space, representations of space, and spaces of representation has proved too hard to put into operation empirically. The crucial link between the construction of place in representation and at the level of everyday experience has not been demonstrated, and so long as this link has not been made, work in this vein does not advance beyond studies – such as those of Raymond Williams – of the way that places are given symbolic meanings.

## 6.3   Urban meaning and 'aura'

Much of Walter Benjamin's writing in the last years of his life, from around 1925 to his death in 1940 constituted an attempt to learn how to 'read' cities. It is therefore strange that although widely discussed within literary studies he has been ignored within urban sociology. This is regrettable since Benjamin's thought avoids some of the problems in understanding urban meaning which have been discussed above.

Benjamin's point of departure was resolutely the urban form as it is experienced and viewed by its observers. For Benjamin the crucial issue is how an urban landscape can be interpreted and its meanings located in the context of every individual's experiences. He began his autobiographical 'A Berlin Chronicle' by reciting how he was brought  up in Berlin's streets, recounting how he came to find his way around them. His concentration on how individuals gain a sense of the urban from their own experience, with the help of 'guides' and maps, posits  the sense of places as integral to personal experiences and feelings, such that urban meaning is interpreted through one's life happenings.

Benjamin's conceptualisation of the individual's experience of the city took a distinctive form. Usually dissections of people's experiences of urban living have had either positivist or existentialist roots. Positivist geographers charted people's cognitive awareness of their physical landscape, by asking questions about the types of mental maps people have of their environment, their knowledge of place-names and the like. Existential approaches, such as that of Lowenthal (1961), explored people's imaginative understandings of place. Yet in both cases the individuals themselves were treated as if in a cultural vacuum, without considering how their values and understandings of places were related to wider cultural and social forces. This was Benjamin's project, to establish the relationship between experience and cultural symbolism, not to favour one more than the other.

Benjamin argued that the city is a repository of people's memories and past, and is also the receptacle of cultural traditions and values. Whereas Simmel had emphasised the separation of the culture of modernity from that of previous eras, Benjamin concentrated on what Frisby (1985) calls the 'prehistory of modernity', recovering the past buried in the built form. Simmel thought that urban life caused us to intellectualise and develop forms of reserve; Benjamin postulated the primacy of unconscious and dream processes and their association with the urban environment. Hence, reading the urban text is not a matter of intellectually scrutinising the landscape: rather it is a matter of exploring the fantasy, wish-processes and dreams locked up in our perception of cities. Benjamin revealed his general aims thus:

> I think of an afternoon in Paris to which I owe insights into my life that came in a flash, with the force of an illumination. It was on this very afternoon that my biographical relationships to people, my friendships and comradeships, my passions and love affairs, were revealed to me in their most vivid and hidden intertwinings. I tell myself it had

to be in Paris, where the walls and quays, the places to pause, the collections and the rubbish, the railings and the squares, the arcades and the kiosks, teach a language so singular that our relations to people attain, in the solitude encompassing our immersion in the world of things, the depths of a sleep in which the dream image waits to show the people their true faces (Benjamin, 1978, p. 318).

For Benjamin, people's memories lay bound up in their experience of built forms, so that specific buildings can take on very different meanings from those intended by their builders. Yet Benjamin was also an objec- tivist. He did not see meanings as the result of subjective processes alone – as a relativist might do – but as objectively located in specific cultural phenomena (Buck-Morss, 1989; Wolin, 1983). He insisted that architec- ture, for instance, did not just exist in the mind of the beholder, but also as 'the most important evidence of latent "mythology"' (quoted in Frisby, 1985, p. 192). These objective meanings could not be grasped conceptually, through a process of intellectual analysis, but only by imaginary and dream processes. Understanding involved unlocking the hidden, obscured meanings by undermining – shattering – received accounts, placing fresh images and fragments together in a new combina- tion to disclose their meaning. The resulting allegories (Sontag, 1978) offered insight into objective meanings which were otherwise obscured.

Much of Benjamin's work is therefore concerned with the complex relationship between individual and collective memories, objective mean- ings and the forms of cognition – mythologies, ideas, symbols – which cloud true knowledge. The interface between individual experience and cultural traditions is at the heart of Benjamin's concerns, and whilst recognising that every city is unique, he also provided insights into the peculiar nature of urban interpretation, in relation to other forms of artistic appreciation. Thereby he delineated some central forces con- structing urban culture.

Benjamin's intention was to recognise that objective meanings can be located in cultural forms, but also that people interpret these cultural artefacts themselves. But how does this translate into method? The key concept is that of 'aura'. Benjamin argued that different types of inter- pretation are possible for varying forms of artistic media, with major implications for their cultural significance. Aura concerns the relationship between an art work and tradition. For Benjamin, before works of art could be mechanically reproduced – through printing, photography, recording, and so on – each piece was uniquely located in time and space, and hence retained a distinctiveness and distance from the viewer. Once art works are mechanically reproduced, however, they lose this specificity and perceptions of them change.

> The uniqueness of a work of art is inseparable from its being embedded in the fabric of tradition. The tradition is alive and extremely changeable . . . the existence of the work of art with reference to its aura is never entirely separated from its ritual function . . . in the age of mechanical reproduction . . . for the first time in world history, mechanical reproduction emancipates the work of art from its parasitical dependence on ritual (Benjamin, 1973, pp. 225–6).

The rise of mechanically reproduced art released it from a specific tradition and allowed it to be deployed in other, more political ways. This both liberates and weakens it. Liberation comes from expanding the uses of art, and from its use in non-traditional ways. But by removing the art work from its own specific tradition it is deprived of its context and unique meaning.

Might the city-as-text be regarded as auratic? Benjamin gave no simple answer. In some ways the city retains an aura, in other ways not. Benjamin regarded film as the archetype of mechanically reproduced art, but literature (mass production of books, etc.), and painting (prints) are also susceptible. The city, by contrast, cannot be mechanically reproduced. Specific buildings might be copied but entire cities cannot: London is London, Paris is Paris. While people might claim some knowledge of most art-forms without having seen an original, it would be inconceivable in respect of cities. It would be curious if someone described Istanbul (for instance) as an attractive city without ever having been there. The uniqueness of cities in space marks them out from other art-forms, and gives them distinctive qualities *vis-à-vis* each other. Yet in another way cities lack aura. Their location within specific traditions is tenuous. Cities have spatial, but not temporal distinctiveness. Whilst virtually all other art forms were composed at a specific moment in history, and hence can be located within a tradition, cities are generally the product of centuries of construction and deconstruction, as new buildings turn to ruins. Their buildings originate in different historical periods, and exhibit many styles. They are frequently marked by evidence of sharp ruptures – as was the case in Paris with Haussmann's reconstruction in the 1870s, and in the redevelopment of Vienna in the same period. Rather than being related to an external tradition, cities are their own tradition: that is to say, the specific historical mixture of styles, forms and functions characterising a city defines its own distinctive tradition. Cities therefore have specific textual properties compared with other forms of art. Spatially unique and unreproducible, they range across time, each with its own aura.

Benjamin saw this distinctive aspect of urban landscape as having certain qualities in relation to other cultural forms. Benjamin was concerned with the potential of different forms of art to challenge received, traditional views of history which propagated a conservative view of social evolution. He saw history, and historical knowledge, as fundamentally conservative, a celebration of the victors in battles between oppressors and oppressed. 'There is no document of civilisation which is not at the same a document of barbarism; barbarism taints also the manner in which it was transmitted from one owner to another' (Benjamin, 1973, p. 258). This is because only cultural artefacts used and developed by the historically successful are preserved. To give a trite example, the city of Troy, for instance was virtually reduced to rubble by the Greeks, hardly a trace survives, whilst there are extensive ruins of most classical Greek cities. In a similar way architectural styles which grow out of fashion may be pulled down, but those which endure do so because they are preferred by powerful groups. Because of the complicity between enduring cultural artefacts and powerful groups, revealing the possibility of political change in the present necessitated the disruption of orthodox historical knowledge so as to expose the perpetual possibility of social change. This notion fascinated Benjamin. Even dismantled buildings may leave traces, and frequently buildings lie derelict after being abandoned. By exploring the ruins of the urban landscape, as much as the celebrated urban centres, it is possible to reveal the range of possibilities which existed in other periods, and to disclose the dreams and hopes implicit in now neglected urban forms. Hence, for Benjamin, exploring the city as a cultural form allows the force of tradition to be disrupted.

Disruption of the urban text was also facilitated by another feature of artistic perception. Benjamin argued that art can be absorbed either through concentration or distraction (Benjamin, 1973, pp. 240ff). Buildings are usually perceived in distraction:

> A man who concentrates before a work of art is absorbed by it . . . in contrast the distracted mass absorbs the work of art. This is most obvious in regard to buildings. Architecture has always represented the prototype of a work of art the reception of which is consummated by a collectivity in a state of distraction (Benjamin, 1973, p. 241).

People usually perceive buildings in passing, on their way to other business – a marked contrast to engagement with paintings or literature. This 'distracted' perception of the urban form was a positive feature, since it, too, helped to disrupt conservative cultural traditions based upon concentrated perception of auratic art. Benjamin's 'Arcades project' (see Buck-Morss, 1989) explored the modes of experiencing urban land-scapes, in the hope of recovering ways of experiencing buildings which might disrupt received cultural traditions and expedite social change. The site was nineteenth-century Paris. He elaborated the distracted nature of perception by focusing on social types with distinct ways of experiencing the urban. The most famous of these was the *flâneur*, or stroller, who wandered in unsystematic way around the city, especially its shopping centres. The *flâneur* was 'above all, someone who does not feel comfortable in his own company' (Benjamin, 1969, p. 48), someone who sampled aspects of urban life in an unpremeditated and voyeuristic way. The distracted nature of urban perception allowed 'involuntary memory' to operate and the present to be incorporated into the past. Drawing upon Proust, Benjamin argued that in a state of distraction memories from the past could be ignited by a current event, so that the present and past united. This was not possible where perception was concentrated, for the attentive frame of mind ruled out the remembrance of involuntary thoughts.

Benjamin's ideas are complex and at times obscure. However, a number of general points emerge:

1.  because each city is unique in space and retains a degree of aura, the extent to which we can talk about urban culture in general is re-stricted. For Benjamin, each city has its own traditions and values, and the particularities of urban cultures are as important as any generic traits they may possess.
2.  urban culture is rooted not only in famous sites (the city centre, the monuments, the tourist attractions) but also in the 'interstices' of urban life – the run-down subway station, the children's playground, the shopping centre. Here people are most likely to perceive the city in distraction and conjure up the images which permit the apprecia-tion of objective meaning.
3.  the city is an interface between individual experience and cultural representation and, hence, the site where received cultural values can most easily be displayed, and therefore subverted. The urban experi-ence is especially conducive to the shattering of cultural aura because it can happen as we go about our daily business.

4. urban cultures cannot be grasped by purely cognitive or intellectual processes – in the way supposed by positivist geographers – but also through fantasy and dream processes.

## 6.4   Urban culture and post-modernity

The post-modernity debate, the question of whether we now live in post-modern times, became, during the 1980s, the most central field for contemporary theoretical development. It raised profound questions about self-identity and social scientific knowledge, social progress and political programmes, throwing into doubt many entrenched personal, intellectual, social and political commitments. The debate has reverberated through many disciplines, philosophy, literature, aesthetics and media studies, and it has been widely taken up in urban sociology.

The term 'post-modernism' is an extremely flexible one. For some writers its use is primarily epistemological, a critique of the rationalist assumptions underlying the 'enlightenment project'. In Lyotard's (1979) influential discussion, post-modernists criticise the modernist use of 'meta-narratives' in which to ground claims about truth and justice. Lyotard claimed that the problem about meta-narratives is that they ignore the contextual nature of knowledge, the fact that all statements gain their meaning only in specific contexts and 'language games', and if abstracted from these and grounded by general principles they become totalitarian (see Connor, 1989). We do not find claims about postmodern epistemologies convincing, and we are more concerned to evaluate the idea of an emerging 'condition of post-modernity'. This is more of an ontological claim about the way that the social world is changing in the contemporary period, and is linked to debates about the rise of post-industrialism (Lash, 1990; Smart, 1992), 'disorganised capitalism', (Lash and Urry, 1987), flexible accumulation (Harvey, 1989) and the like. Among the shared key-themes of many accounts of the post-modern condition are included a new radical scepticism about the role of scientific knowledge; a new concern with aesthetics rather than morality; enhanced reflexivity on the part of individuals about their identity and the grounds for their conduct; a magnified importance for mass media in the framing of everyday life; an intensification of consumerism, the demise of socialist politics and its replacement by the local and personal politics of new social movements.

As this brief discussion of post-modernity indicates, there is major confusion and disagreement about both the way that the condition of post-modernity can best be defined and its implications for understanding urban cultural differentiation. One perspective, derived from architecture argues that the development of post-modern architecture allows a much greater attention to urban difference and specificity. Architecture was one of the first areas where the term post-modern was applied (Jencks, 1984). Post-modern architecture claims to be a rejection of the uniformity of modernist practice, which was held responsible for the creation of a bland uniform style of building characterised by high-rise flats, shopping centres, and standardised plans. Modernist architecture was also blamed for the creation of styles of building insensitive to context (most notable in the 'international style' of Gropius and Mies van der Rohe) and hence seemed to perpetuate uniformity of urban cultures as all city centres came to be dominated by similar high-rise glass and concrete buildings.

In one of the most notable accounts, *Learning from Las Vegas*, Venturi, Scott Brown and Izenour argued that architects had to learn from local vernacular traditions, and abandon the pretensions of the uniform modernist style. Post-modern architecture claimed to celebrate multivalence (many meanings), over univalence (one meaning), and to promote a fresh aesthetic borrowing from different architectural styles from various historical periods. Between 1970 and 1990 many city centres have seen massive building and redevelopment projects, many of which are deliberately grand and lavish, announcing their own uniqueness and presence. One of the first of these was the AT&T building in New York, a skyscraper designed like a Chippendale chair, so that its roofline was of curious, non-functional appearance.

Post-modern architecture celebrated local variety and reasserted the importance of urban differentiation. There are however grounds for scepticism. Post-modernist architects consciously reacted against modernist uniformity and functionality. However, it is doubtful that modernist architecture can really be seen purely in these terms. Although Le Corbusier's claim that 'buildings are machines for living in' has become notorious, many modernist projects of urban grandeur and specificity had similar objectives to the post-modernists. It thus seems that Jencks's post-modernist attack on Mies van der Rohe's architecture is not because of its supposed functionality or univalence, but because it was an architecture of 'confusion' in which Mies upset architectural convention, by building a boiler-house like a cathedral, for instance (see Jencks, 1984, p. 16).

This point bears out Connor's (1989) observation that in reality as opposed to rhetoric, post-modernist architecture cannot be radically distinguished from its modernist forbears. Just as modernist architecture claimed to be new and 'modern', so post-modern architecture gains its following from being a departure from orthodoxy, and hence 'state of the art'. Clearly there are some changes in architectural style which might usefully be labelled post-modern – for instance, its concern to re-evaluate past styles and traditions, and to develop a greater aesthetic and playful sense. However, not all contemporary architecture is post-modern. 'High-Tech' architecture, itself a mutated form of modernism – such as expressed in the Lloyds building in London does not easily fit – the label of post-modernism. Much building continues to be in a more modernist style. It might hence be argued that alongside the much-heralded post-modern architecture of corporate office blocks and prestigious developments the 1980s saw the rise of a bland architecture of uniformity and functionality – the architecture of the warehouse, retail and factory unit and the shopping mall.

It is precisely these sorts of rather bland, functional buildings, that have been scrutinised by other commentators on post-modernism. David Harvey, for instance, while arguing that there is a distinct post-modern architectural style also pays attention to the creation of 'new urban spaces'. Harvey argues that the condition of post-modernity can best be seen as related to 'time–space compression' in contemporary capitalism (see Chapter 3). For Harvey, the most important development brought about under conditions of flexible accumulation is the growing ease of spatial mobility of people and artefacts. In this situation the condition of post-modernity is largely concerned with the development of a new 'placeless' urban environment.

Harvey's argument is elaborated by his analysis of 'new urban spaces'. These are the characteristic sites of urban development in the 1980s and 1990s – the out-of-town hypermarket, the shopping mall, and the motorway network have gained new prominence in urban living, appearing to herald a new 'placeless' city. Once inside a shopping mall, or on a motorway interchange, one could be almost anywhere in the world; links to others parts of the urban fabric seem tangential and haphazard.

Shopping malls are particularly interesting examples. Most widespread in North America where they have largely eclipsed central shopping venues, but also found throughout Europe, they offer a self-contained, roofed and enclosed environment in which shoppers move off the city streets and enter an environment geared exclusively to the selling of products. In some malls, such as one of the world's largest at West Edmonton in Canada (Shields, 1989), references to other countries and cities are made inside the mall itself, so that the visitor is wrenched even further away from the culture of the specific city in which it is located, into a new, imaginary realm.

Shopping malls are only one instance of emerging interchangeable urban spaces divorced from local context. Similar architectural styles – based on the manipulation of concrete and glass – are used in most cities. Many British and North American cities sport 'waterfront' developments, in which leisure facilities and middle-class housing – sometimes in the form of warehouse conversions, sometimes newly built – intermingle. Where high streets continue to flourish, each contains branches of the same major retailers. Private housing estates on the outskirts of large conurbations seem indistinguishable from one another, as do motorway systems.

These new urban spaces have been seen as distinctive, not simply in terms of their architecture, but also in terms of the cultural values they embody. Perhaps the most important of these are concerned with the redefinition of social boundaries such as the distinction between inside and outside is clouded. Frederic Jameson (1984, 1991) claims that post-modern architecture has a number of distinct features: 'the strange new feeling of an absence of inside and outside, the bewilderment and loss of spatial orientation in Portman's hotels, the messiness of an environment in which things and people no longer find their place (Jameson, 1991, pp. 117–18). In his study of the Frank Gehry House in Santa Monica, California, Jameson shows how parts of the house are glassed over and so open to the outside gaze, whilst the house itself has an older and newer part, each in very different styles, so undermining the integrity of the interior.

Shields makes a similar point, that 'post-modern spatialisation' means that:

> boundaries may be becoming more than lines defining the enclosed from the unenclosed, the ordered from the unordered, the known from the unknown. Boundaries have marked the limit where absence becomes presence. But such boundaries appear to be dissolving. They appear less as impermeable barricades and more as thresholds, limen across which communication takes place and where things of different categories – local and distant, native and foreign, and so on, interact (Shields, 1992, p. 195).

This new form of urban space has led Frederic Jameson to call for fresh forms of 'cognitive mapping', in order to restore critical sense to our understanding of the modern urban environment. Yet the extent to which there has been such a dramatic change in the nature of urban boundaries is questionable. For although some areas may have lost a clear boundary between the inside and outside, others have gained it. The increasing fitting of security doors in blocks of flats has meant that the staircase and lobby, a previous example of a realm between the inside and outside has been reduced in importance. Furthermore the idea that there ever has been a clearly defined public realm in stark opposition to a private realm is itself problematic, as Habermas's idea that the public realm was defined by the bourgeoisie, or feminist observations about the male-defined nature of this terrain indicate.

Many examples of new built forms in which boundaries are blurred are in fact high-status developments, built for wealthy individuals or corporate clients. Perhaps behind these new forms is the tendency for ostentatious display of wealth, partly in order for it to function as cultural capital. This is the line of argument taken by Mike Davis (1985) who sees post-modernism as the architectural product of a *laissez-faire* political regime. In this context Shields's argument that 'presence and proximity is no longer an indicator of inside status, of citizenship, of cultural membership' (Shields, 1992, p. 195) seems erroneous. As we saw in Chapter 4, there is very little evidence that social segregation is in decline, and the rise of gentrification appears to mark the rezoning of cities to accommodate specific groups defined both by gender and class – gentrified areas do not have a social mix except in the very early stages when older residents have not been entirely displaced.

The fact that some boundaries are being redrawn is not in doubt. What is doubtful is whether the changes taking place in the present day are any different in scale from those which have occurred constantly throughout the history of the modern city. Benjamin himself saw the precursors of today's shopping malls – the Paris Arcades – as an allegory for the modern city, the shopping mall can simply be seen as the development of this. Equally, Benjamin recognised that the experience of being lost in vast and complex urban space characterised our perception of the modern city. Paris, for Benjamin, 'was a maze not only of paths but also of tunnels. I cannot think of the underworld of the Metro and the north–south line opening their hundreds of shafts all over the city without recalling my endless *flâneries*' (Benjamin, 1978, p. 299, see also Frisby, 1985). In this line of thought the shopping mall is simply the last in a long line of tunnels, which need to be reconnected, by the wanderer, back into the urban landscape. If the shopping mall appears new and placeless today, this is because it has not yet been integrated back into its surrounding urban fabric, either by wear and tear, by feats of imagination, or by reputation. Urban-dwellers of the nineteenth-century regarded innovations such as the subway as heralding a new, placeless realm. Today these have been moulded into their contextual environments. We should therefore be cautious about assuming that the shopping mall has revolutionised urban culture.

Sharon Zukin (1992) attempts another way of formulating the idea of the post-modern city. She has identified two important types of post-modern spaces: gentrified areas and the new fantasy theme-parks such as Disneyland. She claims that these new developments mark a major break from older urban structures. In traditional and modern cities landscape – the city spaces of the culturally and politically dominant – stands opposed to the vernacular – the spaces of the dispossessed and powerless. Zorbaugh's contrast between the Gold Goast and the slum is perhaps the perfect example. In the post-modern city, Zukin argues the distinction between landscape and vernacular breaks down. Gentrification implies the revaluation of formerly run-down areas of the city – the vernacular becomes part of the landscape.

More generally, Zukin depicts the post-modern city as increasingly commodified and as the site of consumption. This relates to a broader conception of the post-modern city developed by Harvey and others, which sees it as primarily the site for a new consumerism, in contrast to the modernist city – such as Chicago – which was primarily defined by its role in industrial production. The idea that post-modernism can be seen as the culture of consumerism has been developed by Frederic Jameson (1984) and echoed by Harvey (1989), Featherstone (1987) and many others. One way of developing this argument in relation to urban development is to relate it to the expansion of tourism. Tourism also has a long history, but it has grown markedly in recent years, and places are increasingly forced to sell themselves in order to attract trade (Urry, 1990a). Promoters of tourism use urban symbols to attract visitors. A celebrated example of the successful use of urban imagery is the case of Glasgow in Scotland, which launched a campaign in the mid-1980s to improve its image. The campaign, 'Glasgow's Miles Better', involved using an easily reproducible logo and the use of *art-nouveau* decorative styles on buildings, pictures and letterheads which could be associated with the Glasgow architect, Charles Rennie Mackintosh (who was ironically largely ignored by Glasgow patrons during his lifetime). This symbolic strategy succeeded in boosting tourist numbers from 700 000 to 3 million in less than a decade (Wishart, 1991). Many other European cities have pursued equivalent strategies (Bianchini, 1991).

The problem, however, with characterising the post-modern city in terms of consumption is that the modern city could equally plausibly be defined in the same way. Benjamin argued precisely this when, in his reflections on the Paris Arcades, he perceived the commodity as the clue to the lost dream-worlds of the inhabitants of the modern city. Berman likewise maintained that the experience of modernity suffused the shopping streets of the Nevsky Prospect. Similarly, whilst tourism has expanded massively in scope, it seems in many ways simply to represent the extension of the *flâneur*'s role which Benjamin again saw as symptomatic of modernity (see Urry, 1990a). As Buck-Morss (1989, p. 344) writes, 'the Utopian moment of *flânerie* was fleeting. But if the *flâneur* disappeared as a specific figure, the perceptive attitude that he embodied saturates modern existence, specifically the society of mass consumption'. Hence, it appears that the post-modern can be seen only as a quantitative rather than a qualitative shift within modernity.

Finally, notwithstanding the major interest in new forms of urban development, whether high-prestige office-blocks, shopping malls, warehouse conversions or whatever, many older parts of the urban fabric remain – and decay. Benjamin laid particular stress on the importance of these sites of dereliction and his lead has been taken up by a number of cultural critics who search for meaning amongst the rubbish. The foremost of these is Patrick Wright (1991), who has shown how it is possible to read contemporary social change through the scrutiny of our urban ruins. One example is the way that a now-forgotten 'Town Guide Cabinet' listing municipal services, now largely closed down, can be used to indicate the decline of state welfare.

In general, then, we are sceptical about claims about the post-modern city. This is not to say that there are not important urban changes taking place, but rather we believe that labelling them post-modern is unhelpful, since it implies that they represent new developments, rather than being the contemporary manifestation of the contradictory nature of modernity. Our position is therefore closer to that developed by Giddens who argues for the persistence of modernity. Within the voluminous literature on modernity, his theoretical work has had considerable appeal in urban studies, his conceptual framework having often been applied by social geographers and social historians. The city plays an important role in

Giddens's thought and specifically in his conception of modernity. In *A Contemporary Critique of Historical Materialism* Giddens used an analysis of the changing role of the city to understand everyday life. He observed that 'life is not experienced as "structures", but as the *durée* of day-to-day existence . . . the continuity of daily life is not a "directly motivated" phenomenon, but assured in the routinisation of practices' (ibid, p. 150). He then argued that tradition loses its capacity to routinise practices for three reasons: the commodification of labour; the 'transformation of the "time–space paths" of the day' (ibid, p. 153); and the commodification of urban land which results in 'created space', the manufactured environments of the modern world. In such societies, the routinisation of day-to-day practice is no longer bound by tradition and is therefore not strongly normatively embedded: 'the moral bindingness of traditionally established practices is replaced by one geared extensively to habit against a background of economic constraint' (ibid, p. 154). The modern condition of personal anxiety and insecurity emerges from a deficit of legitimacy which appears as normative uncertainty. This condition emanates from the normative disembedding of the routine practices rather than from control over labour, reification or material aspects of commodification. For Giddens, cities are not fundamentally the products of capitalist economic forces, but rather those of a search for meaning.

In Giddens most recent work (1990, 1991), these themes recur as central to his understanding of modernity. The existential and social problems of the age are concerned with developing sufficient trust in others to allay the fears inspired by the ever-present risks of life in an uncertain world. Thus he explores the dynamics of personal intimate relationships and addresses the risks posed by nuclear war and ecological catastrophe. He argues, nevertheless, that the present is better grasped as high modernity rather than as post-modernity. There is no abrupt transformation. The tribulations of the 1990s represent perhaps an intensification of the paradox of modernity but no qualitative break.

## 6.5  Conclusion

The approaches to urban meaning considered in this chapter offer stimulating insights into the old question of urban culture. Rather than seeking some universal cultural characteristics of all cities, they propose that meanings vary from group to group and that there are plural interpretations of the symbols and images visible in cities. They suggest that cities and neighbourhoods are appreciated for their unique and distinctive, rather than their common, features. Nevertheless meanings have to be constructed and sustained, for they remain open to challenge. The radical doubt characteristic of modernity induces perpetual re-evaluation of the truthfulness and efficacy of collective perceptions of space. Under such conditions Benjamin's formulation of the way that personal experience and dominant meanings grate upon one another provides an axis for the appreciation of the role of the symbolic in urban social conflict.

Observing the diversity and plurality of images of place reminds us that imagery is created and can be manipulated. Many actors, from estate agents to local authorities, have vested interests in presenting places in their most favourable light. Increasingly, local authorities try to present their own area as appealing, sometimes to tourists, sometimes to affluent households. If people generally can be persuaded to think a neighbourhood 'good', an old town 'historic', or a downtown 'exciting', then a place may attract residents who can pay higher local taxes, new commercial opportunities may arise and additional jobs may be generated. A reputation for distinctiveness and quality is beneficial. The economic strategies of the local state represent the reassertion of the dull compulsion of economic life even in the sphere of memory and the imaginary. Indeed, in the urban manifestations of the consumer-culture may be discerned the coincidence of the relentless impulse of capital accumulation and many of the dreams and aspirations of personal life.

As Lefebvre appreciated, urban meaning is a political instrument. The next chapter indicates many of the ways in which contemporary urban politics is infused with the presentation and re-presentation of people's sense of place. For Castells, as also for Lefebvre, urban meaning may be contested politically by the oppressed who seek to define 'belonging' in particular ways. For other citizens, identification with place or region may be becoming a more significant element in their political calculations. For urban élites, the management of image has become a vital aspect of economic policy and political success.

# 7 Urban Politics

Local or regional political authorities with territorial jurisdiction are ubiquitous in Western societies, though their forms vary considerably. Urban politics refers both to what local state agencies do and to the external, mobilised social groups which try to influence their policies. Local states make decisions which affect life in cities; and at the same time, sections of the populations of those cities, through their attempts at influencing local government, in elections, movements and campaigns, reciprocally affect the state and its policies. Often it is difficult to separate clearly what is the effect of local, what of national, agencies, and indeed the proper competences of each is a centuries-old source of dispute. Understanding politics is therefore an essential aspect of a satisfactory urban sociology.

Urban and regional politics are changing rapidly, and urban sociology has responded, in its accustomed fashion, by reconsidering its analysis in the light of new political practices. In the UK, between the Second World War and the 1970s most political forces worked within a 'social democratic consensus' which supported extensive national state welfare services and economic-planning agreements. The rise of the 'New Right' from the mid-1970s challenged assumptions of the benevolence of the welfare state and campaigned for the replacement of state involvement by market provision wherever possible. This was probably the most far-reaching political controversy of the era and it caused intense debate within urban sociology over the relative benefits of 'states *versus* markets': socialists defended the achievements of the welfare state, while sympathisers with the New Right position avowed that privatisation of services and a popular capitalism, whose emblem was home-ownership, offered real individual empowerment. The 1980s also witnessed a second bitter dispute, between central government and local authorities about their respective powers and jurisdictions. Its ramifications included reappraisal of the nature of democratic accountability, the proper powers of local government and the capacity to which local politics could arouse the interest of citizens in local affairs in a world where most important economic and political decisions were taken at national or international level.

Recent urban political analysis, and the conceptualisation of local political practice, has developed in a rather mechanical way, mostly trying to isolate the functions or purposes of local governance. Four different views of the local state can be distinguished:

- as provider of welfare;
- as regulator of the local economy;
- as intermediary in the formation of collective identity;
- as coercive agent of social order and discipline.

These tend to have been explored separately and this chapter is organised as a review of the literature and issues occasioned by each of these approaches. However, we also seek to argue that these might be better integrated if considered not as alternative theoretical accounts, but as the systematic and unintended outcomes of contradictions inherent in capitalist economic arrangements and the condition of modernity. Each of the four theses about the local state contains internal tensions which emit political dilemmas. The welfare and economic interventionist roles of the local state arise from problems of managing capitalist development; those of identity and order are more matters of dealing with the consequences of modernity. The contrary demands, imposed upon local states by the operations of these conflicting roles, produce permanent fluctuations in the nature of political problems and what might be appropriate solutions. In many respects, amelioration of one set of problems makes another set worse. For instance, the fiscal crises of states, national and local, since the 1970s, emanate from the contradictory requirements of reconciling policies for economic growth with those for social maintenance.

Most Western governments in the 1980s have sought to reduce public expenditure, particularly on social welfare. This was partly because, it was said, demand for services were inexhaustible – no matter what level of service was provided, organised groups of potential beneficiaries would campaign for improvement and extension. The effect was 'overload', an incapacity of state revenues to meet escalating demand. Moreover, it was argued, funds made available for welfare diminished expenditure directed to productive economic activity, hampering the economic growth that eventually had to finance social services. However, as many authors also argued, welfare provision was essential to societal reproduction, both for humanitarian reasons tied up with the legitimacy of Western societies and in order to educate and maintain the health and efficiency of the labour force (see O'Connor, 1973; Offe, 1982). Welfare provision contained contradictions.

Economic management itself also contained specific tensions. Capitalist states are obliged to encourage the operation of markets and investment of capital in specific locations. Yet, being part of a world system, investment can, in principle, be directed to any country; totally free markets pose problems for national governments since essential new investment may be lost abroad. At the same time, mobile capital can be attracted by inducements and subsidies, whether by direct grants, efficient cheap urban infrastructure or a highly skilled and educated labour force. Inducements require state intervention, however, which entail raising revenue through taxation and, in important ways, interfering with market mechanisms. The logic of this process is contradictory: the state must preserve and facilitate market mechanisms, but must supplement market mechanisms by offering subsidised provision. This dilemma occurs in many spheres.

Capitalism generates a variety of effects on work experience, industrial organisation, geographical unevenness and, above all, an unequal distribution of rewards and privileges, but it is inherently neither orderly nor disorderly. To be sure the capitalist economy is highly dynamic, pushed on by competition between firms and conflicts between social classes with antagonistic interests in the process. But as corporatist and social democratic forms of the state have shown, these matters can be handled in a highly orderly way. Other capitalist regimes exhibit, by contrast, more markedly unruly, lawless and disorderly social relations. By the same token, the condition of modernity is not necessarily or inherently one that produces divisive inequalities. It is, as recent authors propose, a world of individual competition, a state in which people are compelled to assert their individuality, exercise personal autonomy and in the process create their own selves (see Bauman, 1988; Giddens, 1991). These activities of the presentation of self entail only that people construct themselves as different; it does not necessarily follow that differences are hierarchical, that some have more prestige or power than other. That this is usually the case is a function of the fact that people enter this process with unequal resources. Difference gives way to distinction. The dilemma specific to the condition of modernity arises from the paradoxical nature of its dominant mode of experience.

Modernity is double-edged. It displays a paradox of self-development, where the potential for change is both welcomed as exciting and shunned as threatening. It promises much – fun, novelty, stimulation, improvement; but change may be for the worse, implying risk and anxiety. Modern people desire both freedom and security, which cannot both be maximised. Savage (1987a) argued that much political campaigning this century has been concerned with reducing insecurity, typically through entitlements to multifarious welfare provision. However, what for one generation was security for another becomes burdensome and compromises personal autonomy. There is again a dilemma for the state which, whether it gives priority to security or enterprise will disturb many of its citizens.

Modernity is intrinsically disorderly because it obliges individuals to experiment, to hope, to gamble and to be ambitious. Its social life lacks the predictability and the certainties that characterise societies governed by tradition. Individual creativity is exchanged for the security of calculable social obligations and the sense of belonging that emanate from fixed social bonds. Recent accounts of the paradoxes of modernity have concentrated unduly on individual self-identity to the neglect of understanding the foundations of collective identity in the contemporary world: for while individual and collective identities are practically inseparable, analytic attention has been devoted to how individuals create 'a self' (e.g. Giddens, 1991). This is not helpful in understanding political behaviour because political agendas and effective political mobilisation are conditional upon collective action. Political demands are presented as the concerns of social categories – citizens, businesses, local ratepayers, conservationists. Individuals *per se* do not make claims. Yet modernity renders collective identity problematic: indeed it corrodes collective identities to the same degree that it enhances individual choice. Attaching people to a collectivity, organising them, becomes a key political task. The labour movement exemplified this at one time by organising people around class identity thus providing a sense of belonging that was supported by an ethic of cooperation and a programme of enhanced collective security. It provided a basis for orderly belonging and hope in a world of individual anxieties.

Governments in recent years have tried to influence the formation and organisation of collectivities of citizens – whether based on characteristics like class, ethnicity and gender, or campaigns over single issues. On the one hand, it is desirable to reduce the effectiveness of these groups for they are sources of claims for resources, rights and services – one cause of 'overload'. There are thus reasons for seeking to disorganise such people, to fragment and individualise the social body. Yet such disorganisation also has negative consequences, causing apathy and disaffection with political processes and the sort of individualistic instrumentalism that is expressed as criminal behaviour. There is, hence, a need to encourage reorganisation in different collectivities, but again these cannot be prevented from formulating and expressing their joint interests and bringing pressure to bear on the state. Thus, for example, to the extent that class identities waned in the 1980s, ethnic and local ones flourished.

One final politically relevant aspect of the condition of modernity is its effect upon those who fail to make a success of the opportunities it presents for self-development and autonomy. In many respects the categories of people who are presented as socially problematic – for instance, vagrants – are, from one point of view, just those who have been unable to benefit from a competitive personal freedom for self-growth, whether because of insufficient resources, ill-health, poor education or bad luck. Modernity, an ethic for restlessness and insecurity, itself produces disorderly failed selves. It also produces the disorganisation associated with the excluded – people who are not integrated into acceptable institutions or conventions of behaviour. For most of the time they are treated as problematic pathological individuals, called delinquent or deviant as they deploy the personal options offered by modernity in ways unacceptable to established authorities. However, in some circumstances the socially disconnected, who are almost always simultaneously the socially under-privileged, express resentment collectively, not in the organised ways of pressure groups but through sporadic, demonstrative, sometimes violent, protests. From this arises one further role for the state agencies, to control the dispossessed in the name of law and order.

This framework allows many of the debates concerning urban politics to be put into fresh perspective. Section 7.1 considers the changing form of state welfare provision through a detailed consideration of the 'new urban sociology' of the 1970s, which first placed the question of the state at the forefront of urban sociology. This literature reveals the shifting emphasis from the apparent inevitability of state intervention in urban welfare services in the 1970s to arguments concerning new forms of privatised consumption which allow some social groups to by-pass public provision. Many of the more general contradictions in the way the state deals with the tensions of capitalism and modernity are revealed through this debate.

Section 7.2 considers how the local state affects economic development and urban economic fortunes. We show how the global scope of capitalism has forced political agents to develop strategies for attracting inward investment, which have wider implications.

Section 7.3 examines place and collective identity, as it affects local political alignments. We examine the trends towards spatial polarisation in voting patterns in British elections, and explore the possible reasons for the revival of place as an axis of political identity.

Section 7.4 explores the role of the local state in the regulation of law and order. The losers in the distributive stakes in urban conflicts, the unemployed, the homeless, the poor, the drifters – precisely the same social groups with which sociologists in the early twentieth-century were concerned – also pose issues of political management. In part they were people whom Castells thought would join urban social movements – squatters, disgruntled tenants, people oppressed by the conditions of congested cities. But often discontent appeared in more rudimentary outbursts of disobedience or riots. Local mobilisation, whether poor people's movements, environmentalist protest or concerted class- or gender-based movements, are activities by means of which ordinary citizens try to bring pressure to bear on the state and government in order to improve the quality of their lives.

## 7.1   States, markets and welfare

### 7.1.1   *Collective consumption*

Classic works of the Chicago School, investigating the world of the transient urban poor, saw cities as a maelstrom of social disorder. The Chicagoans themselves were involved in local reform politics devoted to expanding state support for the problems they diagnosed. In succeeding years, not only in the USA but also throughout the developed capitalist world an increasing range of state welfare provision began to be directed at the urban population. Public housing, state educational and health agencies, planning and zoning controls, and public leisure facilities appeared to transform the urban landscape into one regulated by state welfare provision.

It was thus unsurprising that when urban sociologists in the 1960s and 1970s turned to the city they were increasingly struck not by the chaotic urban life dissected by Simmel and the Chicagoans, but the planned, regimented and controlled life apparently ushered in by the welfare state.

British urban sociologists following Rex and Moore (1967) developed an approach sometimes termed 'urban managerialism' which argued that 'gatekeepers' – key managers in bureaucratic institutions – played a vital role in distributing resources to different groups within the city. Rex and Moore (1967) emphasised the way that housing managers, housing visitors, planners, building-society managers and the like could affect people's lives. One example concerns the way in which building-society managers could 'red-line' an area; by deciding that a particular part of a city was disreputable and hence a bad financial risk, they could refuse to give mortgages on property in it. As a result these areas were starved of new investment and fell into greater decay, so realising a self-fulfilling prophecy.

Urban managerialism was much debated in the 1970s (see Saunders, 1986), and seemed to offer a new way of seeing the city as the product of bureaucratic action. Increasingly, however, this interest dissolved into an obscure debate about whether urban gatekeepers had real autonomy in their decision-making or whether their actions were the inevitable product of the bureaucratic structures in which they worked. Ultimately it was the new urban sociology developed initially within French Marxism in the 1970s which took up some of the useful emphases of urban managerialism in a more rigorous way. The new urban sociology can be seen as a theoretical reflection on the significance of state welfare provision both for capitalism as a system, and also for urban politics and conflict. Its importance lies not so much in its specific ideas and arguments, most of which have now been undermined, as in its role in developing a concern with the role of the state and market in organising processes of consumption.

The key book of the 'new urban sociology' was *The Urban Question*, written by Manuel Castells and published in English in 1977. It was both a critique of older urban sociology and an attempt to reformulate urban sociology around the issue of state welfare provision. Castells maintained that the distinctive social function of the city in late capitalism was as the principal site for the reproduction of labour power. Cities had become central to processes of 'collective consumption' rather than production or exchange (in the way Harvey might argue, for instance). Castells's two most distinctive concepts were reproduction of labour power and collective consumption.

The idea of the reproduction of labour power pointed to the fact that capitalism does not simply rely on physical resources, but also depends upon the existence of a healthy labour force, able to work effectively in order to produce commodities for their employers. Hence, capitalism can only survive if the labour force can be reproduced – clothed, kept healthy, educated and such like. Castells's argument was that the reproduction of labour power depended upon state intervention, since in many areas it is not profitable for capitalists themselves to provide the welfare services necessary for the reproduction of labour. Thus the state organises and subsidises housing and transport, it runs a health service, and it provides a huge complex of educational, training and research facilities. In general these services play a vital role in the maintenance of the existing workforce and the creation of the next generation of healthy, skilled and socialised workers. In this way, the state guarantees certain essential functions for the continuance of effective capital accumulation.

This process was described as the collectivisation, or socialisation, of the reproduction of labour power, hence the concept 'collective consumption'. A distinction was drawn between individual and collective consumption. Individual consumption involves the acquisition of consumable goods acquired through market exchange; people buy, and personally own and use, food, clothing, and consumer durables. On the other hand, people collectively use certain services. Parks, hospitals, roads and schools are not usually personally acquired or individually used, yet access to them substantially determines the quality of life for an individual and is a *sine qua non* of the maintenance of the system and relations of economic production. The state increasingly came to play a vital role in organising and running these forms of collective consumption.

Castells claimed that the fundamental characteristic of the city was that it was the spatial unit within which collective consumption was organised in monopoly capitalism. He suggested that the city is the most efficient and convenient form of organisation of collective consumption since the concentration of the population around centrally located services minimises the costs of reproducing labour power. For Castells this process was the basic cause of spatial form in the contemporary city. It was not the only function of the city, but the distinctive current one. The function of the city was different in feudal society, for instance, where administrative or political elements were dominant. Its function has also altered with different stages of capitalism, for Castells argued that the spatial form of the capitalist city depends upon the period in which it develops.

Castells maintained that state welfare provision of services was an inherent feature of contemporary capitalism, and that cities were increasingly defined in terms of their roles as sites of collective consumption, rather than in their role as a site for production. He argued that the impact of industry and its geographical dispersion occurs at the regional level rather than, as in earlier periods of capitalism, at the city level.

Castells went on from his analysis of collective consumption to a discussion of the way that it led to urban contradictions and 'urban social movements'. The main urban contradiction which Castells discussed is that of fiscal crisis. As the state pays for the services which the private sector will not touch because they are unprofitable, so it is forced to raise revenues to finance them. There are, however, limits to how much can be raised through taxation without causing popular unrest or undermining the profitability of capitalist firms, and there are also limits to how much financial institutions are prepared to lend. As a result the state faces constant pressures to cut back spending. As it does so it runs the risk of raising opposition from the urban dwellers who rely on state-organised welfare provision, and this can lead to 'urban social movements', as they band together to campaign for improvements in public services. Castells explored the importance of urban social movements in various European cities in the 1960s and 1970s, looking at the rise of tenants' movements, neighbourhood campaigns, and the like as an indication of the way in which the developing urban contradictions were increasingly putting urban social movements at the vanguard of radical political movements more generally.

Thus, Castells offered a rudimentary (and here much simplified) account of the role of the city in contemporary capitalist society. He identified a major function, the organisation of collective consumption; he showed that it related to industrial production and the accumulation of capital but that the city is now less important in this respect than before; and he suggested way that this gave rise to urban problems and to resistance from the urban movements. In short, Castells proffered a theoretical account of contemporary urban change.

Castells is no longer committed strongly to the ideas that once proved so controversial. Nonetheless, his work inspired more interest in issues concerned with the significance of public welfare in cities. One line of development was the ·geography of state provision, exploring spatial inequalities in welfare (Pinch, 1985). For instance Dickens *et al.* (1985) show that there were major differences in the geography of council-house building in different parts of Britain. Between 1974 and 1982 there were some areas where 77 per cent of all houses were built by the council, whilst in others the figure was as low as 18 per cent. The recognition of such differences led to attempts to explain the differences in levels of public provision (Dickens *et al.*, 1985; Mark-Lawson *et al.*,

1985). There was also more research into the significance of urban protest such as tenants' movements (Lowe, 1986).

Despite this, Castells's general framework has been heavily criticised from all sides. Orthodox Marxists, like Lojkine (1976), argued that Castells underestimated the continuing importance of the city to the process of production, an objection which also underlines the work of other Marxists emphasising the continuing centrality of production processes, such as David Harvey or Doreen Massey.

Another line of attack was on the concept of collective consumption and its role in urban development which was deemed imprecise (see Dunleavy, 1980). Pahl (1978) argued that Castells failed to give a satisfactory explanation of why consumption becomes socialised in the first place. There are, Pahl pointed out, a number of plausible explanations of the expansion of public welfare services. It could be seen as inevitable, a pragmatic response to urban conditions and increasing population size of large cities. It could be seen as rationalisation of previous, inefficient, state-subsidised services. It might be considered in terms of profit maximisation, that it was cheaper in the long run for capital to have state provision of necessary services. It could be that consumption was socialised because of political pressure from the representatives of the apparent beneficiaries – the working classes. Or, finally, the growth of welfare might even be seen as a step on the road to socialism. Castells failed to be clear which of these lines of reasoning he was following. Pahl also pointed out that Castells always stressed the negative distributional consequences of collective consumption, whereas in fact the impact of state provision is not always bad and indeed varies from country to country, city to city. Collective provision is not simply a function of the logic of capital accumulation and it is important to recognise that the level of provision varies, and hence cannot be seen as the inevitable result of capitalist needs. Pahl summed up his criticisms by saying that it is artificial to limit the 'urban' to collective consumption and that Castells in many ways could not account for the political aspects of the expansion of collective consumption.

A third critique came from feminist scholars who objected because the concept of the reproduction of labour power tends to confuse biological, physical and social reproduction. More pertinently, it also tends to explain the practices involved in reproduction solely in terms of the logic of capital, hence ignoring gender inequalities inherent in the ways reproduction of labour power is socially organised. Castells's notion of collective consumption is contrasted with individual consumption assumed to be based on buying services on the market, whereas in fact the domestic arena is a third, highly important, way of obtaining services which is completely neglected in this schema.

Finally, the implications for city politics were also criticised. Castells equivocated about the relationship between urban social movements and the labour movement (Castells, 1978, ch. 8). In his writings in the 1970s he clearly expected urban movements (squatters, tenants' groups, opposition to planning proposals for urban renewal and new roads, demands for better urban services, etc.) to succeed in transforming the political system, but only in association with labour movements based on old-established social classes. In particular, as a supporter, he thought that the Communist Party needed to play a leading role if urban social movements were to succeed. He envisaged some sort of alliance between urban movements, trade unions and left-wing parties because he believed that the urban movements could not succeed alone.

Castells was strongly criticised, but also extensively re-adapted, by neo-Weberian scholars. The political importance of state provision of the means of collective consumption is undeniable. What the idea of collective consumption did was to allow a new angle on the politics of welfare services, one which made explicit links between local and central provision of services. The role of the local state in the provision and delivery of welfare remains a significant political issue but one that is not often closely examined. In the context of the growth of fiscal problems for local city administrations from the 1970s onwards the role of expenditure on welfare services became a prominent axis of political activity.

But perhaps the major problem with Castells's analysis is that it seems no longer applicable in an age when the social democratic consensus has all but disappeared. There is a dated ring about arguments concerning the inevitability of state welfare and their functional value for capitalism following a decade of major restructuring and considerable diminution of welfare provision, both in Britain and the USA. Castells did not appreciate sufficiently the contradictory nature of state intervention. He assumed that people have a vested interest in always struggling for more state services, when in fact they might prefer to obtain services in other ways. People might also prefer to trade-off security against personal excitement.

## 7.1.2 *From collectivised to privatised consumption*

If Castells's work was an attempt to theorise urban politics from the perspective of the significance of state welfare, that of Peter Saunders approached the subject via privatised consumption. What Castells was to the 1970s, Peter Saunders was to the 1980s. The rise of 'popular' capital-ism, the growth of home-ownership, privatisation, the expansion of market provision of services, the decline of planning and so forth were the pressing issues of the contemporary political agenda raised forcefully by Saunders in his contributions to the analysis of urban politics.

The progress of Saunders' work charts the changing agenda for urban politics. More influential in Britain than elsewhere, since his empirical research and the political issues he addresses arise immediately from British experience, his importance derives partly from his preparedness to reject central assumptions of British sociology. His early research on Croydon (Saunders, 1979) was primarily an attempt to refine Castells and to explore the local politics of consumption, but he was already con-cerned with home-ownership. His essay, 'Beyond housing classes', (Saunders, 1984) advanced the claim that home ownership brought about far-reaching social change, offering a powerful critique of prevailing social-democratic assumptions about housing. In subsequent years he has become more absorbed by the politics of the New Right and expressed increasingly critical views of the dominant liberal and left standpoints of British sociology about social justice, equality and citizenship. This has sometimes led to his incorporating reactionary themes about the biolo-gical basis of human behaviour and on many other occasions it has produced defiant defences of the market mechanism against state plan-ning. His critiques have usually been framed as a repudiation of Marxism and Marxist influences: thus in *A Nation of Home Owners* (Saunders, 1990) theoretical preambles and chapter summaries are almost always framed as refutations of Marxist scholarship, though the actual contents of the chapters are much more nuanced. He thus offered a glimpse of an intelligent sociology written from a free-market liberal perspective.

While Castells had very little to say about services not provided by the state, Saunders insisted that privatised consumption was of increasing social importance, and – *contra* Castells – that there is no inevitability about the state provision of services. Saunders maintained that there is a new division between those people who can afford to purchase their own services individually, on the market, and those who are forced to rely on state welfare. This new division, or 'cleavage', tends to lead to the decline of social class and its replacement by consumption-based divisions as the main axis of political conflict.

For Saunders, analysis of urban inequality is particularly bound up with the social and political importance of owner-occupation. As we discussed in Chapter 4, Saunders argued that access to housing cannot be linked in any simple way to social class or other economic divisions. He maintained that owner-occupation is a superior tenure to public (and private) renting. It allows money to be made through capital gains, it gives greater control to its owners, and provides greater psychological security: it allows an 'expression of personal identity and [is] a source of ontological security' (Saunders, 1984, p. 203). Furthermore, Saunders postulated that we increasingly derive our satisfaction not from work, but from consuming goods and services, so that our enjoyment of housing is of major significance. He therefore sees the increase in owner-occupation in Britain as having almost revolutionary implications, allowing the majority of the population to gain a 'stake in the country'. Certainly owner-occupation in Britain has expanded rapidly. The number of council houses has reduced sharply in Britain; some 1.4 million houses, almost a quarter of the stock, have been sold since 1981 (*Independent*, 8 October 1990). Levels of owner-occupation in Britain – almost 70 per cent – are now almost as high as those of USA, Canada and Australia, and are significantly higher than in many European countries. What is in doubt is whether this process has the widespread social and political implications claimed by Saunders.

Saunders suggested that divisions in housing relate to the development of a wider 'cleavage' between those reliant on public provision and those who enjoy private provision. People consume in two broadly different ways, some use 'privatised' modes, others 'collectivised' ones. There is in Saunders's work an implicit ideal–typical opposition between these two modes which looks something like Table 7.1.

**Table 7.1**  *Privatised and collectivised modes of consumption*

| Mode | Privatised | Collectivised |
|------|-----------|---------------|
| Property rights | Ownership | Non-ownership |
| Access | Purchased | Allocated |
| Control | Consumer | Bureaucratic |
| Sector | Market | State |
| Quality/ satisfaction | Good | Poor |

*Source*: A. Warde, 'Production, Consumption and Social Change', *International Journal of Urban and Regional Research*, 14, 2 (1990).

This schema is deemed applicable to other consumption practices besides housing, such as health care, education, transport, and so forth. Privatised consumption involves consumers purchasing what they choose through the market and this generally provides a good service. Collectivised consumption denies people ownership, and they become clients of the state, receiving bureaucratically allocated, poor-quality services. This is the basis of consumption-sector cleavages:

> [the] main division arising in the process of consumption in these [capitalist] societies is between those who satisfy their main consumption requirements through personal ownership (e.g. through purchase of a house, a car, nursery schooling, dental treatment, medical insurance, pension schemes and so on) and those who are excluded from such forms of ownership and who thus remain reliant on collective provision through the state (Saunders, 1986, p. 312).

As collectivised services become fewer, and poorer people make most use of them, they will deteriorate further in quality.

Saunders proposed this on the basis of a periodisation of consumption practices. He distinguishes three stages of development from a market mode (in the nineteenth-century), to a socialised mode (the era of state welfare which Castells had discussed), and now, increasingly, to a privatised mode. The distinctiveness of this last mode is the role of state subsidy for private consumption. The universalism of the post-war European welfare state has been undermined by a crisis of public expenditure associated with socialised provision and by increasing demand for privatised provision. As increased standards of living make it possible for people to meet their consumption needs through (subsidised) purchase, a self-propelling decline in the use of, and quality of, services directly provided by the state will ensue. One consequence will be 'polarisation', where

> [the] majority satisfies most of its consumption requirements through private purchase (subsidised where appropriate by the state through income transfers, discounts, tax relief or whatever), while the minority is cast adrift on the waterlogged raft of what remains of the welfare state (Saunders, 1986, p. 318).

Saunders's work has proved highly controversial (see Burrows and Butler, 1989; Hamnett, 1989; Harloe, 1984; Warde, 1990, for critiques).

There are a number of initially attractive features of his account. First, he correctly challenged the assumption that there is no alternative to direct state provision of services and registered the importance of private service provision. Second, his propositions appear to gain credibility from developments in political alignments. There has been much discussion in Britain about class de-alignment, the idea that political division is less based around social class than in the 1950s and 1960s. This debate is immensely complex (see Crewe and Sarlvik, 1981; Dunleavy, 1990; Heath *et al.*, 1985; Marshall *et al.*, 1988; Robertson, 1984, amongst others). The apparent inability of the Labour Party to win office and the desertion of many skilled manual workers to the Conservatives – precisely the group who are likely to own their own homes and cars – seems *prima facie* support for Saunders's contentions. Third, he also offered a rationale for explaining the strong anti-statist culture which the Conservative Party – and other right-wing political forces throughout the developed world – adumbrated in the 1980s.

Nonetheless, despite their apparent ability to account for current political development, some key claims do not survive closer scrutiny. His analysis depends heavily on the social and political implications of home-ownership. Yet housing is a distinctive commodity. It is not, in its form, mode of delivery or relation to human need, directly parallel with medical, educational or transport services – the other major means of consumption analysed. Individuals can buy entire houses but not entire hospitals or roads. Saunders conflates the control which people have when purchasing their houses with the control which people have when purchasing specific services on the market. But this is not a useful comparison. Indeed many people who are committed owner-occupiers strongly support the state provision of educational and medical facilities. Similarly, houses are distinctive, as Saunders has shown, in that they can be bought and sold at a profit, and he makes much of the money which people can accrue in this way. Leaving aside the question as to whether such gains are as widespread as Saunders suggests (see Chapter 4), it is important to recognise that few other artefacts, for instance motor cars, have this potential.

Saunders's conception of the relationship between consumption divisions and social class is also problematic. Section 4.2 advanced evidence that the divisions arising out of consumption are related to social class. Saunders has made much of the fact that housing tenure seems a good guide to voting patterns with owner-occupiers tending to vote Conservative, and council-tenants Labour. Yet because access to tenures continues to be associated with social class, it is difficult to establish that differences in voting behaviour are caused by tenure rather than by social class. Most council-tenants are working class, and live in strongly working-class-identified areas – often fairly homogeneous council estates. It is likely to be this factor, rather than that of their tenure, which induces them to vote Labour. Saunders himself was forced to admit that his own survey evidence shows that 'the electoral significance of housing tenure is secondary to that of social class' (Saunders, 1990, p. 234).

At a more general level Saunders failed to develop a viable analysis of the way in which states and markets are related. He operated with a sharp distinction between state provision of services and provision on the market even while recognising that the state cannot currently be divorced from regulating the provision of services on the market. Owner-occupation, for instance, is crucially affected by state policies ranging from tax relief on mortgages, through planning controls, to inducements to buy council houses under 'Right to Buy' legislation. It is true that the dominant political rhetoric in the 1980s in Britain concerned 'rolling back the frontiers of the state' and 'releasing market forces'. In the early years with Margaret Thatcher as Prime Minister strategic emphasis was on cutting state expenditure, particularly on welfare services. The selling of council houses was one of the most prominent policies. Privatisation of state-owned industry also became important in the mid-1980s when many of the largest and potentially profitable companies, like British Telecom and British Gas, were sold. However, one of the paradoxes of the Conservative programme was that while it reduced state involvement in some areas, its intervention increased in others. Edgell and Duke (1991) noted that more parliamentary legislation was passed in the 1980s than ever before. Moreover, along with reductions in social-security provision went increases in spending on law and order. One influential description of Thatcherism was 'authoritarian populism', which partly captured the mix of augmented state intervention in the field of social control and an appeal for reductions in state operations to permit cuts in income taxes in others. The overall effect was not to reduce state expenditure but to restructure spending. This effectively masked some of the ways in which the state supported the accumulation of private capital, property ownership, and market transactions.

Developments in the 1980s do not mark the rise of market over state provision. Rather, the important transition is between different forms of state intervention, with a shift from direct control to a sponsorship of market provision. The state apparatus has not been dismantled, but state power is used for different ends than had been the case during the consensus of the post-war settlement.

Finally, as with Castells, perhaps the ideas of Saunders are products of the experiences of one decade. Many of the trends which fascinate Saunders – house price inflation, the decline of the Labour Party, and privatisation are probably unrepeatable. For instance, high rates of house-price inflation might well be a temporary historical phenomenon of the 1970s and 1980s caused by a very rapid rise in the number of households entering the tenure, causing high demand, so pushing up prices. It is also likely that since levels of owner-occupation have reached 70 per cent they cannot go much higher, and hence the resulting fall-off in demand will ensure that house prices never rise at earlier rates. In sum, whilst Saunders diagnosed well some of the problems in the state provision of services, he should not assume that the market provision of services is without contradiction. Indeed, according to his own arguments it was the problems of market provision of services which initially led to the rise of the welfare state earlier this century! The uneasy balance between market freedom and state regulation is an inherent feature of capitalist societies, not amenable to any permanent resolution.

## 7.2 Local states and economic development

Castells saw urban politics as the structurally determined politics of collective consumption. We showed in Section 7.1 that the main flaw of this was to generalise a theory of the state in advanced capitalist societies from specific types of state welfare provision of the 1960s and 1970s. Largely in reaction to structural Marxist accounts more recent debates about urban politics have become centred on questions of the autonomy of local politics, and the role of the local state in economic development rather than consumption.

One development was the recognition of the immense diversity of forms of local governance. It was clear, for instance, that the forms of urban politics in the USA differed from those in Britain. Gottdiener (1987 and 1989; see also Cox, 1991) argued strongly that the experience of the USA is very different from that of European states. Moreover, there are differences within the European Community. The nature of local government, or of political units with internal territorial jurisdiction, varies from country to country. Hence the scope and powers of local governments vary, as do the sorts of political and administrative positions which are elected or appointed. Nevertheless, throughout the Western world there are invariably local governments, usually having responsibility for public services – like education, roads, policing, fire-fighting and garbage collection – and also having the right to raise taxes locally to pay for those services.

There are also different systems for financing local government. The proportion of local expenditure paid for by grants from central governments varies. In the USA grant-aid is comparatively small and some cities and counties levy tax on sales and income as well as property. Access to services has been a major source of fiscal crisis and political conflict; particularly contentious was the issue of residents of adjacent suburban local authorities benefiting from the extensive and expensive services of the central cities, the population of which include a disproportionate number of poor people with limited potential for raising revenues. In Britain the block grant from central funds is larger, though it is declining, and there is currently much uncertainty about the local taxation system working alongside. The Community Charge (popularly known as the 'Poll Tax'), introduced in Scotland in 1988 and England and Wales in 1989, which moved from a property tax (rates) to a fixed capitation tax, caused enormous dissent and has subsequently been transmuted to a differential household, but still regressive, tax. In Sweden by contrast, a local income tax operates.

Action by local authorities is, importantly, a result of what they are empowered to do. This varies according to the institutional structures. In Britain, for instance, local governments traditionally have had an 'executant' role, with considerable discretion about how to implement central government policies (Pickvance, 1990). A considerable proportion of public employees have, as a result, been employed by the local rather than the central state (38 per cent as compared with 10 per cent in the more centralised France). This effectively allowed local authorities more autonomy, witnessed by at least their temporary room for manoeuvre in the face of Thatcherite attempts to exert more control over them.

Such considerations helped to establish the variability of political institutions. Simultaneously the presumption that urban politics was concerned primarily with welfare issues was challenged. Attention shifted to the politics of local economic development, mostly inspired by American writers, where the role of the local state in encouraging investment was well-established. Their theoretical starting-point tended to come from Harvey, with his emphasis on the way in which capital accumulation in the built environment was a crucial element of capitalist economies, and they hence developed an interest in the ways by which such investment took place (see Chapter 3). However, American political economy approaches of the 1980s were at pains to distance themselves from economic determinist accounts of what local states do. Instead they stressed the role of local political processes in formulating locally differentiated policies. This ran in parallel with the increasing favour found by neo-Weberian approaches in urban politics, which insisted that the state apparatus – bureaucrats and their organisations – have interests at stake too in local politics.

Logan and Molotch, key writers in this vein, argued that local political regulation and intervention for reasons of economic development is of major importance in urban politics (Logan and Molotch, 1987). They explored the significance of 'growth coalitions' in American cities. Growth coalitions they defined as groupings of influential actors who seek local growth at almost any cost. Borrowing from Harvey, *rentiers* were identified as standing to gain from more intensive use of their land and property, and therefore tending to form coalitions to apply pressure through local government in support of their interests. This entails encouraging urban expansion which will lead to the more intensive use of their natural monopoly, land. This may be achieved by attracting mobile capital (and the in-migrants who follow), securing amenable planning decisions, or subsidising new buildings and urban infrastructure. The interests of such *rentier* groups, who, according to Logan and Molotch, aim to pursue increases in 'exchange-value', may not coincide with the interests of most existing residents, who might seek use-values like a non-congested city. However, political forces and the political machinery work generally in favour of growth coalitions. Members of the coalition tend to take an active part in local government, partly because they have more to gain directly than most other people. But they generally also manage to persuade others that growth is in everyone's interests. Trade unionists and workers are likely to be persuaded that growth brings jobs, though in fact, as Molotch (1976) demonstrated, rates of unemployment are not correlated with rates of increase in city size. There are as many areas of high unemployment in the expanding Sunbelt in south-west USA as in the old US north-eastern manufacturing belt. Consensus on the value of growth is shared not only by local government, but also local newspapers which have the material incentive that they can only improve their sales if there are more people around locally. The implication is that a small proportion of the population gain from growth, while environmental amenities may deteriorate for many residents. Within any place, some residents, usually already the more privileged, get a better deal than others – for example, when the costs of growth have been the destruction of inner-areas working-class communities. This has indeed recently created degrees of resistance among local populations, with 'no-growth' movements emerging frequently. Another effect has been to create competition between local governments for footloose investment. However, that competition is of the 'beggar-my-neighbour' kind, for when all involved authorities offer inducements, relative positions in the national urban hierarchy are not improved.

Logan and Molotch's ideas have been criticised effectively by Cox and Mair (1989) who argue that it contains ambiguities. First, in the course of analysis the category of *rentiers* tends to dissolve, discussion covering an amorphous mass of all sorts of property interests. Logan and Molotch cannot consistently identify a fraction of business with a primary interest in increasing land-rent as opposed to other forms of capitalist investment. Second, the key distinction between use-value and exchange-value is insufficiently subtle to sustain the argument. Owner-occupiers, for example, also have interests in exchange-values and these seem more often to be the basis of political conflict with developers than the protection of use-values. Cox and Mair assert that the origin of these defects is to be found in the idealism and voluntarism of a neo-Weberian theoretical framework and an associated simplistic account of capitalist accumulation.

Cox and Mair offer an alternative explanation of the existence of growth coalitions. It is primarily geographically immobile capital, rather than just anyone with an interest in land-rent, which provides the core of local coalitions. These groups are 'locally dependent' and hence have distinct interests in developing the local area. In America where banks are legally prohibited from operating in more than one state, and where gas and electricity utilities are local, and privately owned, the expansion of their business does indeed depend on encouraging other enterprises (and subsequently more people) to locate in the area.

All agree that in the USA, 'boosterism' – support for economic development through urban growth – has been a fundamental driving force in urban politics. Moreover, local politics are about advancing the material interests of different sections of the population. Logan and Molotch, while giving considerable weight to political machinations at the local level, argue that the outcome is usually to favour the interests of a small group. As such their argument continues the older community-power debate which was also concerned with examining whose decisions held sway, whether power was in the hands of a small unrepresentative élite, or whether there were a number of effective interest groups in the community. This debate now shows signs of reviving with analysis revolving around a concept of urban political regime (Stone and Sanders, 1987).

One of the lessons of the older debate is that the nature of local power is both spatially and historically specific. In the UK, the most influential of local elected representatives in the nineteenth-century tended to be wealthy property-owners, leading employers or small businessmen. Landed and large industrial capitalists became steadily less prominent during the early twentieth-century as small local property-owners came to predominate, though increasingly in political contest with councillors representing the Labour Party who were either workers or, especially, union officials. After 1945 professionals – often state-employed rather than fee-earning – became prominent. These shifts in the composition of local councils reflect, in part, the changing stakes in local politics – the newly recruited categories having welfare-related interests whose policies for expansion of social programmes often pitted them against local capitals which sought support for trade and commerce and/or low rates. Actual compositions of councils varied from area to area. Large traditional manufacturing centres, like Newcastle upon Tyne, Sheffield or Glasgow, were likely to have had firmly established Labour Parties, while seaside resorts and commercial towns were more likely to have Conservative (or until the 1960s Independent) administrations led by *petit bourgeois* groups.

As the community-power debate revealed, formal representation through electoral channels does not necessarily coincide with effective power. The extent to which organisations or groups exert influence behind the scenes through other channels is a key issue, both practically and methodologically. Which issues are admitted to be political, and which are placed on the agenda for discussion and decision, are key questions in understanding the operation of local power. Crenson's (1971) account of Gary, Indiana, where US Steel had such a reputation for power that the pollution from their factories was neither regulated nor contested, was a much-quoted case-study of the operation of covert power (see Lukes, 1974). This was a case where the dominant local employer, without formal representation in local politics, pursued commercial policies that negatively affected the local population but without creating opposition or resistance. This may have been an extreme case, though one which has often been repeated in communities where the economic power of a dominant employer renders local people so dependent that they are effectively powerless to offer overt resistance. This has been demonstrated especially in geographically isolated industrial sites, as with the miners of the Appalachian mountains (Gaventa, 1980) or the textile workers of Manchester, New England (Hareven, 1982). These extreme cases are useful for indicating clearly that power can be exercised informally and covertly; the extent to which it is so exercised will vary with local conditions.

If we place Logan and Molotch's and Cox and Mair's arguments within the context of this wider debate, it is noteworthy that Cox and Mair by implication suggest that local politics is reverting to a much older pattern where leading local capitalists play a crucial role in urban governance. The players may have changed – from the textile and engineering employers to the corporate banks and utility companies – but the processes are similar. In the same vein, Logan and Molotch's emphasis on the part of property capital has historical parallels with the political significance of the urban *petite bourgeoisie* (Hennock, 1973).

All these writers emphasise the role of economic motivations behind political processes. Mollenkopf (1983) by contrast advances a rather different argument that links together the political strategies of national parties and the ways in which cities have pursued urban development. Extensive federal urban development programmes, emerging from the New Deal, were a conscious attempt by the Democratic Party to establish a new social base and new political alignments:

> National and local political entrepreneurs, for the most part Democrats, constructed new political alignments and new coalitions around the framework of federal urban development programmes. These programmes provided a means by which diverse local constituencies, all of which had some stake in stepping up the rate of urban development, could be brought together in new 'progrowth' coalitions (Mollenkopf, 1983, p. 15).

What Mollenkopf insists upon is that 'Politics runs on votes as well as money' (ibid, p. 9); the need to win electoral support also affects the types of policies which local states could develop.

The American concern for the urban politics of economic growth has not been reflected in British research. Nonetheless in the 1980s similar policies can be detected. Urban development has been an objective of local authorities in Britain since the middle of the nineteenth-century, where it was embedded in competing notions of Civic Virtue and

Municipal Socialism. The emphasis was on providing services and facilities for residents, from gas and water to parks and roads. However, local authorities until recently had almost no role in specifically economic development, though there are some interesting exceptions, such as the way in which seaside towns developed a tourist infrastructure and advertised the delights of holidaying in Morecambe or Bridlington. Attempts to intervene to counteract uneven economic development in the UK began to be formulated in the 1930s, largely at the instigation of central government, and these spawned regional rather than local policies. Various forms of policy for regional aid and development were tried after the Slump and again in the 1960s and 1970s when the reappearance of unemployment showed strong regional variations. Only since the 1960s, however, have local authorities in Britain begun to be seriously involved in economic development, providing land for industry, sometimes producing promotional literature and even less frequently industrial premises or financial assistance (Pickvance, 1990). Their activities expanded more quickly from the late-1970s, due to worsening levels of unemployment and to the desire of Labour-controlled local authorities to resist the imposition of Thatcherite central government economic policies. The slogan, 'restructuring for labour', rather than for capital, identified the political motivation involved among the radical Labour administrations of some metropolitan counties like Sheffield and the Greater London Council. These attempted to implement on a local level some of the features of Labour's national *Alternative Economic Strategy*, with planning agreements covering working conditions and types of product in exchange for financial assistance (see Wainwright, 1987). More moderate Labour councils, like Swindon (see Bassett *et al.*, 1989; Bassett and Harloe, 1990) or Middlesbrough (Hudson, 1990) formed growth coalitions but with much less direct involvement by business than in the US. These have been understood in the British urban politics literature as 'spatial' or 'territorial coalitions', the cross-class, consensual, social bases for local economic regeneration. The differences between the two countries are probably due to the fact that the extent of 'local dependence' by capital is much weaker in Britain than in the USA, because of the greater likelihood that firms are controlled from outside any specific place.

One of the main differences between Britain and the USA is that it is difficult to find any evidence in Britain that there are local social forces pressing for development. In Britain policies appear to be largely developed by political parties, or by local state professionals (Urry, 1990b). One of the most interesting demonstrations of this point is Susan Halford's analysis of women's initiatives in local government (Halford, 1989). In the 1980s a number of local councils developed a series of feminist-inspired initiatives, including women's committees, equal opportunities policies, women's training schemes, and grants to women's groups. Although some of the strongest of these – especially in central London – were found in areas with powerful traditions of feminist politics, and in particular where there were large numbers of women in professional and managerial jobs, Halford argued that their extent and success were not due to the character of local social relations, but to the internal politics of the local councils, and especially bureaucratic processes within differing local authorities (Halford, 1992).

The implication is that local policies should be seen not only in the context of the wider urban social structure, but also in terms of internal politicking, both between different interest groups within the state and also between local and central government. This idea has been developed by Pickvance in his analysis of the changing relationship between central and local government in Britain. In Britain there has been a major restructuring of local government in the 1980s. Pickvance (1990) summarises concisely the policies designed to reduce local authority autonomy during the 1980s. Central government began by trying to reduce local spending, to control the amount of income generated (by rate-capping), to insist that local services were contracted out rather than being provided by local authority employees and to sell assets like council houses. These policies had both an economic rationale – to reduce public expenditure – and a political rationale – to reduce the power of local authority trade unions, to privatise economic activities and to penalise Labour councils. That these projects largely failed, because of local authority resistance, Pickvance sees as indicating the considerable strength of local autonomy. That power was based partly in the expertise of the local authorities with a strong executant role – their officials had the knowledge essential to the implementation of government policies such that the central state was incapable of directly imposing its policies. In addition, as local government has become fully partisan (there being few Independents elected to councils since the 1970s), the threat of electoral unpopularity at the local level could have consequences for fortunes in Parliament.

More recently the Conservative governments have therefore tried institutional reforms as a way of exerting greater control. Altering the system of local finance, from rates to the poll tax was one way of trying to reduce local discretion, though one which backfired when its enormous unpopularity had highly negative effects for the Conservative government nationally. The abolition of the GLC and the other six large metropolitan authorities in 1986 removed one focus of significant political opposition, for they had been amongst the most recalcitrant of authorities. However, they tended to have legitimacy locally and the overtly political reasons for abolition were unmistakable. A third strategy was to try to by-pass local authorities. Sometimes this has meant removing existing institutions from local authority jurisdiction. In the educational sphere polytechnics were removed from local control in 1988, City Technical Colleges were set up that were funded centrally, and schools were permitted to opt out of local control and become self-governing under the 1988 Education Act. Circumventing local authorities has also been significant in the field of economic policy where the creation of Urban Development Corporations (UDCs) and Enterprise Zones instituted new authoritative bodies, not subject to local electoral control, designed to encourage private investment in areas with economic problems.

Urban Development Corporations were set up in twelve places in Britain, the first two in Liverpool and London Docklands in 1981, the rest in two subsequent waves in areas including Tyneside, Manchester and Glasgow. The creation of UDCs was one of a long series of initiatives for resolving some of the problems of inner-city regeneration faced particularly by old industrial manufacturing centres. UDCs have appointed boards, mostly composed of local business people, and without any direct representation from local councils or trade unions. The brief is to encourage private capital investment, and incentives include making large tracts of land available (through compulsory purchase where necessary), financial investment by the UDC in infrastructure and the abolition of normal planning restrictions (the UDC is its own planning authority). In most instances the outcome has been that any inward private capital investment has taken the form of property speculation, with large cleared and prepared sites offering opportunities for the construction of shopping centres and new up-market dwellings: little new employment has been generated and much of that has come from nearby. In such places the public costs have vastly outweighed the forthcoming private investment. The only instance where extensive private investment has emerged has been in London Docklands where not only has the economic prognosis been gloomy but the environmental and social consequences have been profound. Disinherited local working-class communities lie alongside new gentrified enclaves (Foster,1991); the congestion incurred by situating new plant and offices has required enormous, unanticipated public investment in transport infrastructure; and considerations of social welfare, arguably the core of inner-city problems, are completely neglected since this is not a UDC function and nor are there any formal means whereby local populations can influence their programmes.

The experience of UDCs has several implications. The first is the extent to which local authorities, elected or appointed, can effectively intervene to manage or attract flows of private capital in a global economy. At present local authorities dare not cease to advertise their attractions, cajole mobile capital and provide limited incentives, largely because other places are doing these things. The result is probably expensive, essentially futile, competition, as the location decisions of capital are not much influenced (most accounts of regional economic policy suggest this) and anyway success mostly means taking investment that would have gone somewhere else in the UK, thus not increasing national economic production or national employment. Second, it alerts us to the existence of non-democratically accountable, spatially defined, agencies of the state. This might lead to reconsideration of the concept of 'the local state'. For as Cox (1991) argues, there are many state agencies which have localised but non-coincident (*ad hoc* or arbitrarily defined) jurisdictions. There are regional bodies and many local quangos (quasi-autonomous non-governmental organisations) whose policies are neither democratically accountable nor coordinated. There is, arguably, not a local state, but a plethora of state institutions with different spatial scopes.

In Britain, for part of the 1980s, local authorities used their accumulated powers, resources and expertise to frustrate attempts to impose central control over their behaviour. They nevertheless have lost control over a range of welfare functions. They did, however, accrue some new economic functions as they became more involved in trying to encourage new capital investment. However, during the decade, central government became more adept in usurping control.

Similar patterns can be found in the USA. There Gottdiener (1987) dates the decline of urban politics from the 1960s. It is often believed that local politics was an arena for active participation and control, by citizens, of the affairs immediately affecting them. According to Gottdiener, that was probably true, but by the 1950s a pluralist democratic culture that was focused on the governance of cities was disappearing because of suburban dislocation and the emergence of regional metropolitan growth. Affluence, a new preparedness to commute, and the changing size and shape of living quarters ended the dominance of the city as a locus of politics. The role of the federal state was considerable in the creation and sustaining of urban growth, through awarding suburban defence contracts, mortgage tax relief, inter-state highway building and so forth. Three crises finally upset old city politics: the ghetto riots of the early 1960s, which rendered apparent ethnic inequalities of income and power, induced federal policies for amelioration and alleviation; second, urban fiscal crises also required federal intervention; and third, deindustrialisation, the decline of manufacturing, hit the cities hardest. A mixture of federal involvement and disillusionment with political outcomes led to a decline of confidence in local representation. As non-democratically (locally) controlled authorities proliferated and redistributive policies failed, political participation, at least as measured by turnout in elections, reduced.

The nature of urban politics, then, has changed enormously in the 1980s and 1990s. Conflict between central and local government is intense, and the emphasis on the local politics of service provision has been supplemented, and at times been replaced by, an interest in the politics of investment. But there is a danger that new accounts have exaggerated the variability of local state activities and their autonomy in relation to their environments. At times, Pickvance adopts a similar method to that of orthodox political scientists, focusing on procedures and policies, and does not place the local state within a broader context. Hence, whilst local politics cannot be reduced to the local social structure in any deterministic way, the conflict between central and local government does have its roots in the nature of uneven development under capitalism. Duncan *et al.* have developed this argument, by showing that:

> Because social relations are unevenly developed there is, on the one hand, a need for different policies in different places and, on the other hand, a need for local state institutions to formulate and implement these variable policies. Local state institutions are rooted in the heterogeneity of local social relations, where central states have difficulty in dealing with this differentiation. But . . . this development of local states is a double-edge sword – for locally constituted groups can then use these institutions to further their own interests, perhaps even in opposition to centrally dominant interests (Duncan *et al.*, 1988, p. 114).

The implications of this are twofold. First, local authorities cannot be abolished because they perform an essential role in managing spatially uneven development. This is bound up with the fact that local political bodies have a legitimacy and an efficacy that inevitably leaves them with discretion in certain matters. It is unsatisfactory, therefore, to see them simply in terms of the working-out of the logic of capital accumulation. However, it is a moot point whether and to what extent, given the internationalisation of production, local political intervention can have any profound impact. That there are many local economic projects in operation does not guarantee that they work. There is, indeed, a danger of romanticising local differences and local autonomy. As Logan and Molotch (1987) pointed out, cities with existing advantages tend to maintain them in relative terms. Urban and regional authorities have to be seen to be acting, but even for the most successful the gains are relatively minor. Economic cycles, national policy and the power of large organisations usually mean that local initiatives are operating on the margins.

Second, the process of uneven development remains of major significance for politics. As we have seen, globalisation, while reducing local economic control, in some respects heightens the significance of spatial difference. For example, firms make heavily researched location decisions on criteria which include the quality of the urban environment and the character of local industrial relations. This implies a recognition of local political differentiation, including an anticipation of political responses by local communities to industrial restructuring. Uneven development renders places politically distinctive.

These points suggest that the autonomy of urban politics from its economic and social context can be exaggerated. Every now and then politicians and bureaucrats do have to take notice of popular politics, in the form of votes, protest, or even violence. It is to a consideration of popular participation in urban politics that we now turn.

## 7.3   Place and political identification

We have argued that theories of urban politics have to be dynamic in the sense of recognising the historical and spatial specificity of various state activities and policies. In this section we show how state agencies exhibit a problematic relationship with social groups and political forces outside its own confines. As we proposed earlier, the state has good reasons both to organise and disorganise social collectivities. In the contemporary period the disorganisation of nationally coordinated class-based political movements organised through workplace institutions such as trade unions enhances locally based collectivities and increases the pressure on local states from their constituents. This encapsulates what Agnew (1987) refers to as the 'politics of place'.

A political orthodoxy of the 1950s and 1960s was that as societies modernised, local differences in political affiliation gave way to primarily national divisions. Modernisation theory maintained that places became more alike as industrialisation and urbanisation developed. Ways of life, culture and politics would become more homogeneous with a more developed division of labour, centralisation of state functions and the growth of the mass media. As a consequence, political cleavages typical of early modern and pre-industrial societies, those based on religion, region, clan or ethnic group, would subside and industrial divisions, essentially of class, would replace them. Those earlier cleavages might survive to a greater or lesser extent in different nation-states, but the tendency was for spatial homogenisation around a politics that was shaped by economic groups. This became apparent in, for example, voting behaviour – the most common, perhaps because requiring the least commitment, of ways of participating in official politics. The UK, with the dramatic exception of Northern Ireland where religion determines the vote, was thought to be a classic case of the tendency toward the modernisation of politics. Though there were some regional differences in support for the two main parties, this was considered to be largely attributable to the differing social composition of the regions. With more working-class people in the North, more salaried workers in the South-east, it was unsurprising that more Labour MPs came from the former. Region was not an independent source of variation in support, though there have always been some national differences between Scotland, Wales and England.

In the 1980s there was a strong reaction against this view. The reason for this is that the politics of territory – in its various forms – has refused to die away. In virtually all areas of political activity local issues have commanded attention in recent years. That people may become attached to places, and can be mobilised to defend 'their' spaces, is witnessed by activities as different as the organisation of gangs to defend their 'turf', the activities of football supporters, the creation of local political movements, and wars between nation-states. Sources of collective identity in such cases are many – ideologies of patriotism, the logic of group formation, ethnic identity, shared interests, attachment to certain symbols and myths specific to particular territories.

This is particularly well-attested in studies of voting behaviour. Here, evidence shows that spatial variation is increasing in British electoral behaviour (see Savage, 1987b; Johnston, Pattie and Allsopp, 1988), a tendency also identified in the USA (see Agnew, 1987). Partisanship is becoming spatially concentrated: in Britain both Labour and Conservative parties have steadily increased support in the constituencies where each is strong and so the number of marginal seats has declined substantially since 1955 as a result (Curtice and Steed, 1982, 1986). The Labour Party has become stronger in urban areas and in the North, the Conservative Party in rural areas and in the South. In recent elections, Labour has won very few seats outside London and south of a line from the Wash to the Severn. Despite the fact that Labour has fallen in popularity nationally, Labour's support has actually increased in most of the major cities and urban areas (at least in terms of control of local councils and representation in Parliament). A similar process has been found in the USA where the Democratic Party continues to dominate most urban centres, even whilst unsuccessful in presidential contests.

The British Election Survey report for the 1987 General Election (Heath *et al.*, 1991) showed that in 1987 there were also strong regional differences most particularly amongst working-class voters. Manual workers in the Northern region, Scotland and Wales were much more likely to vote Labour than manual workers elsewhere (see Table 7.2), though there were also regional variations among professional and managerial classes too. These differences cannot be attributed to the different class composition in the regions, for people of the same class in different places voted for different parties. Nor was this effect due to other measured factors like housing tenure or trade-union membership. Even controlling for contextual effects within constituencies (though these are also related to vote), there remained an independent regional effect.

**Table 7.2**    *Region and vote in the working class, 1987*

|  | Conservative | Alliance | Labour | Other | % | (N) |
|---|---|---|---|---|---|---|
| Wales | 14 | 13 | 69 | 4 | 100 | (71) |
| Scotland | 10 | 21 | 62 | 8 | 101 | (92) |
| North | 24 | 16 | 59 | 0 | 99 | (345) |
| Midlands | 38 | 23 | 40 | 0 | 101 | (245) |
| South | 44 | 26 | 30 | 0 | 100 | (281) |

*Source*: A. Heath *et al.*, *Understanding Political Change* (Oxford: Pergamon, 1991) table 7.6, p. 108.

There are a number of possible causes of this. These differences might reflect the existence of contextual effects, whereby individuals are influenced by the political affiliations of their neighbours. Or they might be due to the nature of uneven development, which may have caused polarisation between local economies, and by extension political division too. Or there may exist localised political cultures, at local or regional level. We discuss each briefly.

One of the most frequently invoked causes is that local variations are related to the social context in which voters find themselves. The best-known contextual effect is the so-called 'neighbourhood effect' – whereby people tend to be affected by the politics of their neighbours. Hence, a working-class person living in a strongly working-class town is more likely to vote Labour than an equivalent worker living in a middle-class suburb. Heath *et al.* (1985) show that in the General Election of 1983 23 per cent of working-class individuals in wards with high proportions of 'salaried' workers voted Labour, compared with 61 per cent of working-class individuals in working-class wards (Heath *et al.*, 1985, p. 73). In short, voting does not simply depend on what work you do but also where you live.

There is no doubt that individuals are affected by the political complexion of their neighbourhood, but the question is why and how? Historically, there is good evidence that coercion has been put on people to adopt certain political views. Shopkeepers, for instance, used to be pressurised by their clients to follow their political beliefs, and on some occasions were boycotted if they did not (Savage, 1987a). In Victorian Britain employers used their influence over their workers to encourage them to vote for chosen candidates (Joyce, 1980). However such strong forms of coercion are hardly ever, if at all, found today for voting is secret and social cohesion weaker. Another possible reason is everyday interaction and discussion of political affairs in the neighbourhood and its institutions, which may, without coercion, encourage people to support the dominant politics of the area. However, this is unlikely too, since people from different social classes rarely converse even if they live on the same street, and so it is not clear what arenas exist for political discussion.

One plausible way of resolving this question is to suggest that the neighbourhood effect exists not because of communication processes within the neighbourhood, but because people living in a certain area tend to have certain shared interests which might dispose them to vote the same way even if they never talked to each other about politics, or had the slightest knowledge about the political alignment of their area.

Indeed perhaps the most instantly plausible explanation of local variations in voting patterns is that it reflects the state of the local economy. In a period of major economic restructuring depressed areas tend to be more anti-Government than are prosperous areas. Savage (1987b) argued that the Conservative Party has indeed pulled ahead in those areas where labour and housing markets have been relatively buoyant – notably in areas round the South-east of England – whilst Labour has done best in those areas of high unemployment and industrial decline. There is clearly a lot of evidence in support of this general idea. Johnston, Pattie and Allsopp (1988) show that 76 per cent of the variation in the Labour vote between constituencies in 1987 can be attributed to the differing social complexion of the constituencies (Johnston *et al.*, 1988, p. 39).

What is not clear from such correlations, however, is whether the cause of the association between local prosperity and voting can be seen in purely instrumental terms, or whether other factors are responsible. Johnston and Pattie (1989) argue that voter satisfaction with governments' economic policy and the voter's degree of economic optimism was probably the major influence on changing patterns of voting, 1979–87.

> Because there was a clear geography to satisfaction/optimism – linked to the country's contemporary economic geography – then the changing geography of voting can be identified as a product of the country's changing geography of economic and social well-being (Johnston and Pattie, 1989).

Heath *et al.* (1991), pursuing such an hypothesis, found that regional differences in voting are not the result of differences in regional income, but were correlated with unemployment. This led them to suggest that 'perceptions of the community's economic situation' (Heath *et al.*, 1991, p. 112) is the basis of regional difference. The suggestion is that part of the voting calculation is a consideration, by members of all classes, of the economic predicament of most other people in a certain town or region, rather than a simple individual calculation of economic advantage. This calculation is especially prominent among the working class, perhaps the result of their lower levels of geographical mobility and hence greater dependence on the fortunes of the local economy.

However, this formulation raises a difficult problem, for it might well be that rather than people's degree of optimism or pessimism about their local economy determining their vote, it might be that their political affiliation determines their beliefs about how the local economy is changing for the better or worse. Discovering an association between one's feelings of optimism or pessimism and one's vote is simply redescribing people's political beliefs, not explaining them.

Another way of explaining the local variations in political alignment is therefore to stress the significance of local political culture. The idea here is that different places develop distinct traditions of political affiliation, which tend to mark them out both to their inhabitants, and to outsiders. Thus in the UK in the inter-war years some industrial towns became labelled as 'Little Moscows' because of the peculiar strength of the Left within them (see MacIntyre, 1980). During the 1980s Sheffield became popularly known as the Socialist Republic of South Yorkshire because of its radical policies (such as cheap, subsidised public transport, and municipal intervention in economic policy). To its Conservative opponents, Sheffield, along with other Metropolitan and old industrial Labour-controlled districts, were branded as 'loony left' authorities. Other examples might include the Welsh Valleys and Glasgow with historically strong socialist traditions, and Belfast characterised by religious sectarianism.

The idea of local political culture offers an explanation of local variations which does not rely purely on instrumental assumptions about the reasons for people's votes, but also considers how people's expressive and emotional attachments to places might affect political partisanship. This stress has appeared in a number of accounts of recent political change: for instance Massey analysing Labour's performance in London in the General Election of 1987 concluded: 'One thing that we have to recognise is that political cultures, and the labour movement, and what will work to make a labour movement popular and successful, varies between different parts of the country' (Massey, 1987). She is just one of several authors recently to resort to the concept to explain spatial variation in political behaviour (see, for example, Cooke, 1984; Hechter, 1975; and Johnston, 1986a, 1986b). The usual emphasis is that people in a certain area are socialised into particular political beliefs, and once these beliefs are established as locally dominant the socialisation of new generations helps to secure their hegemony. Johnston argued that since political parties are organised locally they may socialise successive generations of voters to support it (Johnston, 1986b, p. 115), the national political system 'may contain within it a mosaic of separate local political cultures' (Johnston, 1986a, p. 50).

Some applications of this concept are problematic. It runs the risk of assuming a degree of cognitive awareness of local politics that most people do not possess. Survey research suggests that most people gain their political knowledge from national events, notably the performance of political parties and their leaders nationally. It is also the case that political alignments can change dramatically quickly, in a way which contradicts the idea of local political cultures where the emphasis is upon the perpetuation of local traditions as successive generations are socialised into prevailing beliefs (Savage, 1987b). To give only a few notable examples from Britain, Liverpool, notorious until the 1960s for the depth of its working-class Tory support, became one of the most left-wing cities in Britain in the 1980s; Glasgow, the centre of 'Red Clydeside', and historically the most militant, socialist area in the UK, has become the centre of pragmatic, moderate Labour politics in the 1980s and although the Labour Party retains control, it faces frequent challenges from the Scottish Nationalist Party (Savage, 1990).

A more general problem with the idea of local political culture relates to our discussion of neighbourhood effects above. It is doubtful if many specifically local sources of socialisation can be found given the importance of nationally and internationally organised agencies in education and the media. Hence the idea of local political culture cannot easily be sustained if the emphasis is upon the way people are socialised into local beliefs through contacts with local inhabitants and institutions in a cohesive community, largely closed from the outside world.

The alternative is to consider how local political cultures can be sustained *alongside* the globalisation of culture and cultural media. One useful approach comes from recent anthropological debates concerning the nature of local cultures. Anthony Cohen (1983) has shown how local identity is rooted symbolically in the processes by which local boundaries are culturally constructed and outsiders and locals distinguished. The advantage of Cohen's formulation is that it helps to explain how local identities can coexist with globalised cultural media. In Cohen's words:

> it would be inadequate to say that a television programme or an EEC directive or a political statement are the "same" for all those who experience or are confronted by them. They are experienced differently in different circumstances: their meanings differ (Cohen, 1983, p. 2).

In this context the new media actually allow symbolic markers to proliferate, and these may be taken up by people, so possibly enhancing their sense of communal identity, even if this is of an imaginary kind. A corollary of this idea might be to investigate how symbolic images are associated with particular political traits, how these are communicated and taken up by people in different areas, and whether they result in distinctly local patterns of political alignment.

There is another general factor of major importance underlying the growing significance of local variations in voting. One way by which the Labour Party came into prominence in the early twentieth-century was the way it created an institutional infrastructure which spanned different working-class areas – through organisations such as trade unions, the creation of national collective bargaining systems, and so forth. The last decade has seen the erosion of working-class organisation at the national level, and some writers have indeed talked about the decline of national-level organisation more generally (Lash and Urry, 1987). The implication might be the greater salience of community and locality as axes of political identification as national cohesiveness subsides. This does not mean that social class itself becomes less important, rather that it becomes important in a different way. In place of political alignments being orchestrated by nationally coordinated collectivities they increasingly rely upon the symbolisation of place and space – with the social class and life-style imagery used in depicting places being of major importance.

Whatever disagreements there might be over the causes of increased variation in voting patterns, the recent trend is clear. As politics polarises on the basis of increased hegemony of conservative politics in affluent areas and the dominance of anti-government forces in depressed urban areas, the potential for conflict to take a spatial form arises. It is possible for the Tories to win parliamentary majorities without getting a single seat from urban areas – so why should they bother developing policies to help people in these areas? People in inner-urban areas might feel increasingly politically frustrated in the knowledge that their political demands can gain strong assent locally but be ignored by the central state. In other words, the trends discussed above lead to the prospect of increasing political exclusion and conflict. It is to the ramifications of such conflict for the city that we now turn.

## 7.4   Urban participation and social order

The extent of popular interest in and action over issues of local politics is much debated. Local democracy seems appealing because, being close to home and on a relatively small scale, it is possible for the citizen to be involved and to influence outcomes. Yet voting turnout is low and involvement in local politics probably decreasing. There are, however, other means of trying to affect outcomes besides using the electoral system, and a good deal of urban politics literature has been concerned with more direct forms of mobilisation.

Different social groups tend to intervene in different kinds of ways. Means of participating in urban politics include lobbying councillors, joining residents' associations, mass movements and rioting. The sort of strategy adopted depends upon what resources are available to particular groups. One type of political movement which has attracted increasing interest is the 'new social movement' in which groups of people combine to press for specific, usually single-issue goals. Examples include the Green movement, conservation politics and so forth. Much has been written on whether these 'new social movements' are forms of middle-class politics, for instance because the middle classes have the knowledge, time, skills and connections which make their protests more effective. 'Poor people's movements', by contrast, are likely to rely on occasional outbursts of protest, like a demonstration or a riot, their lack of resources making it difficult to mount a sustained campaign of any other kind. Moreover, the extent of grassroot participation itself varies from country to country, with direct local participation in movements, like that of the Greens, very high in Denmark but low in Britain, where organised, pressure-group methods are more usual (Halkier, 1991).

Participation through formal channels is uneven. Women participate more in informal and neighbourhood-based actions, a result of the unequal gendered division of labour which leaves them with less time and less resources for attending meetings. Middle-class people join more formal associations and vote rather more often; ethnic minorities, the elderly and the unemployed are less involved. Middle-class presence in social movements is a result of their typically having more flexible time-schedules, organising and campaigning skills and different values. Sometimes their involvement stems from their own material interests: ratepayer and housing associations representing owner-occupiers are usually channels through which middle-class residents claim more services or privileges. As many studies have shown, such groups are likely to be effective in mobilising to achieve planning decisions which will protect their property values (Saunders, 1979; Logan and Molotch, 1987). On other occasions, though, middle-class people (or rather certain fractions of the middle class) are likely to be principal actors in Green, feminist or peace movements, where they, as Offe (1985) put it, promote 'the politics of a class but not for a class'.

The role of urban movements in causing change is contentious. As we mentioned above, in his early work Castells envisaged a grand role for urban movements which, in contesting issues around collective consumption, might profoundly alter the social relations of contemporary societies. He believed that the multitude of protests that persistently emerge in cities over housing, transport, access to public facilities, planning decisions and so forth, might be coordinated through alliances with labour movement organisations. In his scenario, urban protest might be elevated to an urban social movement with the potential to transform fundamentally the urban structure. However, despite high levels of protest in the cities of the advanced societies in the 1970s, such radical urban social movements directed towards the alteration of the material inequalities associated with the organisation of collective consumption did not transpire. Critics concluded that Castells's analysis was wrong. He was considered too tied to a Marxist interpretation of the centrality of class struggles, oblivious to the gender and ethnic bases of urban discontent, ambivalent about the relationship between urban protests and the class politics of the labour movement, and insufficiently appreciative of other political issues besides those arising from material inequalities.

Castells's later work, especially *The City and the Grassroots* (1983), acknowledged many of these criticisms and, abandoning many elements of his structuralism, tried to develop an alternative theoretical approach to urban social movements. The book proceeds from an analysis of various large-scale movements in particular cities – the Glasgow Rent Strikes of 1915, the Gay Movement in San Francisco, squatters in the capital cities of South America, the Citizen Movement of Madrid – on the basis of which a less monolithic account of urban mobilisation is developed. Here he acknowledges that:

> although class relationships and class struggle are fundamental in understanding urban conflict, they are not, by any means, the only primary source of urban social change. The autonomous role of the state, gender relationships, ethnic and national movements, and movements that define themselves as citizen, are among other alternative sources of urban change (Castells, 1983, p. 291).

Castells distances himself from reductionist Marxist accounts, using the work of Lefebvre and the action-approaches to social movements of Touraine and Melucci, and reinterprets urban politics as conflict over 'urban meaning'. Urban meaning is concerned with the role which the city is assigned at different periods in history, that role being fought over between dominant and subordinate social groups. Such a concern allows much greater flexibility in interpreting what is at stake in urban protest, for people may want quite different things from a city. While *rentiers* and property-developers might want opportunities for investment, the unemployed want work, the young excitement, the homeless adequate housing and mothers, suitable child-care facilities. What constitutes a good city to live in is an issue that engenders multifarious conflicts of interest. For that reason urban protest remains fragmented. Indeed, even protest against the Poll Tax in Britain, a tax which a great many people refused to pay, which resulted in hundreds of people arrested in demonstrations in many places, and which was ultimately successful insofar as the government changed its legislation, remained localised and fragmented.

The Anti-Poll Tax movements were a classic instance of protest against the state and its right to tax the population. Many protest movements make the state, rather than capital, the principal focus of opposition. Some understandings of the Greens, and quite obviously anti-nuclear protest, are directed against a state which is thought too powerful and beyond reasonable control by their citizens. Social criticism of the state takes different forms among different groups. While the new middle classes involved in contemporary social movements pursue participatory, small-scale, democratic association as an alternative to central state direction, poorer and weaker groups have other grievances and agendas.

One, indirect, source of change in the cities of the USA in the 1960s was the rioting that induced new, ameliorative urban policies. Riots in British cities in the past decade were likewise felt to require fresh schemes of social intervention. There is some disagreement as to whether riots are 'political'. Some would maintain that they are merely wanton disorder, deviance and lawlessness. It is, however, difficult sociologically to deny that they are an expression of protest and discontent. The fact that only some groups engage in riotous behaviour, and they are those without easy access to established political channels, is not incidental. Sites of riots in Britain have been ones where the poor live and where relations between local young people and police forces have been hostile and embittered. Often these have been places where ethnic minorities are prominent and visible, but one recent series of incidents, on the Meadow Well estate in North Shields on Tyneside, was among an entirely white population but where, it is estimated, 86 per cent of the residents were unemployed (*Guardian*, 1 October 1991, p. 4). Young, unqualified white males, whose prospects for legitimate involvement in a consumer culture are severely restricted, have perhaps come to form yet another marginalised and excluded social category whose means of protest is limited to attacks on property and resistance to the police. Responses to these incidents are instructive: some authorities point to a need to relieve social deprivation, others to a need for more policing. During the 1980s riot shields and CS gas, wielded by police, became a feature of life in parts of British cities, as well as in mining communities during the national strike of 1984–5.

What these examples suggest is that informal political mobilisation and protest remain a major feature of urban life, and that this poses significant problems for the state. The state is therefore forced to intervene to retain authority and control of urban sites. Gottdiener has emphasised the importance of the state's role in enforcing social control (see also Cockburn, 1977). Gottdiener begins from the premise that 'the principal function of the local state is its role as the socially legitimated guardian of property expropriation. As such its fundamental purpose is social control.' (Gottdiener, 1987, p. 195) Such an approach is especially apposite to the USA where the state has intervened relatively infrequently in comparison with the unitary states of Europe. According to Gottdiener, there has been relatively little direct state intervention in economic life (e.g. of corporatist types), or in reproduction of labour power:

> the US is a poor case to argue for the uniqueness of the state's role in labour's reproduction or that urban politics centers around the local state's role in the socialization of capital. One cannot assert that the local State functions in a necessary sense in this capacity in the US. Indeed, the principal role which local governments seem to play with regard to labor is in managing the urban underclass – those sections of the population so marginalized by the march of capitalist development as to constitute a permanent population relegated to life outside the mainstream of society. While this social control function of the State is necessary and increasing in scope, it is hardly a role associated with labor's reproduction (Gottdiener, 1987, p. 203).

Gottdiener's argument is insufficiently elaborate, but it is suggestive of another important way of seeing local states. In his view one could see both the conflict between the police and poor people in terms of state preservation of the fundamental security of property, both its own and that of private individuals. For one of the strong points of Gottdiener's analysis is his insistence that the state itself is a propertied body, that people frequently become resentful and that, as in tax revolts, contestation ensues. The state, it should be appreciated, often acts to expand its own powers. This may sometimes result in state-led social reform for which there is no pressing social demand, on other occasions may mean the further expansion of bureaucratic agencies like the police force whose collective interest is its own expansion.

Historically, one set of obligations on local authorities was the maintenance of law and order within their areas of jurisdiction. In the UK, police forces used to be local agencies, though policing has become more centralised during the twentieth-century. In the UK there are now fifty-two police authorities, whereas there were over 250 in 1951 (Fyfe, 1991). Once, like asylums and workhouses, they were the responsibility of individual authorities. In the USA there are still about 25 000 separate police forces. Wilson's study of comparative policy in different US cities found that police departmental styles linked to distinct types of local political regime (reported in Fyfe, 1991, pp. 262–3).

It is not, however, that the police are capable of securing safer streets. One of the principal forms of gender inequality in the modern city concerns violence against women, many feminist accounts pointing out the extent to which women are afraid to go out alone in evenings, especially after dark. This seems to be a greater fear in the USA and UK than in, for instance, Greece, (Vaiou, 1991). Where there are well-used spaces, and where there is a vibrant public life, as in the Mediterranean countries, women's fear of violence on the streets is reduced.


## 7.5   Conclusion

We have argued that the terrain of urban politics shifts over time. Attempts to theorise the distinct function of urban politics, whether around consumption, or boosterism, or even social control, fail to recognise the dynamic and reactive character of urban politics. We have argued that the contradictions of capitalism and modernity preclude political stasis. Nevertheless some general conclusions can be drawn about the changing nature of urban politics in advanced capitalist societies since the 1960s. The era of state welfare saw an urban politics of collective consumption. This state-welfare provision can be seen as the end product of major historical struggles by working-class movements, feminists and other social groups to achieve a basic level of security within capitalism. Yet during the 1970s and 1980s this political edifice was eroded in the course of massive economic restructuring and state policies to deal with financial deficits through welfare cuts and the promotion of popular capitalism.

The politics of urban boosterism is a concomitant of the globalisation of the economy, with the resulting need for political intervention to attract footloose investment. Yet we have also seen that such a politics in some ways marks a return to much older political formations, with local élites playing important roles. Alongside state retrenchment and economic restructuring, political alignments have become more localised as the political forces created to organise social groups nationally attenuate. The result is to enhance a fragmented politics, in which local protest can take a variety of forms, some of them violent. Increasingly the state's role as law-enforcer and agent of social control is emphasised to deal with such problems.

It is wrong to see the recent period as the triumph of 'markets' over 'states'. The state continues to be at the heart of current forms of urban politics, as *organiser* of new forms of investment, market regulation, new forms of control and policing and as *disorganiser* of old forms of welfare provision and social collectivity. The state cannot resolve the problems of capitalism and modernity, with the result that one set of solutions becomes another set of problems. The move away from state welfare and towards market provision was a response to the problems of fiscal crisis and the increasing demands made on the state for facilities and resources. But it is likely that the shift to market provision will create new problems, of social justice and the maintenance of law and order.

# 8 Conclusion: Urban Sociology, Capitalism and Modernity

The past twenty years have witnessed a growing doubt about the status of scientific knowledge. The problem, the philosophers observe, is one of finding some foundational grounding for affirming knowledge true and certain. Enlightenment philosophers of the eighteenth-century believed in the capacity of Reason to understand the world, whereupon planned interventions might secure human Progress. Western social thought developed largely under the wing of such a modern rationalist view, though there was always philosophical dissent. Today, the dissenters are in the majority. Post-modernists and post-structuralists deny that there can be any grounds for sustaining the narrative of Progress, of a singular, universal and developing core of knowledge to which science once pretended. We live in an age of radical doubt. While this condition might seem to undermine traditional histories of science as steadily approaching perfect understanding, it makes little difference to giving an account of urban sociology, which has always been characterised by discontinuity, uncertainty and rediscovery.

Our review of debates has identified many significant issues and important findings, illustrating the diverse concerns that have been addressed under the auspices of urban sociology. Yet that diversity poses again the question of what it is that constitutes urban sociology as a subdiscipline.

We take the view that there can be no satisfactory delimitation of the concept of the urban. The often confusing and obsessive debate in the field since the 1970s reached an appropriate conclusion that it is impossible to develop a scientifically useful concept of the 'urban'. In that sense, 'urban sociology' is mostly a convenient label. Nevertheless, it has a core set of concerns and practitioners of urban sociology have developed a distinctive and specialised corpus of knowledge. The historic core of urban sociology is best appreciated as a contextualised investigation of capitalist modernity.

Historically, the attention of urban sociology was mainly, if implicitly, concentrated on modernity, its capitalist aspect being the subordinate theme except in the 1970s. Much of the most valuable work arose from interpretive, and often impressionistic, attempts to dissect 'the experience of modernity'. The ethnographic fieldwork of the Chicago School on the nature of social order in an industrial city, Simmel's analysis of the culture accompanying the money economy and Benjamin's account of the relationship between tradition, experience and modernity exemplify the intellectual endeavour. Each was concerned with the texture of collective experience, with personal identity and social relationships in a tumultuous and disarticulated world. All sought to isolate the central, shared threads of everyday experience and the common meanings resulting from developments in Western societies between 1880 and 1940. The distinctive features of mundane experience came to be identified as the hallmarks of urban life. Metropolitan cities were seen as repositories of transitory, fleeting and contingent perceptions and relationships; as the locus of fashion, spectacle and novelty; as sites where new levels of personal anxiety, uncertainty, anonymity and dislocation emerged. These characteristics we now perceive as the traits of modernity.

Like many other people, we believe that urban sociology took a wrong turn in its reception of Wirth's essay 'Urbanism as a Way of Life', a deeply influential intellectual manifesto which masqueraded as a theoretical synthesis of the inquiries of the Chicago School. The mistake, put simply, was to attribute the elements of the experience of modernity to urbanisation. So although Wirth accurately described some pertinent defining characteristics of cities and some of the behavioural traits of city-dwellers, he implied false causal connections between cities, as urban environments, and the social relationships and institutions of modernity. The aspects of human experience once attributed to the city *per se*, are better conceptualised as elements of the experience of modernity.

In the early twentieth-century the ambivalent experience of modernity was still in competition with older, traditional forms of social order. For this reason it made sense to study the large metropolitan city as the place where the culture of modernity was most evident – to use the city as a laboratory, in Park's phrase. It therefore, perhaps, makes sense to distinguish a recent period of late or high modernity, for there are now few parts of the globe not thoroughly trammelled by a capitalist modernity. The experience of modernity has been diffused. It may still be that city-dwellers are the vanguard of social change, since many modalities of the experience of modernity are most strongly manifest in large cities. Their circumstances may thus repay the most intensive study. Cities may still fruitfully be used a laboratories for sociological observation, but they are no longer such privileged sites.

If Wirth confused the urban and the modern, his critics in the 1970s often made a parallel mistake in attributing the same experience of modernity almost entirely to forms of capitalist economic organisation. Marxist concerns with the role of the capitalist state in the maintenance of the social relations of economic production was a powerful corrective to those investigations of everyday life, like the community studies for instance, which tended to ignore external economic and political determinations. Uneven economic development on a global scale was dissected, showing that the process of industrial restructuring was passing beyond the control of the nation-state, increasing economic insecurity for many. The social power accruing to owners of land and capital, the connections between the logic of accumulation and welfare provision, the effects of class position on private consumption and the impact of residential segregation on life chances were all identified as important material determinants of social inequalities. The Marxist project uncovered submerged aspects of the capitalist structuring of everyday life.

However, although there is surely some elective affinity between capitalist economic arrangements and the experience of modernity, the one is not reducible to the other. Nor is it the case that class divisions, however important, are sufficient to account for the struggles and contradictions of the modern experience. Berman suggests that the modern experience cuts across other social divisions – of nationality, class, religion, etc. This is correct. However, currently there seems some danger that the universal aspects of the experience of modernity will again eclipse interest in the material bases of social divisions.

Sociological theory might be seen to oscillate between concerns with social inequalities and social disorganisation. The origins of social inequality lie primarily in differential access to material resources. Simplifying greatly, this is primarily attributable to the way in which private property, capital and labour markets operate to distribute rewards unequally between nations, regions, social classes, men and women, ethnic groups and age groups. Capitalist economic arrangements create material inequalities, though forms and levels of inequality are profoundly affected by political intervention and cultural representation. Welfare facilities, international trade agreements, class cultures, regional identities, etc., are effective components of the global structuring of resources. Urban sociologists have documented, explored and explained such inequalities at a localised level. Social segregation, the analysis of private and collective consumption and the politics of growth coalitions are important elements in a multifaceted understanding of inequalities and their effects on everyday life.

The specifically modern integument of capitalist relations creates a second set of political and cultural problems which we term social disorganisation. As was pointed out in Chapter 7, political issues of social order cannot all be reduced to ones of material inequality. Indeed, some of the major 'urban problems' of the late twentieth-century, concerning the environment, congestion, crime, etc., are more easily understood as the effects of the experience of modernity. In a cultural world where the search for excitement, power, joy and self-transformation (rather than acquiescence, security, reproducibility and self-maintenance) are central legitimate individual aspirations, harmonious social reproduction is inevitably rendered problematic. Material affluence secures neither restraint nor contentment; indeed it just as much encourages competitiveness, fashion, mobility, restlessness, the search for novel experience – the very traits that classical urban sociologists saw as creating a difficult and fragmentary social world.

The social inequalities of capitalism and the social disorganisation of modernity are symbiotic. A precise and adequate formulation of the dialectic of capitalism and modernity has yet to be devised. One way of stating the paradox of modernity is that it constantly confronts people with a choice between opportunity and security. At one level we have, in the modern world, unparalleled freedom to change and develop, since, compared with other times, the force of legal, social and personal ties is much diminished. One cause of this is the fact that capitalist economic forms do not bind people together in permanent or personal ties. At the same time, however, such change and development threatens to remove the securities achieved through routine involvements and relationships. Insecurity and uncertainty may thus arise from our own actions. Moreover, we are liable to have our plans and hopes crushed, since the same forces that increase opportunities tend to reduce levels of social control and allow other people similar freedoms, so that their behaviour becomes unpredictable and unreliable. Insecurity is the other side of opportunity.

In an unequal society, insecurity and freedom are felt in different ways depending upon a person's place in a material hierarchy. This means that by and large, the well-resourced select the best means of minimising the risks and maximising the potential of modernity. In a sense, the middle-class retreat to the suburbs was a way of obtaining security and reducing the risks of life in central locations, where there are more dangers and unwelcome interactions with other social groups. Gentrifiers, by contrast, seek to maximise another of the potential gains of modernity, its excite-ment, its fashions, its amenities, etc., by increasing their access to work, services and facilities, but this time protected from many of the negative aspects of inner-city living. By the same calculation, young working-class men looking for excitement, who become described as delinquent, are also maximising some of the possibilities of modernity, but under the constraint of more limited resources.

Many of the specialist contributions of urban sociology arise from the detailed examination of the localised intersection of capitalism and mod-ernity. For example, it gives rise to the principal form of urban politics – that concerned with collective security, providing a framework of welfare for expanding the opportunities of all citizens. Similarly, inequal-ities of condition both create and are reproduced through residential location: living in 'better neighbourhoods' gives opportunities to enjoy pleasant residential surroundings, ease of living in a concentration of people in similar material circumstances, acceptable journeys to work, better leisure facilities and less exposure to risks of theft and pollution. These inequalities affect not only mundane material existence but are also to do with cultural belonging, solidarity and identity.

Many so-called urban problems arise precisely because of the simul-taneity of opportunity and insecurity. Although there is no useful the-oretical application of the concept of the urban, there is a perfectly meaningful descriptive and practical dimension, which is the basis for the existence of interdisciplinary urban studies. Certain urban political and demographic features inevitably pose problems of management. Most simply, the city is a political jurisdiction in Western states with varied responsibilities for handling matters like congestion, hardship, homeless-ness, crime and social intolerance which arise more or less directly from the dense concentration of heterogeneous groups of people. There is thus a need for information, planning, policy and regulation which is supplied by urban managers and professionals, who have an inescapable practical role. This provides the basis for a normal science of urban demography and policy, the domain of urban studies. Urban sociology contributes in varying degrees to this venture, but is not premised upon, nor provided with an intellectual rationale by, urban studies.

Urban sociology has exhibited a distinctive relationship to social theory. It tends to take a new turn when social theory throws up new theses that can be explored using the city as a research site. Waves of theoretical speculation about modernity, at different periods, have provided such occasions. Association and disorganisation are opposite sides of the experience of modernity. This central dilemma of forms of life in capitalist modernity has been developed by many social theorists. It is a process on which the specialised inquiries of urban sociology have gained some purchase. Some of the best studies in urban sociology implicitly bring abstract social theory to earth, or at least closer to the grounds of everyday experience.

Urban sociology is a fragmented and somewhat unstable subdiscipline precisely because many of the key practices of everyday life are contextual and configurational. It is context – the social interactions of individuals and groups – that is the backcloth to action. In previous urban sociologies context has often been reduced to, or conceived in terms of, its spatial dimensions. Gans (1984, p. 303) has argued, very plausibly, that: '[urban sociology] has remained a field partly because it alone among sociological endeavours has emphasised spatial concepts, variables and factors'. But as we have seen, some of the ways in which it has conceived of space have been counter-productive. Context is more than spatial configuration. One aspect of the temporal experience of modernity is the normality of rapid changes of social context. As the social interactionist tradition in sociology has pointed out, deciding on an appropriate form of behaviour depends upon actors jointly recognising the social context in which their mutual responses are called forth. In a world of fleeting encounters this requires a considerable range of repertoires of behaviour, strategic reflection and flexibility in mundane situations. Inventive and adaptive responses make for a huge variety of encounters, the content of which is not, or at least not easily, subject to generalisation. The specificity of an event, a situation or a location cannot be grasped abstractly, which is why ethnographic methods proved so essential to understanding modern experience as it transpired in everyday life in the metropolis. Many aspects of that experience cannot be appreciated using statistical methods. Rather the sympathetic reconstruction of everyday meanings accomplished by studies of small groups, subcultures, neighbourhoods, communities and localities provides the means to identify social organisation in modern situations. Such inquiries in part uncover unique configurations, which our analysis of place has recognised. At the same time, the unique dramatic episodes of everyday life constitute the fundamental and common characteristic of the experience of modernity.

# Bibliography

Abrams, P. (1968) *The Origins of British Sociology 1834–1914* (Chicago: University Press of Chicago).

Abu-Lughod, J. (1980) *Urban Apartheid: A Study of Rabat* (Boston, Mass.: MIT Press).

Aglietta, M. (1979) *A Theory of Capitalist Regulation: The US Experience* (London: Verso).

Agnew, J. (1987) *Place and Politics: The Geographical Mediation of State and Society* (Boston: Allen & Unwin).

Alexander, J. (1982) *Theoretical Logic in Sociology* (Berkeley: University of California Press).

Alexander, J. (1986) *Twenty Lectures on Sociological Theory* (New York: Columbia University Press).

Alihan, M. (1938) *Social Ecology: A Critical Analysis* (New York: Wiley).

Andersen, N. (1923) *The Hobo* (Chicago: University of Chicago Press).

Anderson, P. (1984) 'Modernity and Revolution', *New Left Review*, 144, 96–113.

Arensberg, C.M. and Kimball S.T. (1940) *Family and Community in Ireland* (London: Peter Smith).

Badcock, B. (1984) *Unfairly Structured Cities* (Oxford: Blackwell).

Bagguley, P., Mark-Lawson, J., Shapiro, D., Urry, J., Walby, S. and Warde, A. (1990) *Restructuring: Place, Class and Gender* (London: Sage).

Bassett, K., Boddy, M., Harloe, M. and Lovering, J. (1989) 'Living in the Fast Lane: Economic and Social Change in Swindon', in P. Cooke (ed.), *Localities* (London: Unwin Hyman), pp. 45–85.

Bassett, K. and Harloe, M. (1990) 'Swindon: The Rise and Decline of a Growth Coalition', in M. Harloe, C. Pickvance and J. Urry (eds), *Place, Policy and Politics* (London: Unwin Hyman), pp. 42–61.

Baudrillard, J. (1986) *Selected Writings* (Cambridge: Polity).

Bauman, Z. (1988) *Freedom* (Milton Keynes: Open University Press).

Beauregard, R.A. (1986) 'The Chaos and Complexity of Gentrification', in N. Smith and P. Williams (eds), *Gentrification and the City* (London: Allen & Unwin), pp. 35–55.

Bell, C. and Newby, H. (eds) (1974) *The Sociology of Community: A Selection of Readings* (London: Frank Cass).

Bell, C. and Newby, H. (1976) 'Communion, Communalism, Class and Community Action: The Sources of the New Urban Politics', in D. Herbert and R. Johnston (eds), *Social Areas in Cities*, vol. 2 (Chichester: Wiley).

Benjamin, W. (1969) *Charles Baudelaire or the Lyric Poet of High Capitalism* (London: New Left Books).

Benjamin, W. (1973) *Illuminations* (London: Fontana).

Benjamin, W. (1978) *One Way Street and Other Writings* (London: Verso).

Benstock, S. (1986) *Women of the Left Bank* (London: Virago).

Bentham, G. (1986) 'Socio-tenurial Polarisation in the UK 1953–83: The Income Evidence', *Urban Studies*, 23(2), 157–62.

Berger, B.M. (1968) *Working Class Suburb: A Study of Auto Workers in Suburbia* (Berkeley: University of California).

Berman, M. (1983) *All That Is Solid Melts Into Air* (London: Verso).

Berman, M. (1984) 'The Signs in the Street: A Response to Perry Anderson', *New Left Review*, 144, 114–23.

Bianchini, F. (1991) 'Cultural Policy and Urban Development: The Experience of West European Cities', paper delivered to Eighth Urban Change and Conflict Conference, Lancaster University.

Bluestone, B. and Harrison, B. (1982) *The De-industrialisation of America* (New York: Basic Books).

Bott, E. (1957) *Family and Social Network: Roles, Norms and External Relationships in Ordinary Families* (London: Tavistock).

Bowlby, S., Lewis, J., McDowell, L., Foord, J., (1989) 'The Geography of Gender', in R. Peet and N. Thrift (eds), *New Models in Geography* (London: Unwin Hyman), pp. 157–76.

Bradbury, M. (1976) 'The Cities of Modernism', in M. Bradbury and J. McFarlane (eds), *Modernism* (Harmondsworth: Penguin), pp. 96–104.

Bradbury, M. and McFarlane, J. (eds) (1976) *Modernism* (Harmondsworth: Penguin).

Branford, V. (1926) 'A Survey of Recent and Contemporary Sociology', *Sociological Review*, XVIII, 315–22.

Branford, V. (1928) 'The Past, Present and Future', *Sociological Review*, XX, 322–39.

Briggs, A. (1963) *Victorian Cities* (Harmondsworth: Penguin).

Buck-Morss, S. (1989) *The Dialectics of Seeing: Walter Benjamin and the Arcades Project* (Cambridge, Mass.: MIT Press).

Bulmer, M. (1984) *The Chicago School of Sociology: Institutionalisation, Diversity and the Rise of Sociological Research* (Chicago: University of Chicago Press).

Burgess, E.W. (1967) 'The Growth of the City', in R.E. Park *et al.* (eds), *The City* (Chicago: University of Chicago Press).

Burrows, R. and Butler, T. (1989) 'Middle Mass and the Pit: A Critical Review of Peter Saunders' Sociology of Consumption', *Sociological Review*, 37, 338–64.

Butler, T. (1991) 'People Like Us: Gentrification and the Service Class in Hackney in the 1980s', Open University PhD.

Byrne, D. (1989) *Beyond the Inner City* (Milton Keynes: Open University Press).

Castells, M. (1977) *The Urban Question* (London: Edward Arnold).

Castells, M. (1978) *City, Class and Power* (London: Macmillan).

Castells, M. (1983) *The City and The Grassroots* (London: Edward Arnold).

Chase-Dunn, J. (1989) *The World Capitalist Economy* (Oxford: Blackwell).

Cho, S.K. (1985) 'The Labour Process and Capital Mobility: The Limits of the New International Division of Labour', *Politics and Society*, 14, 2, 185–222.

Christopherson, S. and Storper, M. (1986) 'The City as Studio: The World as Back Lot: The Impact of Vertical Disintegration on the Location of the Modern Picture Industry', *Environment and Planning D: Society and Space*, 4, 3, 305–20.

Clark, T.J. (1985) *The Painting of Modern Life* (London: Thames & Hudson).

Cockburn, C. (1977) *The Local State: Management of Cities and People* (London: Pluto).

Cohen, A.P. (ed.) (1983) *Belonging: Identity and Social Organisation in British Rural Culture* (Manchester: University of Manchester Press).

Cohen, R. (1987) *The New Helots: Migrants in the International Division of Labour* (Aldershot: Gower).

Connor, S. (1989) *Postmodernist Culture* (Oxford: Blackwell).

Cooke, P. (1984) 'Regions, Class and Gender: A European Comparison', *Progress in Planning*, 22, 89–146.

Cooke, P. (ed.) (1986) *Global Restructuring, Local Response* (London: ESRC).

Cooke, P. (1989a) 'Locality, Economic Restructuring and World Development', in P. Cooke (ed.), *Localities* (London: Unwin Hyman), pp. 1–44.

Cooke, P. (ed.) (1989b) *Localities* (London: Unwin Hyman).

Cooke, P. (1989c) 'Locality Theory and the Poverty of Spatial Variation', *Antipode*, 21, 3, 261–73.

Cooley, C. (1909) *Social Organization* (New York: Scribner).

Corbridge, S. (1986) *The Capitalist World Order* (Oxford: Blackwell).

Corbridge, S. (1989) 'Marxism, Post-Marxism and the Geography of Under-development', in R. Peet and N. Thrift (eds), *New Models in Geography* (London: Unwin Hyman), pp. 224–56.

Cornwell, J. (1984) *Hard Earned Lives: Accounts of Health and Illness from East London* (London: Tavistock).

Cowan, R.S. (1983) *More Work for Mother: The Ironies of Household Technology from the Open Hearth to the Microwave* (New York: Basic).

Cox, K. (1991) 'Conceptualising the Local State', paper delivered to Eighth Urban Change and Conflict Conference, Lancaster University, September.

Cox, K.R. and Mair, A. (1989) 'Urban Growth Machines and the Politics of Local Economic Development', *International Journal of Urban and Regional Research*, 13(1), 137–46.

Crenson, M.A. (1971) *The Un-Politics of Air Pollution: A Study of Non-Decision Making in the Cities* (Baltimore: John-Hopkins).

Cressey, P.G. (1932) *The Taxi-Hall Dancer* (Chicago: University of Chicago Press).

Crewe, I. and Sarlvik, B. (1981) *Decade of De-alignment: The Conservative Victory in 1979 and Electoral Trends in the 1970s* (Cambridge: University of Cambridge Press).

Crompton, R. (1991) 'Three Varieties of Class Analysis: A Comment on R.E. Pahl', *International Journal of Urban and Regional Research*, 15, 1, 108–13.

Crow, G. (1989) 'The Use of the Concept "Strategy" in Recent Sociological Literature', *Sociology*, 23, 1, 1–24.

Curtice, J. and Steed, M. (1982) 'Electoral Choice and the Production of Government', *British Journal of Political Science*, 12, 249–98.

Curtice, J. and Steed, M. (1986) 'Proportionality and Exaggeration in the British

Electoral System', *Electoral Studies*, 5, 209–28.

Dahrendorf, R. (1987) 'The Erosion of Citizenship and its Consequences for Us All', *New Statesman*, 12 June.

Daunton, M. (1983) *House and Home in Victorian Britain: Working Class Housing 1850–1914* (London: Edward Arnold).

Davidoff, L. (1976) 'The Rationalisation of Housework', in D. Barker and S. Allen (eds), *Dependence and Exploitation in Work and Marriage* (London: Longman).

Davidoff, L. and Hall, C. (1983) 'The Architecture of Public and Private Life: English Middle-Class Society in a Provincial Town 1780–1850', in D. Fraser and A. Sutcliffe (eds), *The Pursuit of Urban History* (London: Edward Arnold), pp. 326–46.

Davidoff, L. and Hall, C. (1987) *Family Fortunes: Men and Women of the English Middle Class* (London: Hutchinson).

Davis, M. (1985) 'Urban Renaissance and the Spirit of Postmodernism', *New Left Review*, 151, 106–14.

Davis, M. (1990) *City of Quartz: Excavating the Future in Los Angeles* (London: Verso).

Dear, M. and Wolch, J. (1987) *Landscapes of Despair: From De-institutionalisation to Homelessness* (Oxford: Blackwell).

Dempsey, K. (1990) *Smalltown: A Study of Social Inequality, Cohesion and Belonging* (Melbourne: Oxford University Press).

Dennis, N., Henriques, F.M. and Slaughter, C. (1956) *Coal is Our Life* (London: Eyre & Spottiswoode).

Dickens, P. (1990) *Urban Sociology: Society, Locality and Human Nature* (Hemel Hempstead: Harvester Wheatsheaf).

Dickens, P., Duncan, S.S., Goodwin, M. and Gray, F. (1985) *Housing, States and Localities* (London: Methuen).

Duncan, S.S. and Savage, M. (1989) 'Space, Scale and Locality', *Antipode*, 21, 3, 179–206.

Duncan, S.S. *et al.* (1988) 'Policy Variations in Local States: Uneven Development and Local Social Relations', *International Journal of Urban and Regional Research*, 12, 107–28.

Dunleavy, P. (1980) *Urban Political Analysis: The Politics of Collective Consumption* (London: Macmillan).

Dunleavy, P. (1990) 'The End of Class Politics?', in A. Cochrane and J. Anderson (eds), *Politics in Transition* (London: Sage), pp. 172–210.

Eagleton, T. (1983) *Literary Theory: An Introduction* (Oxford: Blackwell).

Edgell, S. and Duke, V. (1991) *A Measure of Thatcherism* (Brighton: Wheatsheaf).

Ellwood, C.A. (1927) 'The Development of Sociology in the US since 1910', *Sociological Review*, XIX, 25–34.

Fainstein, S. (1987) 'Local Mobilisation and Economic Discontent', in M.P. Smith and J.R. Feagin (eds), *The Capitalist City* (Oxford: Blackwell), pp. 323–42.

Feagin, J.R. and Smith, M.P. (1987) 'Cities and the New International Division of Labour: An Overview', in M.P. Smith and J.R. Feagin (eds), *The Capitalist City* (Oxford: Blackwell), pp. 3–36.

Featherstone, M. (1987) 'Lifestyle and Consumer Culture', in *Theory, Culture and*

*Society*, 4, 1, 55–70.

Featherstone, M. (ed.) (1991) *Theory, Culture and Society*, 8, 3, special issue on Georg Simmel.

Fielding, A.J. (1982) *Counter Urbanisation* (London: Methuen).

Fischer, C. (1975) 'The Study of Urban Community and Personality', *Annual Review of Sociology*, 75. 1, 67–89.

Fischer, C.S. (1982) *To Dwell Among Friends: Personal Networks in Town and City* (Chicago: University of Chicago Press).

Forbes, D. and Thrift, N. (1987) *The Socialist Third World* (Oxford: Blackwell).

Foster, J. (1991) 'Conflict and Conciliation: The Experience of Rapid Urban Change on the Isle of Dogs', paper delivered to Eighth Urban Change and Conflict Conference, Lancaster University, September.

Fox, K. (1985) *Metropolitan America: Urban Life and Urban Policy in the United States 1940–1980* (London: Macmillan).

Frankenberg, R. (1957) *Village on the Border* (London: Cohen & West).

Frankenberg, R. (1966) *Communities in Britain* (Harmondsworth: Penguin).

Frisby, D. (1984) *Georg Simmel* (Chichester: Ellis Horwood).

Frisby, D. (1985) *Fragments of Modernity: Theories of Modernity in the Work of Simmel, Kracauer and Benjamin* (Cambridge: Polity).

Frobel, F., Heinrichs, J. and Kreye, K. (1980) *The New International Division of Labour: Structural Unemployment in Industrial Countries and Industrialisation in Developing Countries* (Cambridge: University of Cambridge Press).

Fyfe, M.R. (1991) 'Police, Space and Society: The Geography of Policing', *Progress in Human Geography*, 15, 3, 249–67.

Gans, H. (1962) *The Urban Villagers* (New York: Free Press).

Gans, H. (1968a) *The Levtittowners: Ways of Life and Politics in a New Suburban Community* (London: Allen Lane).

Gans, H. (1968b) 'Urbanism and Suburbanism as Ways of Life', in R. Pahl (ed.), *Readings in Urban Sociology* (Oxford: Pergamon).

Gans, H. (1984) 'American Urban Theories and Urban Areas: Some Observations on Contemporary Ecological and Marxist Paradigms', in I. Szelenyi (ed.), *Cities in Recession: Critical Responses to Urban Politics of the New Right* (London: Sage), pp. 278–308.

Garfinkel, H. (1967) *Studies in Ethnomethodology* (Englewood Cliffs, NJ: Prentice-Hall).

Gasson, R., Crow, G., Errington, A., Hutson, J., Marsden, T., and Winter, D. (1988) 'The Farm as a Family Business', *Journal of Agricultural Economics*, 39, 1–41.

Gaventa, J. (1980) *Power and Powerlessness: Quiescence and Rebellion in an Appalachian Valley* (Oxford: Clarendon).

Giddens, A. (1971) *Capitalism and Modern Social Theory* (Cambridge: University of Cambridge Press).

Giddens, A. (1981) *A Contemporary Critique of Historical Materialism* (London: Macmillan).

Giddens, A. (1984) *The Constitution of Society* (Cambridge: Polity).

Giddens, A. (1990) *The Consequences of Modernity* (Cambridge: Polity).

Giddens, A. (1991) *Modernity and Self Identity* (Cambridge: Polity).

Girouard, M. (1990) *The English Country Town* (New Haven: University of Yale

Press).

Glass, D.V. (1954) *Social Mobility in Britain* (London: Routledge & Kegan Paul).

Glass, R. (1989) *Cliches of Urban Doom and Other Essays* (Oxford: Blackwell).

Glucksmann, M. (1990) *Women Assemble* (London: Routledge).

Goffman, E. (1959) *The Presentation of Self in Everyday Life* (Garden City: Doubleday).

Goldthorpe, J.H. (1980) *Social Mobility and the Class Structure in Modern Britain* (Oxford: Clarendon).

Goldthorpe, J.H., Lockwood, D., Bechhofer, F. and Platt, J. (1968, 1969) *The Affluent Worker in the Class Structure* (Cambridge: University of Cambridge Press).

Gordon, D. (1984) 'Capitalist Development and the History of American Cities', in W. Tabb and L. Sawyer (eds), *Marxism and the Metropolis* (New York: University of Oxford Press).

Gottdiener, M. (1985) *The Social Production of Urban Space* (Austin: University of Texas Press).

Gottdiener, M. (1987) *The Decline of Urban Politics: Political Theory and the Crisis of the Local State* (London: Sage).

Gottdiener, M. (1989) 'Crisis Theory and Socio-Spatial Restructuring: The US Case', in M. Gottdiener and N. Komninos (eds), *Capitalist Development and Crisis Theory: Accumulation, Regulation and Spatial Restructuring* (London: Macmillan), pp. 365–90.

Gottdiener, M. and Komninos, N. (eds) (1989) *Capitalist Development and Crisis Theory: Accumulation, Regulation, and Spatial Restructuring* (London: Macmillan).

Greer, S. (1962) *The Emerging City: Myth and Reality* (New York: Free Press).

Gregory, D. and Urry, J. (eds) (1985) *Social Relations and Spatial Structures* (London: Macmillan).

Habermas, J. (1989) *The Structural Transformation of the Public Sphere: An Inquiry into a Category of Bourgeois Society* (Cambridge: Polity).

Hakim, C. (1987) 'Trends in the Flexible Workforce', *Employment Gazette*, 95.

Halford, S. (1989) 'Spatial Divisions and Women's Initiatives in Local Government', *Geoforum*, 20, 2, 161–74.

Halford, S. (1992) 'Feminist Change in a Patriarchal Organisation: The Experience of Women's Initiatives in Local Government and Implications for Feminist Perspectives on State Institutions', in M. Savage and A. Witz (eds), *Gender and Bureaucracy* (Oxford: Blackwell).

Halkier, B. (1991) 'Greens in Movement: A Comparative Analysis of Friends of the Earth in Britain and NOAH in Denmark', MA thesis, Department of Sociology, University of Lancaster.

Hall, P. (1988) 'Urban Growth in Western Europe', in M. Dogan and J.D. Kasarda (eds), *The Metropolis Era*, vol. 1 (New York: Sage), pp. 111–27.

Hall, P. and Hay, P. (1980) *Growth Centers in European Urban Systems* (Berkeley: University of California Press).

Halsey, A.H., Heath, A. and Ridge, J. (1980) *Origins and Destinations* (Oxford: Clarendon).

Hamnett, C. (1984a) 'Gentrification and Urban Location Theory: A Review and Assessment', in D.T. Herbert and R.J. Johnston (eds), *Geography and the Urban Environment*, vol. 6 (New York: John Wiley).

Hamnett, C. (1984b) 'Housing the Two Nations: Socio-Tenurial Polarisation in England and Wales, 1961–81', *Urban Studies*, 21, 4, 389–405.

Hamnett, C. (1989) 'Consumption and Class in Contemporary Britain', in C. Hamnett *et al.* (eds), *The Changing Social Structure* (London: Sage), pp. 199–243.

Hamnett, C. and Randolph, B. (1986) 'The Role of Labour and Housing Markets in the Production of Geographical Variations in Social Stratification', in K. Hoggart and E. Kofman (eds), *Political Geography and Social Stratification* (London: Croom Helm), pp. 213–46.

Hannerz, U. (1980) *Exploring the City: Inquiries towards an Urban Anthropology* (New York: Columbia University Press).

Hannoosh, M. (1984) 'Painters of Modern Life: Baudelaire and the Impressionists', in W. Sharpe and L. Wallock (eds), *Visions of the Modern City* (New York: Columbia University Press), pp. 164–84.

Harding, P. and Jenkins, R. (1989) *The Myth of the Hidden Economy: Towards a New Understanding of Informal Economic Activity* (Milton Keynes: Open University Press).

Hareven, T. (1982) *Family Time and Industrial Time: The Relationship between Family and Work in a New England Community* (Cambridge: University of Cambridge Press).

Harloe, M. (1984) 'Sector and Class: A Critical Comment', *International Journal of Urban and Regional Research*, 8, 228–37.

Harloe, M., Pickvance, C., Urry, J. (eds), *Place, Policy and Politics: Do Localities Matter?* (London: Unwin Hyman).

Harraway, D. (1989) *Primate Visions* (London: Routledge).

Harvey, D. (1973) *Social Justice and the City* (London: Edward Arnold).

Harvey, D. (1977) 'Labour, Capital and Class Struggle around the Built Environment in Advanced Capitalist Societies', *Politics and Society*, 6, 265–95.

Harvey, D. (1982) *The Limits to Capital* (Oxford: Blackwell).

Harvey, D. (1985a) *The Urbanisation of Capital* (Oxford: Blackwell).

Harvey, D. (1985b) *Consciousness and the Urban Experience* (Oxford: Blackwell).

Harvey, D. (1985c) 'Monument and Myth: The Building of the Basilica of the Sacred Heart', in D. Harvey, *Consciousness and the Urban Experience* (Oxford: Blackwell).

Harvey, D. (1988) *Social Justice and the City*, 2nd ed. (Oxford: Blackwell).

Harvey, D. (1989) *The Condition of Postmodernity* (Oxford: Blackwell).

Harvey, L. (1987) 'The Nature of "Schools" in the Sociology of Knowledge: The Case of the "Chicago School"', *Sociological Review*, 35, 2, 245–78.

Hausermann, H. and Kramer-Badoni, T. (1989) 'The Change of Regional Inequality in the Federal Republic of Germany', in M. Gottdiener and N. Komninos (eds), *Capitalist Development and Crisis Theory: Accumulation, Regulation and Spatial Restructuring* (London: Macmillan), pp. 331–47.

Hawley, A. (1950) *Human Ecology: A Theory of Community Structure* (New York: Ronald Press).

Heath, A., Jowell, R. and Curtice, J. (1985) *How Britain Votes* (Oxford: Pergamon).

Heath, A., Curtice, J., Evans, G., Jowell, R., Field, J. and Witherspoon, S. (1991) *Understanding Political Change* (Oxford: Pergamon).

Hechter, M. (1975) *Internal Colonialism: The Celtic Fringe in British National*

*Development* (London: Routledge).

Hennock, E. (1973) *Fit and Proper Persons* (London: Edward Arnold).

Herbert, D. and Johnston, R. (1976) *Social Areas in Cities*, vol. 1 (Chichester: John Wiley).

Herbert, D. and Johnston, R. (1978) *Social Areas in Cities: Processes, Patterns and Problems* (Chichester: John Wiley).

Hill, R.C. (1987) 'Global Factory and Company Town: The Changing Division of Labour in the International Automobile Industry', in J. Henderson and M. Castells (eds), *Global Restructuring and Territorial Development* (London: Sage).

Hillery, C.A. (1955) 'Definitions of Community: Areas of Agreement', *Rural Sociology*, 20, 93–118.

Hoyt, H. (1939) *The Structure and Growth of Residential Neighbourhoods in American Cities* (Chicago: University of Chicago Press).

Hudson, R. (1990) 'Trying to Revive an Infant Hercules: The Rise and Fall of Local Authority Modernization Politics on Teesside', in M. Harloe, C. Pickvance and J. Urry (eds), *Place, Policy and Politics* (London: Unwin Hyman), pp. 62–86.

Hudson, R. and Williams, A. (1990) *Divided Britain* (London: Belhaven).

Inglis, F. (1990) 'Landscape as Popular Culture', in S. Pugh (ed.), *Reading Landscapes: City–Country–Capital* (Manchester: Manchester University Press).

Jacobs, J. (1961) *The Death and Life of Great American Cities* (New York: Random House).

Jager, M. (1986) 'Class Definition and the Aesthetics of Gentrification: Victoriana in Melbourne', in N. Smith and P. Williams (eds), *Gentrification of the City* (Boston: Allen & Unwin), pp. 78–91.

Jameson, F. (1984) 'Postmodernism, or the Cultural Logic of Late Capitalism', *New Left Review*, 146, 53–92.

Jameson, F. (1991) *Postmodernism or the Cultural Logic of Late Capitalism* (London: Verso).

Jencks, C. (1984) *The Language of Postmodern Architecture* (London: Academy).

Jessop, B. (1982) *The Capitalist State: Marxist Theories and Method* (London: Robertson).

Jessop, B. (1990) 'Regulation Theories in Retrospect and Prospect', *Economy and Society*, 19, 2, pp. 153–216.

Johnston, R. (1986a) 'The Neighbourhood Effect Revisited: Spatial Science or Political Regionalism', *Environment and Planning D: Society and Space*, 4, 41–55.

Johnston, R. (1986b) 'Places and Votes: the Role of Location in the Creation of Political Attitudes', *Urban Geography*, 7, 103–16.

Johnston, R. and Pattie, C. (1989) 'Voting in Britain since 1979: A Growing North–South Divide?', in J. Lewis and A. Townsend (eds), *The North–South Divide* (London: Paul Chapman).

Johnston, R., Pattie, C. and Allsopp, J. (1988) *A Nation Dividing? The Electoral Map of Great Britain 1979–87* (London: Longman).

Joyce, P. (1980) *Work, Society and Politics* (Brighton: Harvester).

Jukes, P. (1990) *A Shout in the Street: The Modern City* (London: Faber).

Kasarda, J. (1988) 'Economic Restructuring and the American Urban Dilemma', in Dogan and Kasarda (eds), *The Metropolis Era* (Newbury Hills, California: Sage), pp. 56–84.

Kent, R.A. (1981) *A History of British Empirical Sociology* (Aldershot: Gower).

King, A. (1990) *World Cities* (London: Routledge).

Kumar, K. (1978) *Prophecy and Progress* (Harmondsworth: Penguin).

Lal, B.B. (1990) *The Romance of Culture in an Urban Civilisation: Robert E. Park on Race and Ethnic Relations in Cities* (London: Routledge).

Lampard, E. (1965) 'Historical Aspects of Urbanisation', in P.M. Hauser and L.F. Schnore (eds), *The Study of Urbanization* (New York: Wiley), pp. 519–54.

Lash, S. (1990) *A Sociology of Postmodernism* (London: Routledge).

Lash, S. and Urry, J. (1987) *The End of Organised Capitalism* (Cambridge: Polity).

Lebas, E. (ed.) (1982) 'Trend Report: Urban and Regional Sociology in Advanced Industrial Societies: A Decade of Marxist and Critical Perspectives', *Current Sociology*, 30, 1, 1–271.

Lee, D. and Newby, H. (1982) *The Problem of Sociology* (London: Unwin Hyman).

Leitner, H. (1989) 'Urban Geography: The Urban Dimension of Economic, Political and Social Restructuring', *Progress in Human Geography*, 13, 4, 551–65.

Lewis, J. and Townsend, A. (eds) (1989) *The North–South Divide: Regional Change in Britain in the 1980s* (London: Paul Chapman).

Lewis, O. (1951), *Life in a Mexican Village* (Urbana: University of Illinois Press).

Ley, D. (1983) *A Social Geography of the City* (New York: Harper & Row).

Littlejohn, J. (1963) *Westrigg: The Sociology of a Cheviot Parish* (London: Routledge & Kegan Paul).

Lockwood, D. (1966) 'Sources of Variation in Working Class Images of Society', *Sociological Review*, 14, 3, 249–67.

Logan, J. and Molotch, H. (1987) *Urban Fortunes: The Political Economy of Place* (Berkeley: University of California Press).

Lojkine, J. (1976) 'Contribution to a Marxist Theory of Urbanisation', in C. Pickvance (ed.), *Urban Sociology: Critical Essays* (London: Tavistock), pp. 119–46.

Longhurst, B. (1989) *Karl Mannheim and the Contemporary Sociology of Knowledge* (London: Macmillan).

Lowe, S. (1986) *Urban Social Movements: The City after Castells* (London: Macmillan).

Lowenthal, D. (1961) 'Geography, Experience and Imagination: Towards a Geographical Epistemology', in *Annals of the American Association of Geographers*, 51, 241–60.

Lukes, S. (1974) *Power: A Radical View* (London: Macmillan).

Luxton, M. (1980) *More than a Labour of Love* (Toronto: Women's Press).

Luxton, M. (1986) 'Two Hands for the Clock: Changing Patterns of the Gendered Division of Labour', in R. Hamilton and M. Barrett (eds), *The Politics of Diversity: Feminism, Marxism and Nationalism* (London: Verso), pp. 35–52.

Lyotard, J.-F. (1979) *The Postmodern Condition* (Manchester: Mancheter University Press).

MacIntyre, S. (1980) *Little Moscows* (London: Croom Helm).

Marcuse, P. (1989) '"Dual City": A Muddy Metaphor for a Quartered City', *International Journal of Urban and Regional Research*, 13, 4, 697–708.

Mark-Lawson, J., Savage, M. and Warde, A. (1985) 'Women and Local Politics: Struggles over Welfare, 1918–39', in L. Murgatroyd, M. Savage, D. Shapiro, J. Urry, S. Walby and A. Warde, *Localities, Class and Gender* (London: Pion), pp. 195–215.

Markusen, A. (1981) 'City Spatial Structure, Women's Household Work and

National Urban Policy', in C.R. Stimpson (ed.), *Women and the American City* (Chicago: University of Chicago Press).

Marshall, G., Rose, G., Newby, H. and Vogler, C. (1988) *Social Class in Britain* (London: Unwin Hyman).

Marshall, G. (1990) *In Praise of Sociology* (London: Unwin Hyman).

Marshall, G. (1991) 'In Defence of Class Analysis: A Comment on R.E. Pahl', *International Journal of Urban and Regional Research*, 15, 114–18.

Marshall, J.N. *et al.* (1988) *Services and Uneven Development* (London: Macmillan).

Martin, B. (1981) *A Sociology of Contemporary Cultural Change* (Oxford: Blackwell).

Massey, D. (1984) *Spatial Divisions of Labour* (London: Macmillan).

Massey, D. (1987) 'Heartlands of Defeat', *Marxism Today*, July, 18–23.

Massey, D. (1988) 'Uneven Redevelopment: Social Change and Spatial Divisions of Labour', in D. Massey and J. Allen (eds), *Uneven Redevelopment* (London: Hodder & Stoughton).

Massey, D. (1991) 'The political place of locality studies', *Environment and Planning A*, 23, 2, 267–282.

Massey, D. and Meegan, R. (1979) 'The Geography of Industrial Reorganisation', *Progress in Planning*, 10, 159–237.

Massey, D. and Meegan, R. (1982) *The Anatomy of Job Loss: The How, Why and Where of Employment Decline* (London: Macmillan).

Meegan, R. (1990) 'Paradise Postponed: The Growth and Decline of Merseyside's Outer Estates', in P. Cooke (ed.), *Localities* (London: Unwin Hyman), pp. 198–234.

Mellor, R. (1977) *Urban Sociology in an Urbanised Society* (London: Routledge).

Mellor, R. (1989) 'Urban Sociology: A Trend Report', *Sociology*, 23, 2, 241–60.

Mills, C.A (1988) 'Life on the Upslope: The Postmodern Landscape of Gentrification', *Society and Space*, 6, 2, 169–90.

Mingione, E. (1987) 'Urban Survival Strategies, Family Structure and Informal Practices', in M.P. Smith and J. Fagin (eds), *The Capitalist City* (Oxford: Blackwell), pp. 297–322.

Mingione, E. and Redclift, N. (1985) *Beyond Employment: Household, Gender and Subsistence* (Oxford: Blackwell).

Mollenkopf, J.H. (1983) *The Contested City* (Princeton, NJ: Princeton University Press).

Molotch, H. (1976) 'The City as a Growth Machine: Towards a Political Economy of Place', *American Journal of Sociology*, 82, 309–32.

Morris, L. (1987) 'Local Social Polarisation: A Study of Hartlepool', *International Journal of Urban and Regional Research*, 11, 3, 331–50.

Morris, R.J. (1983) 'The Middle Class and British Towns and Cities of the Industrial Revolution', in D. Fraser and A. Sutcliffe (eds), *The Pursuit of Urban History* (London: Edward Arnold).

Mullins, P. (1991) 'The Identification of Social Forces in Development as a General Problem in Sociology: A Comment on Pahl's Remarks on Class and Consumption as Forces in Urban and Regional Development', *International Journal of Urban and Regional Research*, 15, 1, 119–126.

Mumford, L. (1938) *The Culture of the City* (Harmondsworth: Penguin).

Mumford, L. (1961) *The City in History* (Harmondsworth: Penguin).

Munro, M. and Maclennan, D. (1987) 'Intra-Urban Change in Housing Prices',

*Housing Studies*, 2, 2, 65–81.

Murgatroyd, L. and Urry, J. (1985) 'The Class and Gender Restructuring of Lancaster', in L. Murgatroyd, M. Savage, D. Shapiro, J. Urry, S. Walby and A. Warde, *Localities, Class and Gender* (London: Pion), 30–53.

Newby, H. (1977) *The Deferential Worker: A Study of Farm Workers in East Anglia* (London: Allen Lane).

Newby, H. (1979) *Green and Pleasant Land? Social Change in Rural England* (Harmondsworth: Penguin).

Oakley, A. (1974) *The Sociology of Housework* (Oxford: Martin Robertson).

O'Connor, J. (1973) *The Fiscal Crisis of the State* (New York: St Martin's Press).

Offe, C. (1982) *The Contradictions of the Welfare State* (London: Hutchinson).

Offe, C. (1985) 'New Social Movements: Challenging the Boundaries of Institutional Politics', *Social Research*, 52, 4, 817–68.

Olsen, D.G. (1983) 'The City as Work of Art', in D. Fraser and A. Sutcliffe (eds), *The Pursuit of Urban History* (London: Edward Arnold).

Olsen, D.G. (1986) *The City as Work of Art* (London: Edward Arnold).

Owens, J.R. and Wade, L.L. (1988) 'Economic Conditions and Constituency Voting in Great Britain', *Political Studies*, 34, 30–51.

Pahl, R.E. (1965) *Urbs in Rure: The Metropolitan Fringe in Hertfordshire*, Geographical Papers 2 (London: London School of Economics).

Pahl, R.E. (1968) 'The Rural–Urban Continuum', in R. Pahl (ed.), *Readings in Urban Sociology* (Oxford: Pergamon), pp. 263–304.

Pahl, R.E. (1970) *Patterns of Urban Life* (London: Longman).

Pahl, R.E. (1975) *Whose City?* (Harmondsworth: Penguin).

Pahl, R.E. (1978) 'Castells and Collective Consumption', *Sociology*, 12, 2, 309–15.

Pahl, R.E. (1984) *Divisions of Labour* (Oxford: Blackwell).

Pahl, R.E. (1988) 'Some Remarks on Informal Work, Social Polarisation and the Social Structure', *International Journal of Urban and Regional Research*, 12, 247–67.

Pahl, R.E. (1989) 'Is the Emperor Naked? Some Questions on the Adequacy of Sociological Theory in Urban and Regional Research', *International Journal of Urban and Regional Research*, 13, 4, 709–20.

Park, R.E. (1921) 'Sociology and the Social Sciences: The Group Concept and Social Research', *American Journal of Sociology*, XXVII, 167–83.

Park, R.E. (1938) 'Reflections on Communication and Culture', *American Journal of Sociology*, XLIV, 187–205.

Park, R.E. (1967) 'The City: Suggestions for the Investigation of Human Behavior in an Urban Environment' (first published 1915), in R.E. Park, E.W. Burgess and R.D. McKenzie (1967) *The City* (Chicago: University of Chicago Press).

Parsons, T. (1937) *The Structure of Social Action* (New York: Free Press).

Parsons, T. (1951) *The Social System* (New York: Free Press).

Payne, G. (1987) *Mobility and Change in Modern Society* (London: Macmillan).

Peach, C. (1975) *Urban Social Segregation* (London: Longman).

Peck, J. and Tickell, A. (1991) *Regulation Theory and the Geography of Flexible Accumulation*, SPA Working Paper No. 12 (University of Manchester).

Perry, D.C. (1987) 'The Politics of Dependency in Deindustrialising America: The Case of Buffalo, New York', in M.P. Smith and J.R. Feagin (eds), *The Capitalist City* (Oxford: Blackwell).

Pfautz, J. (1967) *On the City: Physical Patterns and Social Structure* (Chicago: University of Chicago Press).

Pickvance, C. (1990) 'Introduction: The Institutional Context of Local Economic Development: Central Controls, Spatial Policies and Local Economic Policies', in M. Harloe, C. Pickvance and J. Urry (eds), *Place, Policy and Politics: Do Localities Matter?* (London Unwin Hyman), pp. 1–41.

Pinch, S. (1985) *Cities and Services: The Geography of Collective Consumption* (London: Routledge).

Pinch, S. (1989) 'The Restructuring Thesis and the Study of Public Services', *Environment and Planning A*, 21, 7, 905–26.

Piore, M. and Sabel, C. (1984) *The Second Industrial Divide: Possibilities for Prosperity* (New York: Basic Books).

Piven, F.F. and Cloward, R.A. (1972) *Regulating the Poor: Functions of Public Welfare* (London: Tavistock).

Piven, F.F. and Friedland, R. (1984) 'Public Choice and Private Power: A Theory of Fiscal Crisis', in A. Kirby, P. Knox and S. Pinch (eds), *Public Service Provision and Urban Development* (London: Croom Helm).

Pollock, G. (1988) *Vision and Difference* (London: Routledge).

Proctor, I. (1982) 'Some Political Economies of Urbanization: Some Suggestions for a Research Framework', *International Journal of Urban and Regional Research* 6, 1, 83–98.

Pryce, K. (1979) *Endless Pressure: A Study of West Indian Life-styles in Bristol* (Harmondsworth: Penguin).

Pugh, S. (ed.) (1990) *Reading Landscape: Country–City–Capital* (Manchester: Manchester University Press).

Raban, J. (1975) *Soft City* (London: Fontana).

Randolph, B. (1991) 'Housing Markets, Labour Markets, and Discontinuity Theory', in J. Allen and C. Hamnett (eds), *Housing and Labour Markets* (London: Unwin Hyman), pp. 16–54.

Redclift, N. and Mingione, E. (eds) (1985) *Beyond Employment: Household, Gender and Subsistence* (Oxford: Blackwell).

Redfield, R. (1947) 'The Folk Society', *American Journal of Sociology*, 52, 293–308.

Reff, T. (1984) 'Manet and the Paris of Hausmann and Baudelaire', in W. Sharpe and L. Wallock (eds), *Visions of the Modern City* (New York: Columbia University Press), pp 131–63.

Reissman, L. (1964) *Urban Process: Cities in Industrial Societies* (New York: Free Press).

Rex, J. and Moore, R. (1967) *Race, Community and Conflict: A Study of Sparkbrook* (Harmondsworth: Penguin).

Riesman, D., with Glazer, N. and Denney, R. (1950) *The Lonely Crowd: A Study of the Changing American Character* (New Haven: University of Yale Press).

Robertson, D. (1984) *Class and the British Electorate* (Oxford: Blackwell).

Rose, D. (1984) 'Rethinking Gentrification: Beyond the Uneven Development of Marxist Urban Theory', *Society and Space*, 2, 47–74.

Rose, D. (1988) 'A Feminist Perspective of Employment Restructuring and Gentrification: The Case of Montreal', in J. Wolch and M. Dear (eds), *The Power of Geography* (Boston: Unwin Hyman), pp. 118–38.

Sassen-Koob, S. (1987) 'Growth and Informalisation at the Core: A Preliminary

Report on New York City', in M.P. Smith and J. Fagin (eds), *The Capitalist World City* (Oxford: Blackwell), pp. 138–54.

Saunders, P. (1979) *Urban Politics: A Sociological Interpretation* (Harmondsworth: Penguin).

Saunders, P. (1981) *Social Theory and the Urban Question* (London: Hutchinson).

Saunders, P. (1984) 'Beyond Housing Classes: The Sociological Significance of Private Property Rights in the Means of Consumption', *International Journal of Urban and Regional Research*, 8, 2, 202–27.

Saunders, P. (1985) 'Space, the City and Urban Sociology', in D. Gregory and J. Urry (eds), *Social Relations and Spatial Structures* (London: Macmillan).

Saunders, P. (1986) *Social Theory and the Urban Question*, 2nd edn (London: Hutchinson).

Saunders, P. (1989) *Social Class and Stratification* (London: Tavistock).

Saunders, P. (1990) *A Nation of Homeowners* (London: Unwin Hyman).

Savage, M. (1987a) *The Dynamics of Working Class Politics* (Cambridge: University of Cambridge Press).

Savage, M. (1987b) 'Understanding Political Alignments in Contemporary Britain: Do Localities Matter?', *Political Geography Quarterly*, 6, 1, 53–76.

Savage, M. (1989) 'Spatial Divisions in Modern Britain', in C. Hamnett *et al.* (eds), *The Changing Social Structure* (London: Sage).

Savage, M. (1990) 'Whatever Happened to Red Clydeside', in J. Anderson and A. Cochrane (eds), *A State of Crisis* (London: Hodder & Stoughton), pp. 231–43.

Savage, M. (1992) 'Women's Expertise, Men's Authority: Gendered Organisations and the Contemporary Middle Classes', in M. Savage and A. Witz (eds), *Gender and Bureaucracy* (Oxford: Blackwell).

Savage, M., Barlow, J., Dickens, P. and Fielding, T. (1992) *Property, Bureaucracy and Culture: Middle Class Formation in Contemporary Britain* (London: Routledge).

Savage, M., Watt, P. and Arber, S. (1991) 'Social Class, Consumption Divisions and Housing Mobility', in R. Burrows and C. Marsh (eds), *Consumption and Class: Divisions and Change* (London: Macmillan), pp. 52–70.

Sayer, A. and Walker, R. (1992) *The New Social Economy: Reworking the Division of Labour* (Oxford: Blackwell).

Schorske, C.E. (1980) *Fin de Siècle Vienna: Politics and Culture* (London: Weidenfeld & Nicolson).

Scott, A.J. (1987) 'The Semi-Conductor Industry in S.E. Asia: Organisation, Location, and the International Division of Labour', *Regional Studies*, 21, 2, 143–60.

Scott, A.J. (1988a) *Metropolis: From the Division of Labour to Urban Form* (Berkeley: University of California Press).

Scott, A.J. (1988b) *New Industrial Spaces: Flexible Production, Organization and Regional Development in North America and Western Europe* (London: Pion).

Sennett, R. (1977) *The Fall of Public Man* (Cambridge: University of Cambridge Press).

Sennett, R. (1990) *The Conscience of the Eye* (London: Faber).

Sharpe, W. and Wallock, L. (1984) *Visions of the Modern City* (New York: University of Columbia Press).

Shields, R. (1989) 'Social Spatialisation and the Built Environment: The Case of the West Edmonton Mall', *Society and Space*, 7, 2, 147–64.

Shields, R. (1991) *Places on the Margin* (London: Routledge).

Shields, R. (1992) 'A Truant Proximity: Presence and Absence in the Space of Modernity', *Environment and Planning D: Society and Space*, 10, 2, 181–98.

Simmel, G. (1950) *The Sociology of Georg Simmel* (edited by Kurt Wolff) (New York: Free Press).

Simmel, G. (1964) 'The Metropolis and Mental Life', in K. Wolff (ed.), *The Sociology of Georg Simmel* (New York: Fress Press), pp. 409–24.

Simmel, G. (1978) *The Philosophy of Money* (London: Routledge).

Smart, B. (1992) *Modern Conditions, Postmodern Controversies* (London: Routledge).

Smith, D. (1988) *The Chicago School: A Liberal Critique of Capitalism* (London: Macmillan).

Smith, M.P. (1980) *The City and Social Theory* (Oxford: Blackwell).

Smith, M.P. and Feagin, J. (eds) (1987) *The Capitalist City: Global Restructuring and Community Politics* (Oxford: Blackwell).

Smith, M.P. and Tardanico, R. (1987) 'Urban Theory Reconsidered: Production, Reproduction and Collective Action', in M.P. Smith and J.R. Feagin (eds), *The Capitalist City* (Oxford: Blackwell), pp. 87–112.

Smith, N. (1979) 'Towards a Theory of Gentrification: A Back to the City Movement by Capital not People', *Journal of the American Planners Association*, 45, 538–48.

Smith, N. (1984) *Uneven Development: Nature, Capital and the Production of Space* (Oxford: Blackwell).

Smith, N. (1986) 'Dangers of the Empirical Turn: Some Comments on The CURS Initiative', *Antipode*, 19, 1, 394–406.

Smith, N. (1987) 'Of Yuppies and Housing: Gentrification, Social Restructuring and the Urban Dream', *Society and Space*, 5, 2, 151–72.

Smith, N. and Williams, P. (eds) (1986) *Gentrification of the City* (Boston: Allen & Unwin).

Smith, S. (1989) *The Politics of Race and Residence* (Oxford: Blackwell).

Society and Space (1988) Special Edition on the New Geography and Sociology of Production, *Environment and Planning D: Society and Space*, 6, 3, 241–370.

Soja, E. (1989) *Postmodern Geographies* (London: Verso).

Sontag, S. (1978) 'Introduction' to *One Way Street and Other Writings* (London: Verso).

Stacey, M. (1960) *Tradition and Change: A Study of Banbury* (Oxford: University of Oxford Press).

Stacey, M. (1969) 'The Myth of Community Studies', *British Journal of Sociology*, 20, 2, 134–47.

Stein, M. (1964) *The Eclipse of Community: An Interpretation of American Studies* (New York: Harper & Row).

Stone, C. and Sanders, H. (eds) (1987) *The Politics of Urban Development* (Kansas: Kansas University Press).

Storper, M. and Walker, R. (1989) *The Capitalist Imperative: Territory, Technology and Industrial Growth* (Oxford: Blackwell).

Strauss, A. (1961) *Images of the American City* (Chicago: University of Chicago Press).

Suttles, G. (1968) *The Social Order of the Slum* (Chicago: University of Chicago

Press).

Suttles, G. (1984) 'The Cumulative Texture of Local Urban Culture', *American Journal of Sociology*, 90, 2, 283–304.

Swenarton, M. and Taylor, S. (1985) 'The Scale and Nature of the Growth of Owner Occupation in Britain between the Wars', *Economic History Review*, 38, 3, 373–93.

Szelenyi, I. (1977) *Urban Inequalities under State Socialism* (Oxford: Clarendon).

Szelenyi, I. (1989) *Socialist Entrepreneurs* (Oxford: Clarendon).

Taylor, B. (1980) *Eve and the New Jerusalem* (London: Virago).

Thompson, E.P. and Yeo, E. (eds) (1971) *The Unknown Mayhew* (Harmondsworth: Penguin).

Thompson, J. (1984) *Studies in the Theory of Ideology* (Cambridge: Polity).

Thompson, J. (1990) *Ideology and Modern Culture* (Cambridge: Polity).

Thorns, D.C. (1982) 'Industrial Restructuring and Change in Labour and Property Markets in Britain', *Environment and Planning A*, 14, 745–63.

Thrasher, F. (1927) *The Gang* (Chicago: University of Chicago Press).

Thrift, N. (1987) 'An Introduction to the Geography of Late Twentieth Century Class Formation', in N. Thrift and P. Williams, *Class and Space* (London: Routledge).

Thrift, N. (1989) 'Images of Social Change', in C. Hamnett et al. (eds), *The Changing Social Structure* (London: Sage).

Timberlake, M. (1987) 'World Systems Theory and Comparative Urbanisation', in M.P. Smith and J. Feagin (eds), *The Capitalist City* (Oxford: Blackwell), pp. 37–65.

Urry, J. (1985) 'Social Relations, Space and Time', in D. Gregory and J. Urry (eds), *Social Relations and Spatial Structures*, pp. 20–48.

Urry, J. (1990a) *The Tourist Gaze* (London: Sage).

Urry, J. (1990b) 'Conclusion: Places and Policies', in M. Harloe, C. Pickvance and J. Urry (eds), *Place, Policy and Politics* (London: Unwin Hyman), pp. 187–204.

Urry, J. (1991) 'Travel and Modernity', paper delivered at Eighth Urban Change and Conflict Conference, Lancaster, September.

Vaiou, D. (1991), 'Gender Divisions in Urban Space: Facets of Everyday Life in an Athenian Suburb', paper delivered to Eighth Urban Change and Conflict Conference, Lancaster, September.

Venturi, R., Scott Brown, D. and Izenour, S. (1977) *Learning from Las Vegas* (Cambridge, Mass.: MIT).

Wainwright, H. (1987) *Labour: A Tale of Two Parties* (London: Hogarth).

Walker, R.A. (1981) 'A Theory of Suburbanisation: Capitalism and the Construction of Urban Spaces in the United States', in M. Dear and A.J. Scott (eds), *Urbanisation and Urban Planning in Capitalist Society* (London: Methuen), pp. 383–430.

Wallerstein, I. (1974) *The Modern World System*, vol. 1 (New York: Academic Press).

Ward, D. (1989) *Poverty, Ethnicity and the American City, 1840–1925: Changing Conceptions of the Slum and the Ghetto* (Cambridge: University of Cambridge Press).

Warde, A. (1985) 'The Homogenisation of Space? Trends in the Spatial Division of Labour in 20th Century Britain', in H. Newby, J. Bujra, P. Littlewood, G. Rees and T. Rees (eds), *Restructuring Capital: Recession and Reorganisation in Industrial Society* (London: Macmillan), pp. 41–64.

Warde, A. (1988) 'Industrial Restructuring, Local Politics and the Reproduction of Labour Power: Some Theoretical Considerations', *Society and Space*, 6, 75–95.

Warde, A. (1990) 'Production, Consumption and Social Change: Reservations regarding Peter Saunders's Sociology of Consumption', *International Journal of Urban and Regional Research*, 14, 2, 228–48.

Warde, A. (1991) 'Gentrification as Consumption: Issues of Class and Gender', *Society and Space*, 9, 2, 223–32.

White, M. (1987) *American Neighbourhoods and Residential Differentiation* (New York: Russell Sage Foundation for the National Committee for Research on the 1980 Census).

Whiteley, P. (1983) *The Labour Party in Crisis* (London: Methuen).

Whiteley, P. (1986) 'Predicting the Labour Vote in 1983: Social Backgrounds versus Subjective Evaluations', *Political Studies*, 34, 1, 82–98.

Whyte, W. (1948) *Street Corner Society* (Chicago: University of Chicago Press).

Wiener, M. (1981) *English Culture and the Decline of the Industrial Spirit* (Harmondsworth: Penguin).

Williams, P. (1986) 'Class Constitution through Spatial Reconstruction? A Re-evaluation of Gentrification in Australia, Britain and the United States', in N. Smith and P. Williams (eds), *Gentrification of the City* (Boston: Allen & Unwin), pp. 56–77.

Williams, P. and Smith, N. (1986) 'From Renaissance to Restructuring: The Dynamics of Contemporary Urban Development', in N. Smith and P. Williams (eds), *Gentrification of the City* (Boston: Allen & Unwin), pp. 204–24.

Williams, R. (1973) *The Country and the City* (London: Chatto & Windus).

Williams, R. (1989) *The Politics of Modernism* (London: Verso).

Williams, W.M. (1956) *The Sociology of an English Village: Gosforth* (London: Routledge & Kegan Paul).

Williams, W.M. (1963) *A West Country Village: Ashworthy* (London: Routledge & Kegan Paul).

Williamson, O.E. (1990) 'The Firm as a Nexus of Treaties: An Introduction', in M. Aoki, B. Gustafsson and O. Williamson (eds), *The Firm as a Nexus of Treaties* (London: Sage), pp. 1–25.

Willmott, P. and Young, M. (1960) *Family and Class in a London Suburb* (London: Routledge & Kegan Paul).

Wilson, E. (1991) *The Sphinx in the City* (London: Virago).

Wirth, L. (1938) 'Urbanism as a Way of Life', *American Journal of Sociology*, XLIV, 1, 1–24.

Wishart, R. (1991) 'Fashioning the Future: Glasgow', in M. Fisher and U. Owen (eds), *Whose Cities?* (Harmondsworth: Penguin), pp. 43–52.

Wolff, J. (1987) 'The Invisible Flaneuse: Women and the Literature of Modernity', in A. Benjamin (ed.), *The Problems of Modernity* (London: Routledge).

Wolin, R. (1983) 'Experience and Materialism in Benjamin's Passagenwerk', in G. Smith (ed.), *Benjamin: Philosophy, Aesthetics, History* (Chicago: University of Chicago Press), pp. 210–27.

Wright, P. (1985) *On Living in an Old Country* (London: Verso).

Wright, P. (1991) *A Journey through the Ruins* (London: Paladin).

Young, M. and Willmott, P. (1962) *Family and Kinship in East London* (Harmondsworth: Penguin).

Young, M. and Willmott, P. (1975) *The Symmetrical Family* (Harmondsworth: Penguin).

Zorbaugh, H.W. (1929) *The Gold Coast and the Slum* (Chicago: University of Chicago Press).

Zukin, S. (1980) 'A Decade of the New Urban Sociology', *Theory and Society*, 9, 4, 575–602.

Zukin, S. (1987) 'Gentrification, Culture and Capital in the Urban Core', *American Journal of Sociology*, 13, 129–47.

Zukin, S. (1988) *Loft Living: Culture and Capital in Urban Change* (London: Radius).

Zukin, S. (1992) 'Postmodern Urban Landscapes: Mapping Culture and Power', in S. Lash and J. Friedman (eds), *Modernity and Identity* (Oxford: Blackwell), pp. 221–47.

# Index

subcultures and 108
Mills, C.A. 84
Mingione, E. 91
mining communities 25, 90
mobilisation, local political 152, 175, 182–6
*see also* urban social movements
mobility research 25
modernisation theory 175
modernist aesthetics 116–17
modernist architecture 139
modernity 149–51, 193
  capitalism and 190–1
  Chicago School 17–18;
    sociation's changing modes
    within 12–14
  culture of 114–20;
    aesthetics 116–17; nature of
    street life 119–20; sexual
    identity 117–18; visual
    115–16
  definition 3–4
  experience of 3–4, 189–90
  maximising potential of 191–2
  paradoxes of 149–50
  Simmel 113–14
  *see also* post-modernity
Mollenkopf, J.H. 168
Molotch, H. 48, 49, 168, 174, 183
  growth coalitions 165–6
money economy 112–13
Moore, R. 68–9, 153
Morris, L. 67, 88
Morris, R.J. 126
Mullins, P. 93
Mumford, L. 124
Munro, M. 73
Murgatroyd, L. 45
museumisation 131

neighbourhood effect, voting
  and 177–8
neighbourhoods, employment 60–1
networks 60
Nevsky Prospect 117, 144
new industrial districts 39–40, 58–60
new industrial division of labour
  (NIDL) thesis 41–5

New London Survey of London Life
  and Labour 22
New Right politics 86, 147
'new social movements' 182
'new urban sociology' 27–31, 153
'new urban spaces' 140–1
New York 43, 80–1, 88, 130
Newby, H. 8, 99, 106
  community 103, 104–5
North Shields 185

Oakley, A. 79
O'Connor, J. 149
Offe, C. 149, 183
Olsen, D.G. 126, 127–8
opportunity, insecurity and 191–2
order, social 32, 149, 191
  post-war urban sociology 22–3, 24
  urban participation and 152, 182–6
  *see also* conflict
overaccumulation 46–7
owner-occupation 69, 77, 87, 163
  consumption and 158–9, 161
  employment and 70–4 *passim*
  state and 162

Pahl, R.E. 2, 88, 89, 93
  collective consumption 156
  household work strategies 90–2
Paris 135, 137, 142
Park, R.E. 9, 11, 17
  human ecology 14, 15–16
  modernity 12–14
  social disorganisation 23
  social laboratory 18, 31
Parsons, T. 9, 22–3
participation, political 152, 175, 182–6
  *see also* urban social movements;
  voting behaviour
Pattie, C. 176, 178
Payne, G. 26
Pfautz, J. 19
Pickvance, C. 164, 169, 170, 173
Pinch, S. 53, 155

220   *Index*

# Economy, Society & Space

Economy + Urban Geographies

Geographies of Industry

---

Approaches to industrial location

Ec. factors in ec. location

Product life cycle // changing structure
                    of industry

Inadequacy of approaches

__focus:__ Urban economies +
          uneven economic development